CHEZ PANISSE FRUIT

CHEZ PANISSE
FRUIT

by

ALICE WATERS

and the Cooks of Chez Panisse
in collaboration with
Alan Tangren and Fritz Streiff

Illustrations by
PATRICIA CURTAN

HarperCollins*Publishers*

ALSO FROM CHEZ PANISSE ❧

Chez Panisse Café Cookbook
Chez Panisse Vegetables
Fanny at Chez Panisse
Chez Panisse Cooking
Chez Panisse Desserts
Chez Panisse Pasta, Pizza, and Calzone
Chez Panisse Menu Cookbook

HarperCollins books may be purchased for educational, business, or sales promotional use. For information, please write: Special Markets Department, HarperCollins Publishers Inc., 10 East 53rd Street, New York, NY 10022.

FIRST EDITION

Designed by Patricia Curtan
Typeset by Bur Davis and Keala Hagmann

Library of Congress Cataloging-in-Publication Data
Waters, Alice.
    Chez Panisse fruit / by Alice Waters and the cooks of Chez Panisse in collaboration with
    Alan Tangren and Fritz Streiff; illustrations by Patricia Curtan
        p. cm.
    Includes bibliographical references and index.
    ISBN 0-06-019957-1 (hardcover)
    1. Cookery (Fruit) 2. Chez Panisse. I. Tangren, Alan. II. Streiff, Fritz. III. Title.

TX811 . W32 2002
641.6'4—dc21

Printed on acid-free paper

02 03 04 05 06 / RRD 10 9 8 7 6 5 4 3 2 1

ACKNOWLEDGMENTS &

Once more, thanks are due first to the Chez Panisse cooks I asked to help me set recipes down on paper for this volume, especially Kelsie Sue Kerr, now a chef in the restaurant downstairs, and Samantha Greenwood Wood, a former anchor of the dessert kitchen; both of them helped shape the book's contents from the beginning. Recipes also came to us from Tracy Bates, Mary Canales, Patricia Curtan, Sarah Egri, Carly Meyer, Jean-Pierre Moullé, Charlene Nicholson, Gilbert Pilgram, Tasha Prysi, Jehnee Rains, Charlene Reis, Alan Tangren, David Tanis, and Anthony Tassinello—all present or former Chez Panisse cooks without whose dedication Chez Panisse could not survive. Our gratitude extends to four great contributors from outside the restaurant: Marion Cunningham, Carol Field, Niloufer Ichaporia, and Shirley Sarvis.

The essays about individual fruits are largely the work of my collaborator, Alan Tangren, the pastry chef at Chez Panisse, whose career at the restaurant has taken him from an early beginning in our kitchens to many years as our "forager"—our procurement officer, so to speak, and as such, the person responsible for forging our relationships with the scores of mostly local growers and suppliers who bring us the beautiful ingredients that, as we boast on our menu, are almost without exception organically grown and sustainably produced. My other collaborator, Fritz Streiff, has once again served as my editorial mouthpiece and mastermind, testing, correcting, writing, and rewriting at every stage of the project.

For their generosity with their expertise, our hearty thanks to Ernie and Chris Bierwagen, Ray Copeland, Darrell Corti, Al Courchesne, Bill Fujimoto, David Karp, C. Todd Kennedy, Andy Sarhanis, Didar Singh, Jonathan and Lucy Tolmach, and Sue at the Racha Café.

As always, my partner, Lindsey Shere, has been a particular inspiration to me. Pastry chef for twenty-six years, she tested recipes and made suggestions that were especially welcome; and the immense influence of her esthetics and perfectionism on her successors is reflected everywhere in this book. Warm thanks arc also owed to the other recipe testers and tasters, among them Thérèse Shere, Yoon Ki Chai, Tomas Salis, Nancy Satoda, and numerous other friends and relatives. And I would especially like to thank Cristina Salas-Porras for her invaluable help in coordinating the logistics of the entire project.

Probably most important of all, *Chez Panisse Fruit* owes the extraordinary beauty and serenity of its illustrations and the clarity and just proportions of its design to Patricia Curtan, who also helped conceive the book almost eight years ago.

Lastly, this book could never have been brought to fruition without the understanding of our editor, Susan Friedland; we thank her again for her enthusiasm, her acumen, and her patience.

CONTENTS ❧

INTRODUCTION 🍃

This is the eighth Chez Panisse cookbook we have published since the restaurant was founded in 1971, and it begins the same way as all the others: I throw open the window, start to flail my arms, and scream: "Pay attention to what you're eating!" And then I calm down a little and try to explain why this matters so much to me.

I did not begin to pay attention to food in earnest until I was nineteen years old. I was luckier than most American children who grew up in the 1950s in that I was exposed to at least some foods that were pure, unprocessed, fresh, and seasonal. My parents planted a vegetable garden in our New Jersey backyard where they grew corn, beans, and tomatoes; my sisters and I foraged for wild blueberries in New Hampshire in July; and our suburban town had not yet spilled out of its borders and buried the small orchards and truck farms that surrounded it.

But nothing I ate prepared me for the food of France, where I went for my junior year of college. There, for the first time in my life, I learned that good food could be a *serious* pleasure and that its pursuit was worthy of the utmost concentration and discrimination. In France people not only gave deep thought to their next meal; they surrendered themselves utterly to its sensual enjoyment.

It was a year of a thousand epiphanies: the bread fresh from the wood-burning oven of my neighborhood bakery; the cheese so unimaginably and ripely various; the staggering bounty of the sea, still glistening and alive at the fishmonger's; the long meals with my new French friends, whose passion for food was so grown-up in its refinement and so childlike in its exuberance.

And then there was the fruit. I will never forget those first fraises des bois scattered on the plate. What are these "strawberries of the woods," I thought; they look awfully tiny. But when I popped one in my mouth and tasted the concentrated essence of high springtime—so sweet, so spicily indescribable—my eyes fluttered shut and I didn't know what to say. It had never occurred to me that strawberries originally came from the woods nor that I was deeply connected with nature. All at once I had a glimmer of understanding of the truth that Wendell Berry would express so well years later: "Eating with the fullest pleasure—pleasure, that is, that does not depend on ignorance—is perhaps the profoundest enactment of our connection with the world."

Long after that year in France, I began to plant fraises des bois in the yard of my Berkeley house, and when my daughter was just beginning to walk, I encouraged her to find her way among the strawberry plants and pick the ripe ones. I watched as her eyes, too, fluttered shut when she tasted one. She grew up in the garden picking strawberries and raspberries—and always only the ones that were perfectly ripe. To this day she would rather have a bowl of berries than a piece of chocolate cake.

Fruit, more than any of the other foods we consume, has this power to go right to the heart of our being. Fruit is sweet. Fruit is beautiful to look at and beautiful to smell. Fruit teaches us the meaning of time and eternity: a tree blooms in the spring and bears fruit, and the fruit falls ripe to the ground in the summer, carrying within itself the seeds of a new plant that will winter over and begin the cycle again. Is it any surprise that the knowledge of good and evil came to us from a fruit?

At Chez Panisse our knowledge of fruits themselves—their varieties, seasons, history, and preparation—has come to us more gradually. From our earliest days it was clear that we had to seek out and cultivate relationships with nearby farmers and orchardists for our produce, and it is thanks to these relationships that we know what we do. Our connections to our suppliers of fruits have also been among our most personally rewarding. Quite early on, neighborhood people started showing up at our kitchen door with Meyer lemons, wild plums, and blackberries for sale. And in our hunger for more and better fruit, we hunted down such relatively rare fruits as mulberries, sour cherries, gooseberries, and currants in backyards and small orchards all over our region of northern California, making lasting friendships while learning just how precious and how ephemeral good fruit can be.

How can we place a value on fruit that is brought to us, hand-picked and selected, by people we love? Every year we keenly anticipate those two-week windows of opportunity when Bob Cannard's cherries will be ripe, or Kimi's peaches, or the Chino family's fraises des bois. For nothing is better than a fruit in its own proper season, perfectly ripened and handled with care by the people who harvest it. We couldn't live without these farmers and foragers; many of them are thanked by name in this book, but there are many more. The thrill of tasting their superb produce is inextricably bound up with the pleasure of knowing them.

As we do at Chez Panisse, you *must* seek out and encourage the artisanal producers of organically grown food who are daring to carry on this noble work despite the encroaching values of a fast-food nation. Start at the nearest farmers' market. Ask questions. Learn what varieties you like and when they come into season. Tell the vendors what you like best and why. When you're out driving in the country, stop at farm stands whether you think you need anything or not. You're sure to learn something. When you shop at grocery stores and supermarkets, talk to the produce manager. Insist that you want the opportunity to buy local, organically grown fruit.

In the kitchen, remember that there is nothing more satisfying at the end of a meal than a perfect piece of fruit, and restrain yourself from doing too much. Naturally, this book is full of recipes, many of them quite precise and some rather elaborate, but do not forget that you are free to adapt them to the fruit you have on hand. We have shied away from providing exhaustive cross-references because we think you can figure out for yourself that peach recipes work equally well with nectarines, for example, and that blackberries can stand in for boysenberries. As always, the most important admonition is to use your taste buds. Resist the temptation to oversweeten—taste critically!

Some of the best uses you will find for fruit in your kitchen will be impromptu and unrepeatable. At my house the dessert I serve most often is a macédoine of whatever seasonal fruits I may have on hand—and because I routinely overbuy, I often have a great deal, all of it ripe or a little overripe. A fruit salad or compote like this is among the best ways to use it up. In the summertime I trim away the bruised parts and cut up a few apricots, say, a nectarine or two, and peaches, all in small pieces; I throw in a few berries if there are some and then look in my refrigerator at what I have in the way of homemade preserves and syrups; perhaps there is some berry jam that I can thin out with a little water, or some rose geranium–infused syrup. I pour in a little and toss the fruit in it and voilà! I always think people are never going to eat one more of these fruit desserts, but every single time they're different, and every time my guests ask for seconds.

We have included a number of recipes for preserving fruit, all of them quite simple and for relatively small quantities. Although an exhaustive treatment of the subject lies outside the scope of this book, we strongly believe in the many benefits of home preserving: not only can you take advantage of the bountiful harvest in this way, but home preserving is also a way to slow yourself down with a task that, despite its tedious aspects, is nevertheless deeply satisfying and, if done with your children, can turn into a beloved home tradition. Best of all, nothing is more pleasurable than the midwinter satisfaction of opening a jar of preserves you put up yourself and tasting the essence of summer; after all, your own preserves will always taste better than anyone else's. For further reading, we highly recommend M. F. K. Fisher's annotated edition of *Fine Preserving,* by Catherine Plagemann; *Putting Food By,* by Ruth Herzberg, Beatrice Vaughan, and Janet Greene; *Preserving,* one of the volumes of Time-Life's *Good Cook* series; and *The Glass Pantry,* by Georgeanne Brennan.

Other recipes included here are drawn from our daily repertoire at Chez Panisse. They are essentially conservative, based on the principle that you don't want to confuse the flavor of good fruit. More rigorously than in our earlier vegetable book, we have adhered to the standard American recipe-writing format, measured spoonfuls and all. To some degree this reflects the actual practice of our pastry kitchen, where precision is perhaps of more necessity than in a home kitchen. But we also still believe that to the real cook, the execution of a recipe requires something more than a paint-by-the-numbers approach. That something more includes the love you feel for those you cook for, your openness to the evidence of your senses, and the reverence you feel before the bounty of creation.

ABOUT THE ILLUSTRATIONS 🕭

.

The original illustrations reproduced in this book are color linocut images drawn, cut, and printed by the artist. As in woodcut relief printing, in linoleum block printing a drawing is first transferred to the block—a layer of smooth linoleum, made from linseed oil and powdered cork, mounted on wood. The linoleum is cut with knives and gouges, to remove the negative space of the image and leave a relief surface of line or solid color. A separate block is cut for each color in the image. The images were printed by hand, one color at a time, on a 10-by-15 Chandler and Price letterpress.

CHEZ PANISSE FRUIT

APPLES ❧

Season: Fresh, late summer through fall; through spring from storage

Every year in the Chez Panisse kitchen we are startled by the earliest ripening apples, arriving as they do at the end of July, long before we expect them. By that point in the summertime, we're always up to our elbows in plums, peaches, nectarines, blackberries, mulberries—almost all of the summer stone fruits and berries, in fact, and all near their seasonal peaks of production. Yet we never fail to be seduced by the rich flavor of Gravensteins and the pastel beauty glowing in the tart skins of Pink Pearls. These two apples are among our favorite varieties for applesauce and galettes, but because neither stores well, we are obliged to use them right away. Fortunately, apple galettes with a sprinkling of blackberries baked on top look quite summery—and we taste and smile, knowing that the procession of apples is only just beginning. Local, freshly harvested, organically grown apples will follow virtually uninterrupted for nearly five months and stored local apples for months more —apples of many varieties, each ripening in its own time, each with its own virtues.

I was born in rural New Jersey in April, when the apple trees were in bloom, and I honestly believe that I have a true memory of their white blossoms falling gently and settling on the mosquito netting draped over my baby carriage. To me, apple trees will always be the most glorious and soothing of flowering trees. To enter a hushed orchard in bloom transports me back to my infancy and calms me down as nothing else can. When my own daughter was about to be born, friends helped me plant two apple trees in my backyard, one a dwarf McIntosh, the other a Gravenstein that bears fruit at just the right time for her birthday. Celebrating with something made with her own apples has become part of her annual August ritual.

Of course, not all of us have apple trees of our own to mark the passage of the seasons with apple-blossom memories and birthday harvests, and because most commercial varieties of apple store so well (many are available year-round, in fact), most of us tend to think of apples as a predictable, ever-ripe, and uniformly rather dull commodity, forgetting that each distinct apple variety has its own season, not to mention its own unique flavor, texture, tartness, color, cooking qualities, ripening time, and cultural history. Something like seven thousand distinct varieties of apples are known to exist. Of these, at least a hundred are produced in quantity in the United States by commercial growers; small farmers and backyard gardeners grow many more.

How sad, then, that over 90 percent of the apples sold in this country belong to one of only fifteen of those seven thousand varieties. Some of these very popular apples, such as the McIntosh or the Jonathan, can be very good. But what about the other 6,985? There must be something about each one that made it worth selecting, naming, and propagating in the first place, and something that might make it worth planting and harvesting today.

Of all our apples, the Red Delicious is the best known: its production outstrips that of all other varieties. It is brilliant red, it is sweet and juicy, and of the top fifteen varieties, it has the most insipid flavor. Farmers in Washington State, where nearly all supermarket Red Delicious apples come from, are finally realizing that their quest for the reddest, most visually flawless fruit has led to a flavor-deficient cardboard copy of an apple, and many orchards are now planting tastier varieties. It should be noted that bland-tasting apples are the predictable result of a large-scale, profit-driven agriculture that necessarily values appearance and keeping and shipping qualities over intensity and quality of flavor. To discover the tastiest apples grown near you, you must seek out small local orchardists who love apples passionately, believe in biodiversity, and practice sustainable agriculture.

In fact, apples far more delicious than most supermarket apples are grown in every one of the continental United States—and in thirty-six states on a commercial scale. Have you tried an Esopus Spitzenburg? This juicy, spicy, fine-textured apple was Thomas Jefferson's favorite; it shows up in our local farmers' market every fall. So does Cox's Orange Pippin, a 170-year-old variety well known in Britain and northern Europe as one of the tastiest of apples, good for cooking, cider-making, and eating fresh. In New York State it is still easy to find the Macoun, a relatively new apple introduced in the 1920s; its smooth green skin is ablush with burgundy and its flesh is fine-grained, pure white, and aromatic. (New York State, long a center of pomological study and experimentation, is blessed with apples. Week after week in the fall, shoppers at New York City's Union Square farmers' market enjoy a multiplicity of varieties exceeding anything we know in northern California. Michigan, Pennsylvania, and Virginia are the other big apple-growing states where dedicated growers are preserving and developing diverse varieties.)

Heirloom varieties are by no means the only ones worth looking for. Jonagold, a cross between the Golden Delicious and the Jonathan, was first developed in the 1940s by Cornell experimenters in Geneva, New York, and made available only some thirty years ago. It is a beautiful greenish-yellow apple blushing with orange-red, and it has a sweet, rich flavor. Very fine for eating fresh and good for cooking too, it is becoming widely available here and is already one of the most popular varieties in European orchards.

Sierra Beauty, introduced in the early twentieth century, is the local apple that has become our standard of excellence. This rather blocky apple has pale green skin handsomely striped with red. When ripe, it has a lovely balance between sweet and tart extremes, with the intense flavor needed for apple tarts. Its crisp juiciness makes it perfect for eating out of hand or in salads. Sierra Beauties are not widely grown, and we can never get enough. Most of our supply comes from The Apple Farm in Mendocino County, north of San Francisco, farmed by Karen and Tim Bates.

Although the apple harvest in most areas starts in August, it really gets going in September. Some of the best varieties to be found at that time are King of Tomkins County, Jonathan, Jonagold, Golden Delicious, McIntosh, and Cox's Orange Pippin. October brings Fuji, Stayman Winesap, Macoun, Rhode Island Greening, Baldwin, Sierra Beauty, Lady, and Rome Beauty. And later still you should look for Arkansas Black, Newtown Pippin, and well-ripened Granny Smith. The later apples are generally the best keepers, something to remember when shopping for apples from storage in late winter or early spring.

Apples are often identified as dessert, cooking, or cider varieties. These definitions can be suggestive, but trust your own taste and experience. For salads, choose a crisp apple that isn't too sweet, such as the Sierra Beauty, Granny Smith, or Newtown Pippin. For delicious applesauce, try Gravenstein, Cortland, McIntosh, Rhode Island Greening, or

Jonathan. For sautéed apple slices and tarte Tatin, use an apple that holds its shape when cooked and caramelized; in our experience, Golden Delicious is the most reliable, but be sure the ones you buy are organically grown and have good flavor. For tarts and galettes, our first choice is Sierra Beauty apples when we can get them, but Jonagold, Golden Delicious, and Winesap are all good.

You can tell a lot about the cooking qualities of an apple with a simple test. Cut a half-inch-thick wedge out of the apple, peel it, and put it in a saucepan with just enough water to cover it. Bring the water to a boil and then simmer until the apple is tender. Probe to see if it holds its shape or turns mushy. Taste to see how much flavor is retained and how much sugar it will need.

At the market, choose organically grown apples that smell fresh. They should have a mildly winey aroma, but avoid those that smell fermented or musty. They should be heavy for their size and feel firm when pressed gently. Their skins should be bright and have good color for their type. If you plan to store apples, avoid those with bruises or other blemishes or punctures in the skin. These will go bad quickly and spoil the lot. Small apples tend to keep better than large ones.

All apples continue to ripen after harvest, and some, particularly the late varieties, are hard and starchy when harvested, unpalatable until they have been stored for a number of weeks. To keep small quantities of apples at home, put them in the refrigerator. Apples will get overripe quickly if held at room temperature.

Apples prepared for a salad should be quartered, cored, and sliced, but not peeled unless the skin is tough; much of the flavor and beauty of an apple is in its skin. If the apples are not to be served right away, forestall browning by tossing the apple slices with a little lemon juice or a bit of the vinegar to be used in the dressing.

Apples that will be cooked are usually peeled first. I find it easiest to quarter the fruit with a large chef's knife before peeling, which I do with a small turning knife. It is then quick to carve out the core at the same time. You can also peel the fruit whole with a knife or vegetable peeler; don't worry too much about the stem or blossom ends of the fruit on the first go-round. Quarter the apple, trim off any bits of skin, and take out the core with a small knife. Apples peeled for tarts, pies, fritters, or sautés can be tightly covered and refrigerated for as long as overnight before using; any browning that takes place will not be noticeable after cooking.

APPLESAUCE

Quarter and core tasty apples. (Peel if you wish, but remember, the skin is full of flavor.) Cut the quarters into ½-inch chunks. Put them in a saucepan and add apple juice or cider to a depth of ½ inch. Simmer, covered, over medium heat, stirring occasionally, for 20 to 30 minutes, until the apples are cooked through, soft, and translucent. If you like applesauce smooth, pass it through a food mill. Taste for sweetness; it may need a little lemon juice. Serve warm with a dollop of crème fraîche or with pan-fried pork chops.

CURLY ENDIVE SALAD WITH CELERY ROOT, APPLES, AND PECANS

> *3 heads very young curly endive*
> *(frisée) no more than*
> *8 inches in diameter,*
> *with tender white centers*
> *⅓ cup pecans*
> *Salt and pepper*
>
> *3 tablespoons verjuice*
> *(page 101)*
> *¼ cup extra-virgin olive oil*
> *½ celery root*
> *2 apples (any crisp, tasty*
> *eating variety)*

Preheat the oven to 375°F.

Tear off and discard any tough green outer leaves from the curly endive. Cut off the root ends and separate the leaves. Wash and dry well.

Toast the pecans in the oven for 7 minutes, cool, and chop roughly.

Combine salt, pepper, and verjuice in a mixing bowl, whisk in the olive oil, taste for acidity and salt, and adjust as necessary. (If the verjuice is too sweet for your taste, you may want to add a dash of white wine vinegar or Champagne vinegar.)

Just before serving, prepare the celery root and apples. Peel the celery root and cut into thin slices. Cut these slices into a fine julienne.

Quarter and core the apples (peeling is optional) and cut into thin slices lengthwise. Add the celery root to the vinaigrette, toss, and let sit for 5 minutes. Add the curly endive, apple slices, and pecans and toss carefully so as not to break the apple slices. Arrange prettily on a plate and serve.

Serves 6.

SPIT-ROASTED PORK WITH ONION-AND-APPLE MARMALADE

The really great pork we use comes from small farms where pigs are given ample living room and fed an organic diet unsupplemented by antibiotics and hormones. You can taste the difference.

3 medium onions
½ cup verjuice (page 101)
¾ cup white wine (Pinot Blancs
   and dry Rieslings are nice
   choices) or hard cider
Salt and pepper
3 apples (Gravensteins, Sierra
   Beauties, Cox's Orange
   Pippins, Granny Smiths, etc.)

1 cup water
2 tablespoons honey
2 tablespoons unsalted butter
1 standing 6-rib pork loin roast,
   chine bone removed

To make the onion-and-apple marmalade, first peel and slice the onions and put them in a heavy-bottomed pan with the verjuice, wine, and a big pinch of salt. Bring to a boil, reduce the heat, and simmer until the liquid has been absorbed, about 20 minutes.

Meanwhile, peel, core, and slice the apples. Add the apples and water to the onions and cook for another ½ hour. Stir occasionally to be sure the marmalade does not stick and burn. When the onions and apples are soft and melted together, the marmalade is done. Stir in the honey and butter. The marmalade can be made a few days ahead of time. Re-warm gently when ready to serve.

Season the pork loin generously with salt and pepper. Tie the roast securely between each rib bone with cotton twine to help ensure even roasting. Refrigerate for a few hours or overnight. Take the roast out of the refrigerator 1 hour before roasting.

Build a fire to develop an ample bed of coals; a healthy fire behind low, steady coals produces the best roast. Impale the loin on the spit length-wise. Roast, turning slowly and continuously, about 1½ hours, until the internal temperature registers 135°F. Use an instant-reading thermome-ter for accuracy. Keep feeding the fire as the roast cooks, raking the coals forward as the ones in front die down. Remove the pork from the fire, cover loosely with foil, and let rest in a warm place for 20 minutes before carving. (During the 20-minute rest the internal temperature will rise to at least 140°F.) To serve, remove the strings and cut crosswise between the ribs, carving the roast into chops. Serve each chop with a dollop of the warm marmalade.

Serves 6.

Note: If you don't have a way to roast the loin on a spit, roast it in a 375°F. oven for about 1½ hours, until the internal temperature registers 135°F.

Cabbage Salad with Apples and Walnuts

1 small savoy cabbage
⅓ cup walnuts
2 tablespoons cider vinegar
1 tablespoon lemon juice
Salt and pepper
½ cup olive oil

2 tablespoons crème fraîche or
   heavy cream
2 apples (any crisp, tasty eating
   variety, such as Sierra Beauty,
   Granny Smith, or Fuji)

Preheat the oven to 375°F.

Tear off and discard the tough outer leaves of the cabbage. Cut it in half and cut out its core. Slice the halves crosswise into a fine chiffonade.

Toast the walnuts in the oven for 8 minutes. While they are still warm, first rub them in a clean dishtowel to remove some of the skins, then chop or coarsely crumble them.

To prepare the dressing, mix the vinegar with the lemon juice, some salt, and a generous amount of pepper. Whisk in the olive oil and then the crème fraîche or cream. Taste and adjust the acid and salt as desired.

Quarter, peel, and core the apples. Slice the quarters lengthwise fairly thin and cut these slices lengthwise into a julienne. Toss the cabbage, apples, and walnuts with the dressing and an extra pinch of salt. Let the salad sit for 5 minutes, taste again, adjust the seasoning as needed, and serve.

Serves 6.

Poulet à la Normande

This simple supper dish from the Norman countryside is one of those French classics that we tried to make over and over in the earliest days of the restaurant. It wasn't until years later that we understood what a great dish it can actually be. What made the difference? The chickens. To be great, dishes like this one have to be made with organically fed, free-ranging, flavorful chickens—like the ones we get from the Hoffman family farm in the Central Valley.

1 chicken (about 3½ pounds)	*1 cup chicken stock*
Salt and pepper	*1 cup crème fraîche*
2 onions	
2 carrots	GARNISH
2 tablespoons unsalted butter	*30 pearl onions*
2 tablespoons pure olive oil	*4 tablespoons (½ stick)*
3 sprigs thyme	* unsalted butter*
1 bay leaf	*Salt and pepper*
½ cup Calvados	*2 or 3 medium apples*
1 cup dry hard cider	

Cut the chicken into 8 pieces. First remove the legs and cut them into thighs and drumsticks. Next cut off the wing tips, leaving the rest of the wings attached to the breast. Then cut the breast off the backbone and divide it in half down the middle of the breastbone. Finally, cut each breast piece in half diagonally, making the piece with the wing a bit smaller than the other. Save the backbone and wing tips for stock. Season the chicken well with salt and pepper. This can be done a day ahead if the chicken is then covered and kept in the refrigerator.

Peel and dice the onions and carrots.

In a heavy-bottomed pot, melt the butter with the olive oil over medium heat. When hot, add the chicken pieces, skin side down, and brown well on all sides. Do this in batches, if necessary. When all the chicken pieces are golden brown, remove them from the pan and set aside.

Pour off most of the fat left in the pan, add the diced carrots and onions and the thyme sprig and bay leaf, and cook until the onion is translucent, about 5 minutes. Pour in the Calvados and warm before igniting carefully—it will flame up, so stand back while doing this. When the Calvados has finished burning, add the cider, stirring and scraping up any brown bits still sticking to the pan. Bring to a boil and reduce by half. Pour in the chicken stock, return the chicken pieces to the pan, and turn down the heat. Simmer, covered, for 15 minutes. Remove the breast pieces and cook the legs and thighs another 15 minutes. When the chicken pieces are done, remove them to a dish and keep covered in a warm place while you finish the sauce.

While the chicken is cooking, start to prepare the garnish. Soak the pearl onions in warm water for a few minutes before peeling them; their skins will come off much more easily.

Melt 2 tablespoons of the butter in a heavy-bottomed pan and add the peeled onions with a pinch of salt. Cook over low heat, tightly covered, until tender and translucent, about 20 minutes. Shake or stir them now and then and add a touch of water if they are threatening to burn.

Peel and core the apples and slice each one into 8 wedges. Melt the rest of the butter in a sauté pan over medium-high heat. Add the apples, season with salt and pepper, and cook for about 10 minutes, tossing them now and then, until they are golden and tender.

Strain the Calvados sauce, pressing on the vegetables to extract all the liquid, and pour it back in the pan. Skim well and bring to a boil. Pour in the juices that have collected in the dish holding the chicken pieces; stir in the crème fraîche. Reduce the heat and simmer until the sauce is reduced by a third or until it coats the spoon. Taste and adjust the seasoning as needed. Return the chicken to the sauce to warm through.

Serve the chicken in its sauce, garnished with the apples and onions —reheated, if necessary, either together or separately.

Serves 4.

Sautéed Duck Foie Gras with Caramelized Apples

Eating the fattened livers of overfed ducks or geese is an expensive extravagance that can be justified only for very special occasions. What's more, to the best of our knowledge, even here in northern California there exists no local, certified organic source for them. The best ones come to us from France, thanks to the southwestern French connections of our longtime chef Jean-Pierre Moullé. For a recent cooking demonstration, Jean-Pierre was even able to produce a foie gras still in the duck's abdomen, and I thought immediately of the passage in *Simple French Food* in which Richard Olney relates how he "once listened in amazement to a Périgord farmwife describing—in what was intended to be a vehement denial that the raising of geese destined to produce foie gras involves cruelty to animals—the tenderness and gentleness with which the birds are treated and, with mounting enthusiasm and in the most extraordinarily sensuous language, the suspense and the excitement experienced as the moment arrives to delicately slit the abdomen, to lovingly—ever so gently—pry it open, exposing finally the huge, glorious, and tender blond treasure, fragile object of so many months' solicitous care and of present adoration. One sensed vividly the goose's plenary participation, actively sharing in the orgasmic beauty of the sublime moment for which her life had been lived."

1 fresh duck foie gras (about 1 pound)	*¼ cup Sauternes or other sweet white wine*
Salt and pepper	*3 tablespoons unsalted butter*
3 apples (Sierra Beauties, Granny Smiths, Cox's Orange Pippins, etc.)	*3 tablespoons Armagnac*
	¼ cup chicken stock
	8 thin slices bread (preferably pain de mie)

Separate the two lobes of the foie gras. Scrape off any green bile and cut away any veins from the area where the two lobes were joined. Cut into ½-inch-thick slices. Season with salt and pepper and refrigerate while you prepare the apples.

Peel and core the apples. Cut into 8 wedges, season with salt and pepper, and toss with the Sauternes. Let the apples marinate for 10 minutes.

Preheat the oven to 350°F.

Heat the butter in a heavy sauté pan over medium-high heat, add the apples, and cook for 10 minutes, tossing frequently; the apples should turn golden and tender. Pour in the Armagnac and warm before igniting carefully—it will flame up, so stand back while doing this. When the Armagnac has finished burning, add the chicken stock, stirring and scraping up any brown bits still sticking to the pan. When the sauce returns to a boil, remove from the heat. There should be just enough juice to create a slight sauce with the apples. Keep warm while you make the toast and cook the liver.

Cut off the crusts from the bread and cut each slice in half diagonally. Place on a baking sheet and cook in the preheated oven until crisp but not golden, about 8 minutes. Keep warm, covered with a towel.

Heat a heavy sauté pan till quite hot. Sauté the slices of foie gras over medium-high heat for 30 seconds on each side. The liver should be browning quickly but not burning; if the pan is too hot, lower the heat immediately. When done, the slices should be caramelized brown on the outside and soft to the touch. Remove from the pan and arrange on a plate; garnish with the apples and their sauce. Serve immediately with the warm toast.

Serves 8.

CALVADOS APPLE CUSTARD TART

1¾ pounds Sierra Beauty or
   Pippin apples
2 tablespoons unsalted butter
¼ cup plus 2 tablespoons
   granulated sugar
⅛ teaspoon ground cinnamon
5 tablespoons Calvados
1 prebaked 11-inch pâte sucrée
   shell (page 296)

2 egg yolks
2 tablespoons plus 2 teaspoons
   unbleached all-purpose flour
⅔ cup heavy cream
¼ teaspoon salt
Powdered sugar for dusting

Quarter, core, peel, and cut the apples into ¼-inch-thick slices. You should have about 5 cups.

Melt the butter in a large sauté pan over medium heat. Add the apples, 2 tablespoons granulated sugar, and the cinnamon and cook for 12 minutes, until the apples are tender. Add 2 tablespoons Calvados and warm before igniting carefully—it will flame up, so stand back while doing this. Once the fire has burned out, arrange the cooked apples evenly in the bottom of the prebaked tart shell.

Preheat the oven to 350°F.

In a mixing bowl, beat the egg yolks and ¼ cup granulated sugar until the mixture is pale yellow and forms a thick ribbon when dropped from the beater. Add the flour, cream, 3 tablespoons Calvados, and salt. Whip this mixture until it is thick and holds soft peaks. Drizzle the custard over the apples and spread evenly over the top. Bake for 15 minutes; dust the top with powdered sugar. Bake the tart another 10 minutes or so, until the top is golden brown. Let cool ½ hour before serving.

Serves 9.

Variation: Don't use quite as many apple slices, and after you've spread the custard over them, evenly scatter a handful of fresh raspberries on the surface and press them down slightly into the custard.

Apple Paste

Fruit pastes are nothing but puréed sweetened fruit that is cooked and reduced to a jellied paste—firmer than jam. Our favorite apples for apple paste are McIntosh and Pink Pearl, but we have used many other kinds successfully. We serve this in thin slices with sheep's-milk cheese or as a post-dessert candy.

3 pounds apples (about 8 medium)
1½ cups sugar plus more for tossing
Juice of 1 lemon

Wash the apples, quarter them, and cut them into 1-inch chunks; they don't need to be peeled or cored. Put the apples in a medium-size heavy-bottomed pot and add water to a depth of about ¼ inch. Cover and cook the apples over medium heat, stirring occasionally, until the fruit is soft and starting to break down, about 15 minutes. Pass the mixture through a food mill or sieve.

Return the purée to the pot and add the sugar. Simmer over low heat, stirring constantly, for about 1 hour, cooking the mixture into a paste. The mixture should be thick and hold a mounding shape; large bubbles should appear. If the mixture starts to stick to the pan before the texture is right, turn off the heat and let it rest for a few minutes before stirring again; when you do, the part sticking to the bottom will release. When the mixture is cooked to the right consistency, stir in the lemon juice and remove from the heat.

Line a shallow pan measuring at least 8 by 10 inches with parchment paper. Lightly oil the paper with light vegetable or almond oil. Pour the paste onto the paper-lined pan, spreading it into an 8- by 10-inch rectangle, about ¼ inch thick. When it has cooled completely, invert the sheet of paste onto another piece of parchment paper. Carefully peel off the upper, oiled parchment paper. Let the paste dry uncovered overnight. (If it is not firm enough to cut at this point, try drying it out in the oven for an hour at 150°F. or the lowest setting.) Once the paste is firm and cool, cut it into 1-inch-square pieces. Store uncovered in a dry place. Just before serving, toss the pieces to coat them with sugar. Keeps for 1 week.

Makes eighty 1-inch-square pieces.

Pink Pearl Apple Galette

People gasp when they see this beautiful tart because the pink blush of the apples is so unexpected and beguiling.

10 ounces galette dough (page 290), rolled into a 14-inch circle
2½ pounds Pink Pearl apples, quartered, peeled, and cored (peels and cores reserved)

2 tablespoons unsalted butter, melted
½ cup plus 5 tablespoons sugar

Preheat the oven to 400°F. Place a pizza stone, if you have one, on the center rack.

Remove the galette dough from the freezer or refrigerator and place on a buttered or parchment-lined baking sheet or aluminum pizza pan.

Slice the apples ¼ inch thick. At the outer edge of the tart shell, arrange apple slices in a slightly overlapping ring 1½ inches in from the edge of the dough. Working inward, arrange the remaining apples in tightly overlapping concentric circles, each smaller than the one before, until you reach the center. Rotate the tart while twisting and folding the overhanging dough over onto itself at regular 1-inch intervals, crimping and nudging the folded dough up against the apples and containing them within a border that resembles a length of rope. Gently brush the melted butter over the apple slices and onto the dough border. Evenly sprinkle 2 tablespoons of sugar over the buttered pastry edge and another 3 tablespoons sugar evenly over the apples.

Bake in the center of the oven (preferably on a pizza stone). Rotate the tart after 15 to 20 minutes and once or twice more as it finishes baking, to ensure even browning of the crust. Bake about 45 minutes in all, until the apples are soft, their edges have browned a bit, and the crust has caramelized to a dark golden brown. Remove the galette from the oven and carefully slide it off the parchment directly onto a cooling rack. Let cool at least 15 minutes before glazing and slicing.

Make the glaze while the tart is baking: Put the reserved apple peels and cores and the remaining ½ cup sugar in a saucepan, pour in just enough water to cover, and simmer for about 25 minutes. Strain the syrup and brush it gently over the finished tart before serving.

Serves 8.

Variation: Serve the galette with a simple huckleberry sauce: Gently heat about 1 cup huckleberries with a little sugar and a splash of water until the berries are soft and juicy. Pass them through a food mill to strain out the seeds and pour a little warm purée over each slice of tart.

GREEN APPLE SHERBET

You need a motorized juicer-extractor and an ice cream maker in order to make this refreshing sherbet, but if you have these machines, this is quick and easy to make. We serve apple sherbet with apple tart or with simple butter cookies. Granny Smith is the apple of choice, but don't hesitate to try it with any good similar variety. The secret is to work quickly—otherwise, you'll end up with brown apple sherbet. Have all your equipment and ingredients ready before you begin cutting the apples.

½ cup sugar　　　　　　　　　*5 pounds Granny Smith apples*
¼ cup water　　　　　　　　　*1 teaspoon lemon juice*
1 egg white

Measure the sugar and water into a small saucepan and stir together over low heat to dissolve the sugar.

Whisk the egg white in a bowl until light and fluffy.

Cut the apples into chunks, removing the cores and pushing the apple chunks through a juice extractor as you go. Quickly whisk together the apple purée, sugar syrup, egg white, and lemon juice. It's okay if the egg white rises to the top; it will be incorporated as the sherbet is frozen. Freeze following the instructions for your ice cream maker.

Makes 1 quart.

APRICOTS &

Season: Late spring through midsummer

The apricot is a prime example of a fruit that has come close to being ruined in the name of "improvement." As recently as the 1950s, fresh apricots had only a brief, fleeting season, in June and July; the rest of the year they could be enjoyed in preserved form: canned, dried, or in jam. But demand for fresh apricots, often the first "soft" fruit of summer, created a powerful incentive for growers and shippers to favor early-maturing varieties, and as too often happens when plant breeders select for only one quality, other virtues were left by the wayside. In their rush to be first to the market, growers chose varieties for neither color, aroma, sweetness, nor flavor, and the apricots that now flood the markets in late spring are usually pale, odorless, tart, and watery. Buy one and prepare to be disappointed. Consumers might reasonably be expected to give up on fresh apricots altogether, and indeed, this seems to be happening: California, which produces the vast majority of apricots in the United States, has seen its apricot orchard acreage decline 30 percent in the last twenty-five years. Inferior varieties predominate, particularly those that were heavily planted in the 1960s. Many of the best of the old apricot varieties have been ripped out or survive only in abandoned orchards.

The apricot was probably cultivated first in China thousands of years ago and spread west from there. Apricots are widely grown today in Turkey, Iran, Afghanistan, and elsewhere in the Middle East, and are used frequently in savory cooking, especially with lamb. As its Latin name, *Prunus armeniaca*, suggests, the fruit was probably introduced into the region of the Mediterranean by way of Armenia. The Spanish in turn brought apricots to the New World and planted them in the mission gardens of California. However, the Blenheim apricot, which was until recently the variety most widely planted here and which many experts regard as the best of all California apricots, comes from England.

The Blenheim apricot was first found in the 1830s in the Duke of Marlborough's gardens at Blenheim Palace. It has medium-size fruit with orange-colored skin and deep yellow flesh that is fragrant, juicy, and richly flavored. Because they have a certain density of texture, Blenheims are perfect for cooking, drying, and preserving. They ripen in early summer and are usually available from late June into July. Even among experts there is much confusion over whether the Royal apricot is exactly the same variety as the Blenheim or a nearly identical clone. Don't worry; by either name it is about the tastiest apricot that can be found. Some growers dodge the issue and label their fruit "Royal Blenheims."

Two other fine varieties ripen a little later than the Blenheim. The Moorpark is a large apricot with a beautiful orange-red blush on its cheeks and deep orange flesh that is juicy and sweet. This delicious variety has lost popularity because it sometimes has green shoulders even when completely ripe. The Tilton apricot, which comes to market in mid-July, was bred in California early in the twentieth century. The trees bear medium-size, fragrant, golden-yellow fruit with a lovely red blush. Try not to be tempted by the early varieties. The Castlebright, for example, never gets really sweet and tends to be watery when cooked.

Whether they are to be eaten fresh, cooked, or preserved, apricots must be allowed to ripen on the tree: they do not improve in flavor after they are picked. At the market, choose organically grown fruit that is plump and fragrant and that gives just a little when gently squeezed. Avoid apricots that feel hard and look pale or greenish; they will never ripen properly. Likewise, shun fruit that feels soft and mushy and fruit that has dark spots or mold.

Ripe apricots that are a little too firm improve in texture if they are stored in a single layer at room temperature for a day or two. Once they start to soften, keep them loosely wrapped in the refrigerator. Apricots seldom need peeling, a difficult project in any case, but they should be washed carefully just before using. To prepare for cooking, cut the fruit in half, using as a guide the "suture" that runs from the stem end to the tip of the fruit, and gently twist the halves apart. Remove and save the pit so that later you can extract its kernel, or *noyau*. Once pitted, apricots can be puréed and frozen into sherbet or ice cream; baked into tarts, pies, or cobblers; cooked down for jam; or preserved by drying.

Apricots preserved by canning are better left unpitted because their flesh absorbs a delicate hint of bitter almond flavor from the kernels inside, the *noyaux*, which also bestow their characteristic flavor on amaretti cookies, liqueurs, ice creams, and custards. To extract the kernels, first roast the pits in a 350°F. oven for ten to fifteen minutes: this makes them easier to crack open and also destroys an enzyme that generates poisonous prussic acid when noyaux are mixed with water. Use a nutcracker, or place the pits on a hard surface and tap with a hammer. To be absolutely sure the noyaux are safe to eat, roast them again for a few minutes after they have been extracted.

MIDDLE EASTERN–STYLE LAMB STEW WITH DRIED APRICOTS

½ pound dried apricots
2½ pounds lamb shoulder,
   cut into 2-inch cubes
Salt and pepper
Olive oil
2 onions, chopped

1 tablespoon plus 1 teaspoon
   finely chopped ginger
1 teaspoon ground coriander
1 teaspoon ground cinnamon
¼ teaspoon saffron
Optional: 1 teaspoon rose water

Soak the apricots in warm water for an hour or so while you prepare the rest of the stew. Season the lamb well with salt and pepper. Put a heavy-bottomed pan over medium-high heat and pour in enough olive oil to generously coat the bottom of the pan. Add the lamb and brown on all sides, working in batches, if necessary. Remove the meat and pour off and discard most of the fat. Cook the onions in the remaining fat until softened, about 7 minutes.

Put the meat back in the pan with the onions, stir in the spices well, and cook for 4 minutes. Add enough water to come just to the top of the meat and bring to a boil, skimming any foam that rises to the top. Turn the heat down to a simmer, cover, and cook for ½ hour.

While the lamb is cooking, drain the apricots, reserving the liquid, and chop them coarsely. Add the apricots to the meat and simmer, partially covered, for another hour or more, until the lamb is tender. Stir now and then, checking the level of the liquid and adding some of the reserved apricot soaking liquid if the stew is drying out and threatening to burn. When the lamb is tender, skim the fat from the stew, taste for salt, and adjust as needed. Add the rose water, if you wish. Serve with plain rice or a simple rice pilaf.

Serves 6.

LULU'S APRICOT COMPOTE WITH GREEN ALMONDS

This dessert was inspired by Lulu Peyraud, the matriarch of the Domaine Tempiêr; we love it for its simplicity. Use apricots that are ripe but still firm enough to hold their shape after poaching. Green almonds are simply immature almonds still in their fuzzy green skins; they are available only in the spring before the shell hardens. They have an indescribably delicate crunchy texture and a clean, mild almond flavor.

*1 pound fresh apricots, halved,
  pitted, and cut in quarters
2¼ cups plus 3 tablespoons sugar
½ pound green almonds
  (about 12)*

*1½ cups water
One 2-inch piece vanilla bean*

Toss the quartered apricots gently with 3 tablespoons sugar and set aside to macerate for about 1 hour.

With a small knife, cut the green almonds along the crease, then twist to open. Pop out the kernel inside, and using the knife and your fingers, peel away the white skin to reveal an even whiter kernel. Collect all the green almonds in a bowl and discard all the scraps. Cut the almonds into slivers and set aside, covered with a damp towel, until ready to serve.

Stir together 2¼ cups sugar and 1½ cups water in a medium-size nonreactive saucepan. Split the piece of vanilla bean lengthwise and scrape out the seeds into the saucepan, reserving the pods for another use. Bring the mixture to a full boil, stirring frequently to dissolve the sugar and break up the bits of vanilla seeds. Reduce the heat to a simmer, add the apricots, and poach them in the syrup for about 5 minutes, until very tender when pierced with the tip of a sharp knife. Remove from the syrup and let cool. Divide the apricots among 4 dessert plates, spoon a few tablespoons of the vanilla syrup over each serving, and sprinkle the slivered green almonds on top.

Serves 4.

APRICOT SOUFFLÉS

An apricot soufflé was one of the first recipes I ever published, over thirty years ago, before Chez Panisse even existed. It appeared on a broadside designed and printed by my friend David Goines, who illustrated it with a little woodcut of a single perfect apricot. David recycled the picture for our New Year's menu just a few years ago, and here is the recycled recipe, reinvented by Samantha Wood.

⅓ cup finely chopped dried apricots (recipe follows)
¼ cup plus 1 tablespoon granulated sugar plus more for coating the ramekins and sprinkling on top
1 teaspoon kirsch
⅓ cup water
1 tablespoon unsalted butter, melted and cooled slightly
½ cup bitter almond–flavored pastry cream (page 302)

½ cup apricot jam (page 25), puréed in a blender or food processor
1 cup egg whites (7 or 8 eggs, depending on their size), room temperature
1 tablespoon cornstarch
1 pinch salt
¼ teaspoon cream of tartar
Powdered sugar for dusting

Put the chopped apricots in a small saucepan with 1 tablespoon sugar, the kirsch, and water. Simmer for a few minutes to plump the fruit; strain, discarding the liquid, and set aside.

Preheat the oven to 450°F.

Brush the insides of eight 5-ounce ramekins with the melted butter, leaving a generous lip of butter around the inner rim. Pour in some granulated sugar, coating the insides, and tap out any excess. Touch up any uncovered spots with more melted butter and sugar. Set the ramekins aside on a baking sheet.

In a large mixing bowl, stir together the pastry cream, jam, and chopped apricots with a large rubber spatula.

In another clean, dry mixing bowl, whisk the egg whites until frothy. Add the cornstarch, salt, and cream of tartar and beat until the whites are fluffy and hold soft peaks. Add ¼ cup sugar and keep whisking until the peaks are firm and glossy, but not dry. Gently fold the whites into the pastry cream, deflating the whites as little as possible.

Spoon the soufflé mixture into the prepared ramekins, filling them to the brim, just to the lip of butter. Sprinkle the tops with a thin layer of granulated sugar. Drag your finger around the top and outer edge of the rim of each ramekin to clean off any splattered excess soufflé mixture; this ensures that the soufflés will rise straight up ½ inch or more without sticking to the sides.

Bake for 8 to 9 minutes, until the soufflés are tall, golden on top, and still slightly soft to the touch in the center. Remove the baking sheet from the oven and dust the tops of the soufflés with powdered sugar. Serve immediately, on individual plates lined with napkins or doilies (to keep the ramekins from sliding around).

Serves 8.

Variation: Use pulverized amaretti cookies (page 297) instead of sugar for coating the insides of the ramekins and for sprinkling on top before baking.

DRIED APRICOTS

There should be a term that describes organic fruit dried on a small scale at home—"fresh-dried," perhaps—because such fruit has distinctive qualities: it is unsulfured, bright-tasting, and colorful. We found that unsliced apricot halves turn brown in the time it takes them to dry, and now we get the best results when we cut the fruit in half, remove the pits (saving them for noyaux), and slice the apricots before drying. The slices should be a little thicker than ¼ inch. Arrange them on the racks of a dehydrator, not touching one another, and dry for 5 to 6 hours at 140°F. (Peaches, nectarines, apples, and persimmons can all be dried this way.) We usually rehydrate apricots by simmering them gently in syrup that is three parts water and one part sugar. Once rehydrated, they can be added to compotes or puréed for sauce.

APRICOT GALETTE

I love the open-face apricot tarts in French *pâtisseries* that look like they've been baked in a wood oven: the fruit has been cut in quarters and arranged with the pointy ends sticking up so they get nice and caramelized. Even more beautiful are the tarts to which a handful of pitted ripe sour cherries has been added, a practice we follow at the restaurant during the brief moment when fresh cherries and apricots are available at the same time.

10 ounces galette dough
   (page 290), rolled into a
   14-inch circle and chilled
¼ cup almond-amaretti powder
   (page 298)
1½ pounds ripe apricots

¼ cup plus 2 tablespoons sugar
1 tablespoon unsalted butter,
   melted
Optional: Apricot jam
Optional: Vanilla ice cream
   (page 301)

Preheat the oven to 400°F. Place a pizza stone, if you have one, on a lower rack.

Remove the prerolled dough from the refrigerator or freezer and place on a buttered or parchment-lined baking sheet. Evenly sprinkle the almond-amaretti powder over the pastry, leaving a 1½-inch border unsprinkled. Cut the apricots in half (in quarters if they are large), removing the pits. Arrange the fruit, skin side down, in concentric circles on the dusted dough, making a single layer of snugly touching apricot pieces and leaving the border bare. Evenly sprinkle ¼ cup sugar over the fruit.

While rotating the tart, fold the border of exposed dough up and over itself at regular intervals, crimping and pushing it up against the outer circle of fruit, creating a containing rim that resembles a length of rope. Pinch off any excess dough. This rim must act as a dam, preventing juices from escaping while cooking, so make sure there are no folds or wrinkles that would permit such a breach. Brush the border gently with melted butter and sprinkle it with 2 tablespoons sugar.

Bake in the lower third of the oven (preferably on a pizza stone) for about 45 to 50 minutes, until the crust is well browned and its edges are slightly caramelized. As soon as the galette is out of the oven, use a large metal spatula to slide it off the baking sheet or parchment paper and onto a cooling rack. This keeps it from steaming and getting soggy. Let cool for 20 minutes.

If you want to glaze the tart, brush the fruit lightly with a little warmed apricot jam. Serve warm, with vanilla ice cream, if you like.

Makes one 12-inch tart; serves 8.

APRICOT JAM

Our apricot jam is sandwiched between cookies and between the layers of almond cakes, heated and brushed on baked galettes as a glaze, puréed and swirled into soufflés, and spread on tart shells as a filling.

*2½ pounds apricots, pitted
and cut into ½-inch pieces
(about 6 cups)
3 cups sugar*

*Optional: A few apricot kernels
(noyaux, see page 19)
Juice of 1 lemon*

Stir the diced apricots and sugar together in a large heavy-bottomed nonreactive pot. Let the mixture stand at least 30 minutes (or overnight) so the apricots release their juices and the sugar dissolves. For bitter almond-flavored apricot jam, crack open a few apricot pits with a hammer, remove the kernels, chop them up, and add to the fruit and sugar. (These kernels are very strong, so use no more then 10 for a batch this size.) Put a small plate in the freezer to use later to test the consistency of the jam.

Prepare four 8-ounce canning jars and self-sealing lids in boiling water, following the manufacturer's instructions.

Bring the pot of fruit to a boil over high heat, stirring occasionally to make sure it isn't sticking to the bottom. The mixture will bubble up dramatically, rising high up the sides of the pot. Skim off any light-colored foam that rises and collects on the sides. Soon the jam will boil down, forming smaller, thicker bubbles. At this point, start testing for consistency by putting a small spoonful of the jam on the plate. This will cool off the jam sample quickly so you can tell what the finished texture will be like. When the jam has cooked to the thickness you want, stir in the lemon juice. Turn off the heat and carefully ladle the jam into the prepared canning jars, allowing at least ¼ inch of headroom. Seal, following the manufacturer's instructions. The jam will keep for about a year.

Makes 4 cups.

Apricot Hazelnut Tart

This tart is best served in thin wedges, with tea. We usually use apricot jam for the filling, but we've had delicious results with raspberry jam and kumquat marmalade too. This same nutty dough can also be rolled out and cut into rounds for jam cookie sandwiches.

10 tablespoons (1¼ sticks) unsalted butter, room temperature	1 teaspoon vanilla extract
	1 teaspoon orange liqueur (such as Grand Marnier)
¾ cup brown sugar, firmly packed	1½ cups unbleached all-purpose flour
2 egg yolks	2 cups hazelnuts, pulverized
½ teaspoon salt	2 cups apricot jam
1 teaspoon grated orange zest	Powdered sugar for dusting

Cream together the butter and brown sugar in a medium-size mixing bowl. Add the egg yolks and beat until thoroughly combined. Stir in the salt, orange zest, vanilla, and orange liqueur. Add the flour and nuts, mixing just until incorporated. Divide the dough into 2 equal pieces. Press one piece into a 4-inch disk and refrigerate.

Preheat the oven to 350°F.

Press the other piece of dough into the bottom of an 11-inch fluted tart shell, using your fingers and the heel of your hand. The bottom and sides of the tart shell should be covered with an even layer of dough a little less than ¼ inch thick; pinch off any excess. Let the shell chill in the freezer for 10 minutes, then bake on the center rack of the oven for 17 minutes, until golden. Remove the shell from the oven and spread it evenly with the jam.

Place the refrigerated disk of dough on a lightly floured piece of parchment paper. Dust the top lightly with flour and roll the disk into a 12-inch circle, a little less than ¼ inch thick. Cut the circle into ½-inch-wide strips. Arrange half the strips on top of the tart, about ½ inch apart. Arrange the rest of the strips crisscross over the others, making a lattice. Trim off the overhanging strips at the rim of the tart pan. With the dough scraps, make a thin layer of dough around the edge of the tart to cover the prebaked rim. Bake for ½ hour, until golden. Allow the tart to cool completely, dust it with powdered sugar, and serve, sliced in thin wedges.

Makes one 11-inch tart; serves 12.

BANANAS 🍌

Season: Year-round

Bananas are one of the immutable givens of modern life: the most popular fruit in North America and a constant presence in the produce market. But bananas have been changing over the last few decades in subtle and not-so-subtle ways. For one thing, organically grown bananas are probably easier to find than any other kind of organically grown fruit.

The banana exporters' longtime most-favored variety, the thick-skinned, long, tapering Gros Michel, proved susceptible to disease and has disappeared from market shelves. It has been quietly replaced by the Cavendish, a somewhat shorter, blunt-ended banana that is more resistant to diseases and insects and less vulnerable to wind damage—albeit thinner-skinned and more prone to bruising. The Cavendish and its close relatives are now the principal varieties sold in the United States.

A more noticeable change is that many unfamiliar-looking bananas are now coming to market. The most popular dessert banana in Latin America, the stubby Manzano, or apple banana, can often be found in Latin markets and specialty produce stores. There you may also see red or yellow bananas with evocative names like Lady Finger and Ice Cream. And you can often find plantains, a potato-like staple in many tropical countries. These starchy banana relatives are usually cooked before they are eaten—either steamed, fried, or boiled.

Bananas and plantains belong to the genus *Musa,* and all cultivated varieties are hybrids of several wild species native to southern India and Southeast Asia. Bananas have become an important staple food crop in tropical countries wherever growing conditions permit, often grown by small farmers for local consumption. Throughout the tropics, huge companies grow most of the bananas for export on large plantations. In their efforts to fight weeds, insects, and diseases, many of these growers have depended on the heavy use of chemicals, showing little regard for the health of their workers or the environment.

Even so, an increasing number of small growers are practicing sustainable agriculture, working with nature rather than against it. There are healthy small communities in the Caribbean and Latin America where growers have organized to export organically grown bananas to the United States and Europe. In Costa Rica organic growers plant bananas alongside tropical fruits, cacao trees, and other food crops, simulating the diversity of the surrounding rain forest and encouraging the work of beneficial insects. In the Caribbean small landowners are successfully avoiding the use of chemicals and protecting the developing fruit from damage by carefully pruning and clearing away dead leaves from around the plants and keeping the soil healthy with additions of compost.

Following the lead of the organic banana producers, and in response to constant pressure from environmental groups, the big commercial banana companies have started working to reduce the amounts of chemicals used on their plantations. One company that is responsible for fully one-quarter of the world's banana production has already agreed to cut its use of chemicals by adopting the standards set by the Better Banana Project.

Bananas are picked and shipped when they are grass green. Over a period of weeks they slowly ripen as some of their starch changes to sugar. They are usually put out for sale still slightly green, when they are less susceptible to bruising. Leaving them for several days at room temperature, uncovered, will finish the ripening at home. Ripe bananas are yellow from stem to tip, with no green showing. This is the right stage for cooking, but for eating out of hand, wait a day or two longer, when brown flecks appear on the skin, an indication of higher sugar content and the best flavor.

The banana you are most likely to encounter, the Cavendish, is also one of the more fragile kinds, with a soft, smooth texture and a thin peel. At the market, avoid those with dark areas showing through the skin, indicating bruising. Also avoid bananas with split skin or moldy stems. And handle them gently at the store and at home.

Apple bananas come in small bunches. The individual fruit are short, about four inches long, and thicker than other bananas, with three distinct sides to each fruit. Ripe apple bananas are only mildly acidic and have a lovely apple-like flavor, but they are unpleasantly tannic when unripe, so be sure to give them plenty of time to ripen; they are best when almost black. They are delicious cooked, when their flavor becomes more intense, but they can become mushy if overcooked.

Red bananas are typically dark green and maroon when unripe and become more orange or bronze as they ripen, but the most reliable test of ripeness is the squeeze test. If a banana gives when it is pressed gently, it is probably ripe. In any event, the flesh of red bananas is firmer than the flesh of regular bananas, and it has an exotic floral aroma and pale ivory salmon color. Red bananas can be eaten raw or cooked.

Plantains are usually larger and thicker than regular bananas, and have clearly tapered ends. The tough green peel turns black as the fruit ripens, but plantains can be cooked at any stage, from green to brown to black. Riper ones are sweeter, but even the ripest are starchier than regular bananas. Some plantains are sweet and tender enough to be eaten raw, but most are prepared in the same ways potatoes usually are: peeled, cut up, and boiled or added to stews; steamed and mashed with butter or olive oil; or sliced and fried or deep-fried.

Fried Plantains

Plantains are fried and enjoyed as a starchy side dish throughout the Caribbean and Latin America and in parts of Africa. They are best fried in one of two ways, depending on the ripeness of the fruit. Plan on half a large plantain per person. The skin of ripe fruit is very brown, bordering on black, and the flesh is beginning to get soft and sweet. When the fruit is this ripe, it can be peeled easily, cut into ¼-inch-thick slices, and fried on each side in just a touch of oil until brown.

When the skin is yellow with brown freckles, the fruit is on its way to being ripe but is not there yet. To fry plantains like these, first peel them—which is not as easy as you might expect. Cut off the ends and cut the plantain in half crosswise. Next, slice through the skin of the fruit lengthwise and pry it away from the flesh. Once the fruit is peeled, cut it into ½-inch-thick slices on the diagonal. Heat a good amount of oil, to a depth of about 1 inch, or enough to cover the fruit while it is cooking. When the oil is hot, add the plantain slices in batches and fry them until they are just turning golden. Transfer them to absorbent paper and let them cool. Then place them between two sheets of parchment or wax paper and, with the bottom of a heavy glass, smash them into even disks. Return these disks to the hot oil and fry them until they are a deep golden brown. Drain well on absorbent paper and sprinkle with salt. Serve while still warm.

Caramelized Red Banana Tartlets

¾ *cup sugar*
¼ *cup water*
¼ *cup rum*
1½ *cups pastry cream (page 302)*

4 ripe red bananas
6 prebaked 4-inch pâte sucrée
   tartlet shells (page 296)

Measure the sugar and water into a small saucepan. Prepare an ice water bath into which you can plunge the bottom of the saucepan to cool it down fast. Place the saucepan over high heat. Cook until the sugar starts to turn a light gold color and is smoking a bit, swirling the pan occasionally to even out the cooking. When the caramel is amber-colored, remove the saucepan from the heat and put its bottom into the ice water bath. This will stop the cooking immediately. As it cools, the caramel will harden in the pan.

Stir 2 tablespoons of the rum into the pastry cream. Peel and slice the bananas a little less than ¼ inch thick.

To assemble the tartlets, remove the prebaked shells from their pans and place them on a cooling rack. Gently rewarm the caramel over low heat, letting it soften enough so that it forms threads when pulled with a fork, but not become so hot that it starts to burn again. Working close to the stove, use the fork to drizzle thin threads of caramel into the bottom of each tartlet, forming nest-like webs. If the caramel gets too thick to drizzle, return it to the heat; if it gets too hot, return it to the ice bath. Thick droplets of caramel will harden and be difficult to eat. If there are big droplets or too much caramel in a tartlet shell, let the caramel cool; the entire web will release easily and you can try again. Once all the tartlets are lined with a crisp, delicate web of caramel, arrange 3 overlapping slices of banana in the bottom of each shell. Fill each shell with ¼ cup of pastry cream and arrange about 6 more slices of banana on top. Thin out the remaining caramel with the rest of the rum and another ¼ cup water. Heat gently, stirring to blend the sauce. Transfer the tartlets to individual serving plates. Pour some of the rum caramel on top of the tartlets and drizzle a little on the plate as a sauce.

Serves 6.

BANANA FRITTERS WITH RUM HONEY SYRUP

The sprinkling of powdered sugar and drizzle of rum honey syrup notwithstanding, these surprisingly light fritters are not too sweet. The bananas must be perfectly ripe: underripe bananas lack depth of flavor, and overripe bananas become unpleasantly squishy when deep-fried this way.

FRITTERS
½ cup water
½ cup milk
¼ pound (1 stick) unsalted
   butter
1 teaspoon granulated sugar
1 pinch salt
½ cup unbleached
   all-purpose flour
½ cup cake flour
4 eggs

4 medium bananas
1 tablespoon rum
2 egg whites
¼ teaspoon cream of tartar
Peanut oil for frying
Powdered sugar for dusting

RUM HONEY SYRUP
¼ cup dark rum
¼ cup water
1 cup honey

Measure the water, milk, butter, sugar, and salt into a saucepan and bring to a boil. Combine the all-purpose and cake flour and add to the liquid all at once. Beat with a wooden spoon over medium heat until the mixture is smooth and pulls away clean from the bottom and sides of the pan. Remove from the heat and continue beating for a minute to release some of the steam before adding the eggs. Add the eggs one by one, beating each until well blended before adding the next. Transfer to a large mixing bowl and allow to cool.

Peel the bananas and cut them lengthwise into quarters. Cut the quarters crosswise into ½-inch-thick pieces. In a small bowl, drizzle the banana chunks with the rum and toss gently.

In a clean, dry mixing bowl, whisk the egg whites until frothy. Add the cream of tartar and beat until the whites are fluffy and hold soft peaks. Fold the egg whites into the cooled batter, a third at a time. Fold in the banana chunks.

Fill a saucepan or electric fryer at least 2 inches deep with oil and heat to 360°F. Carefully drop heaping teaspoons of batter-covered bananas into the hot oil and fry until golden brown. Don't attempt to fry more than 4 or 5 fritters at a time or the oil temperature will drop and the fritters will absorb too much oil. Drain on paper towels and sprinkle with powdered sugar on all sides. Serve hot with a generous drizzle of rum honey syrup.

To make the syrup, measure the rum, water, and honey into a saucepan and place over low heat just before you start frying the fritters. When the syrup is smooth and homogeneous, remove from the heat and cool briefly before drizzling over the fritters.

Serves 8.

Variation: We use this same dough to make apple fritters, substituting coarsely chopped apples and Calvados for the bananas and rum.

BANANA WAFFLES

2 cups unbleached all-purpose flour	*2 cups buttermilk*
2 teaspoons baking powder	*½ teaspoon vanilla extract*
½ teaspoon baking soda	*¼ pound (1 stick) unsalted butter, melted*
1 teaspoon salt	*4 bananas, peeled and sliced thin*
2 tablespoons sugar	
2 eggs	

Preheat the waffle iron.

Sift together into a large bowl the flour, baking powder, baking soda, salt, and sugar.

In another bowl, whisk together the eggs, buttermilk, and vanilla. Whisk most of the melted butter into the buttermilk mixture, reserving about 1½ tablespoons to use later.

Pour the buttermilk mixture over the flour mixture and stir just until the dry ingredients are moistened, leaving the mixture lumpy.

Before cooking each round of waffles, brush both sides of the waffle iron with the reserved melted butter. To make a waffle, ladle a thin layer of batter over the bottom of the iron, arrange a layer of banana slices about ½ inch apart on top, and ladle another thin layer of batter over the slices, creating a banana sandwich. Cook until crisp and golden. Serve hot, with maple syrup.

Serves 6.

BLACKBERRIES ❧

Season: Midsummer

Blackberries are the most local fruit we serve at Chez Panisse: a wild vine climbs over the fence behind the restaurant, and every August we pick the blackberries that ripen on our side. To us the word "blackberries" almost always means *wild* blackberries, and that is the fruit we discuss in this chapter. Boysenberries, loganberries, olallieberries, and the other cultivated blackberries are given a chapter of their own.

Hundreds of species of wild blackberries grow around North America, and there are many more throughout the world. Blackberries will sprout in almost any open, sunny spot, especially in areas where the natural vegetation has been disturbed by cultivation, fire, or the cutting of forests. The fruit is attractive to birds and mammals alike, and its seeds are widely dispersed in their droppings. Because so much land was cleared as our continent filled up with settlers, wild blackberries are now more widespread in the United States than when European settlement began.

Blackberries and their cultivated cousins are all members of the genus *Rubus,* in the rose family, and every blackberry blossom looks like a miniature wild rose. In the West most of the wild blackberries have long canes that trail along the ground, while eastern wild blackberries grow more upright. There are eleven wild species of blackberries in California alone, four of which were introduced from other places. The best of the native western blackberries, *R. ursinus,* has small, intensely flavorful fruit; its habitat ranges eastward from the Pacific coast up to the western slopes of the Sierra Nevada and Cascade Mountains, and from California north to British Columbia. As its Latin name, *ursinus,* suggests, it is irresistible to bears. More commonly found is *R. procerus,* the so-called Himalaya blackberry, misidentified and misnamed by Luther Burbank. (The real Himalaya blackberry is native to Germany, not Asia, and is larger and not as tasty as *R. procerus*.) Finally, the Evergreen blackberry of England, *R. lacianatus*, is widely planted commercially but has escaped from cultivation and established itself in the wild.

Almost everyone who lives outside the big cities knows where wild blackberries are growing nearby. My friends Susie and Mark have a wonderful place in Bolinas surrounded by wild blackberries, and when I go to visit them, we spend hours picking fruit and eating it. Blackberries are so invasive they can be a nuisance for farmers and gardeners; if you see them growing wild, you can usually get permission from the landowner to pick a few. Braving the thorns and tangles of the vines to get at the fruit can be an adventure, and if you can resist the urge to eat all you pick, you will have lovely berries to show for your efforts—as well as scratches and purple fingers.

The ripest wild blackberries—the ones that fall from the branch when given a gentle nudge—are the sweetest and best. Taste until you can judge ripeness by appearance. When you go picking, have a lot of containers handy and don't fill any too full, unless you are making jam right away, as ripe wild blackberries are very soft and easily damaged. A few markets and farm stands offer wild blackberries for sale. Be sure to inspect them closely; wild berries are very fragile and begin to break down soon after picking. Look for whole, plump, dark berries with a soft sheen. Berries with the "cap" still attached or whose color tends toward red will not be ripe. Also avoid those that look shriveled and dry. Check carefully for mold, which often starts in the stem end of the berry.

Once you get home, whether from field or market, you should try to use blackberries soon. If they are very fresh you can keep them for a day or two in the refrigerator, spread in a single layer on a paper-lined baking sheet. Pick out and discard any soft berries; they are likely to get moldy. Don't wash blackberries unless they are very dusty, and then only with a quick rinse of cold water just before using. Very ripe berries usually require a squeeze of lemon juice to perk up the flavor.

The peak of blackberry season comes in July and August, and their dusky flavor combines very nicely with other summer fruits, especially those with a little acid to balance the sweetness of the blackberries; try them, for example, in simple compotes with tart summer berries such as raspberries or mulberries. Peaches and blackberries are wonderful together: try making a variant peach Melba with blackberry sauce instead of raspberry, or combine peaches and blackberries in a tart, a crisp, or a cobbler. We particularly like the combination of blackberry and peach in a double-crusted crostata made with cornmeal dough. Later in the summer, blackberries contribute their texture and sweetness to tarts made with the first Gravenstein apples.

Peach and Blackberry Crostata

In Italy a *crostata* is something crusty. We use the term for all the tarts we bake using our cornmeal dough recipe.

1 prebaked 11-inch cornmeal
    tart shell (page 293)
1 tablespoon cornmeal
4 medium peaches
    (about 1½ pounds)
2 cups blackberries

3 tablespoons sugar plus extra
    for sprinkling
10 ounces cornmeal dough
    (page 293), rolled into a
    13-inch circle and refrigerated
1 egg yolk
2 tablespoons milk

Preheat the oven to 400°F.

Sprinkle the bottom of the prebaked tart shell with 1 tablespoon cornmeal. Peel, pit, and slice the peaches. Arrange the sliced peaches evenly in the tart shell. Scatter the blackberries over the peaches. Sprinkle the fruit with 3 tablespoons sugar.

Remove the circle of unbaked cornmeal dough from the refrigerator. Peel off the top sheet of parchment paper and invert the dough onto the fruit. Remove the other piece of parchment and let the dough settle over the fruit. Gently seal the tart by pressing around the outside edge of the dough.

Make an egg wash by mixing the egg yolk and milk and brush the top of the tart with it. Sprinkle with sugar (for extra crunch we use crystallized or raw sugar). Bake in the top third of the oven for 45 to 50 minutes, until the top is golden brown. Let cool for 10 minutes and serve warm with ice cream or crème fraîche.

Makes one 11-inch tart.

BLACKBERRY AND GRAVENSTEIN APPLE GALETTE

We bake this galette with a top crust to add the extra crunchy contrast we want when using an apple like the Gravenstein, which is very soft when baked. This pie is equally good for breakfast or dessert. If you don't find Gravenstein, try another tasty apple with a similar texture, such as a good McIntosh or a Jonathan.

Two 10-ounce pieces galette
   dough (page 290)
2 pounds Gravenstein apples
1 tablespoon flour

½ cup sugar
2 cups blackberries
3 tablespoons unsalted butter,
   melted

Roll out the galette dough into 2 circles about ⅛ inch thick, one with a diameter of about 14 inches, the other about 15 inches. Refrigerate the dough with parchment paper or plastic wrap separating the pieces. Quarter, peel, and core the apples, then slice them into ¼-inch wedges.

Preheat the oven to 400°F.

Remove the smaller dough circle from the refrigerator and lay it on a parchment paper–lined baking sheet. Mix together the flour and 1 tablespoon of the sugar and distribute evenly over the dough, spreading with your fingers and leaving a 1½-inch border at the edge uncovered. Spread the sliced apples evenly on top of the flour and sugar mixture, leaving the border bare, and scatter the blackberries over the apples. Sprinkle the fruit with most of the remaining sugar, saving about 3 tablespoons for later use. Brush the exposed edge of dough with melted butter and lay the second, larger piece of dough on top so that it blankets the entire tart. Use a small paring knife to trim away any excess overhanging dough. Gently press around the circumference to seal the top and bottom pieces of dough together, then work your away around the tart, folding over the layers of dough on themselves and crimping to make a sealed rim that resembles a length of rope. Cut 6 evenly spaced holes in the top of the galette so that steam can escape when it is baking. Brush the top with the remaining butter and sprinkle with the remaining sugar.

Bake until the top is brown and caramelized, about 1 hour 15 minutes. Check the tart about halfway through baking to make sure it is browning evenly; rotate if necessary. When done, remove the tart and slide it off the parchment directly onto a cooling rack. Let cool 15 minutes. Slice into wedges and serve warm, with vanilla ice cream.

Makes one 13-inch tart; serves 8.

BLACKBERRY JELLY

Excellent as a glaze for fresh berry tarts; irresistible on a peanut-butter-and-jelly sandwich. Blackberries don't have much pectin of their own, so we cook them with apple, which adds gelling power naturally.

6 cups ripe blackberries	*2 cups sugar*
1 apple	*Juice of 1 lemon*

Rinse the berries and pick over them, discarding any moldy ones. Put the berries in a large heavy-bottomed nonreactive pot. Chop the apple into ¼-inch pieces—skin, core, seeds, and all—and add to the pot. Cover with water to a depth of about ½ inch and slowly simmer this mixture (the "mash") for about 10 minutes over medium heat, crushing the berries with a potato masher or a wooden pestle until they all appear to have popped and released their juices.

Strain the mash through a jelly bag or very fine strainer into a clean glass bowl. If you want the jelly to be perfectly clear, let the mash sit in the strainer so that the juice drips out on its own without being forced through; it is fine to let it drain overnight if necessary. If you don't care whether or not the jelly is a little cloudy, go ahead and push the juice through the strainer with the back of a spoon. Discard the mash when you have extracted as much juice from it as you can.

Measure the juice (there should be about 4 cups) and return it to the jelly pot. For every cup of juice, add ½ cup sugar. Add the lemon juice. Over high heat, bring the mixture to a boil and skim off any white foam. Boil the mixture until it becomes syrup. If you monitor the temperature with a candy thermometer, when it reaches 220°F., it's definitely done. If you don't have a thermometer, use the cold plate test: put a teaspoonful on a refrigerated or frozen plate and put it back in the refrigerator for a minute; the texture should be like very thick syrup. (It is better to err on the loose side with jelly because it can easily get rubbery. If it's really too thin, you can always cook it a little more the next day.)

While the jelly is boiling, prepare four 8-ounce canning jars and self-sealing lids in boiling water, following the manufacturer's instructions.

When you have determined that the jelly is cooked to your liking, carefully ladle the hot liquid into the prepared canning jars, allowing at least ¼ inch of headroom. Cover and seal, following the manufacturer's instructions. The jelly will keep for about a year.

Makes 3½ cups.

Blackberries in Rose Geranium–Red Wine Syrup

Blackberries and rose geraniums are magic together, especially over ice cream or with pound cake.

1 cup red wine
½ cup sugar, plus more for sprinkling
4 rose geranium leaves
3 cups blackberries

Cook the wine and the sugar together in a small saucepan until reduced by half. Pour the hot syrup over the geranium leaves and cool. Sprinkle the blackberries with a little sugar and let sit for a few minutes until they release their juices. Pour the syrup over the berries and serve immediately.
Serves 6.

BLUEBERRIES 🫐

Season: Late spring through summer

Native wild blueberries are widespread throughout the wilds of eastern North America. When I was a child, in the summer my dad would take my sisters and me in a little putt-putt motorboat out to the islands in the middle of Squam Lake in New Hampshire to pick wild berries. He would cut the motor, the boat would drift into the thick overhanging blueberry brambles at water's edge, and we would climb out and start picking. It was difficult work, and we always came home tired, our feet wet and our bodies covered with scratches. No blueberries have ever tasted so good to me as those we picked ourselves for my mom to stir into her pancake batter.

Wild blueberries were tamed by Elizabeth White, a cranberry grower's daughter from the Pinelands of southern New Jersey, who selected local wild plants with desirable qualities and, with the help of a plant breeder, developed the first cultivated varieties in the early 1900s. Since then cultivated blueberries have become enormously popular. North America is the largest producer by far.

Blueberries were an important source of food for Native Americans. They were eaten fresh, to be sure, but much of the summer harvest was laid out and dried in the sun, then stored for winter use. The dried berries were pounded to a powder and added to stews and porridge.

We have not experimented with dried blueberries at Chez Panisse, and we use fresh blueberries in desserts but not in savory dishes. Their rich, sweet-tart flavor has a particular affinity for nectarines, and we like to combine the two in crisps and cobblers. Our favorite blueberry tart plays off that rich flavor against lemon curd. A little acidification with lemon or lime juice brightens blueberry flavor in ice creams and sherbets too.

There are many species of native blueberries. Lowbush blueberries, *Vaccinium angustifolium*, still grow wild in northeastern North America. Thousands of acres of wild plants in Maine and eastern Canada are carefully tended and harvested. The bushes are low indeed, usually less than eighteen inches tall, but thanks to underground runners, a single plant can spread out to a diameter of forty feet. The fruit, which is very small, is harvested by hand with berry rakes. Highbush blueberries, *V. corymbosum*, produce larger fruit. The most widely cultivated modern varieties belong to this species, descendants of the plants Elizabeth White selected. More recently plant breeders have crossed highbush and lowbush varieties in the effort to produce cultivated varieties with more wild blueberry flavor. Rabbit eye blueberries, *V. ashei*, so called because of their pink color before ripening, are native to the Southeast. Many specialized varieties that grow well in the South have some rabbit eye parentage.

Confusingly, many varieties of wild blueberries are often called huckleberries. However, the true huckleberry genus, *Gaylussacia*, can easily be distinguished from blueberries if you remember that true blueberries have multiple small seeds and huckleberries have only ten, which are larger and harder than blueberry seeds.

Blueberry season starts in May in the South and moves north to New Jersey in July and August. August is the peak of the season in Michigan, which grows the most blueberries, and in the West the harvest begins in California in June and lasts into July and August in the Northwest. Most growers plant varieties that mature at different times so they can have a succession of crops through the season. Blueberries are generally sold without being labeled with the name of their variety, despite real differences in flavor. Some popular varieties lack acidity and can taste quite bland. But Bluecrop, which happens to be popular with growers, has excellent flavor, as do Earliblue, Collins, Stanley, and a lowbush cross named Northsky. Rancocas is a variety with particularly outstanding flavor, although its small berries and clinging stems make it hard to pick; this is the one we wait for, grown locally by a conscientious organic grower in Sonoma County, the Sebastopol Berry Farm. Ask at your farmers' market for the best-tasting varieties in your area. And remember that although the blueberry harvest on most large farms is done with expensive hand labor or mechanical harvesters, many farms allow consumers to come and pick their own at a bargain price.

On the farm or at the market, search for firm blueberries with smooth skin that still has a lovely waxy bloom. Don't buy berries that are shriveled or hard. Most blueberries don't have much aroma, but smell them before you buy anyway, to detect the off-odors of spoilage or mold. Blueberries are actually less likely to develop mold than other berries, and they keep quite well—up to a week in the refrigerator. Moreover, they are embarrassingly easy to prepare: just pull out any stems that may still be attached and rinse the berries in cold water. To make a quick and delicious sauce, cover blueberries with water, add sugar to taste, and cook until the berries are tender. To make syrup, cook until completely soft and strain through a fine strainer.

BLUEBERRY BUTTERMILK PANCAKES

This is Marion Cunningham's buttermilk pancake recipe. In Marion's words: "Among buttermilk pancakes, I don't think you can beat these." To our taste, they make great blueberry griddlecakes. For a heartier version, substitute ½ cup buckwheat flour for ½ cup of the white flour.

2 cups buttermilk
2 eggs
6 tablespoons (¾ stick)
    unsalted butter, melted
1½ cups unbleached
    all-purpose flour

1 tablespoon sugar
1 teaspoon salt
2 teaspoons baking soda
1½ cups blueberries

Beat the buttermilk and eggs together with a fork in a large mixing bowl. Stir in the melted butter. Sift together the flour, sugar, salt, and baking soda. Gently stir the flour mixture into the buttermilk mixture until the ingredients are just combined; the batter will be a little lumpy.

Heat a skillet or griddle to medium hot. Grease lightly with oil or butter and spoon on the batter, about 3 tablespoons per pancake. Sprinkle blueberries on each pancake and press them into the batter with the back of a spoon. Cook the pancakes until a few of the bubbles on top have broken, then flip them over and cook until golden brown on both sides. Keep the pancakes warm, letting them accumulate until there are enough to serve everyone at once. Have butter and maple syrup on the table. Refrigerated leftover batter will keep for a day or two.

Serves 6.

BLUEBERRY AND LEMON TART

LEMON CURD
Grated zest of 2 lemons
Juice of 2 lemons
    (about 6 tablespoons)
3 tablespoons water
½ cup sugar
¼ pound (1 stick) unsalted
    butter
¼ teaspoon salt

3 whole eggs
3 yolks
1 prebaked 11-inch pâte sucrée
    tart shell (page 296)

BLUEBERRY TOPPING
3 cups blueberries
¼ cup sugar
2 tablespoons water

To make the lemon curd, put the lemon zest (removed with a zester or a fine grater), lemon juice, water, sugar, butter, and salt into a 1-quart heavy-bottomed nonreactive saucepan. Heat slowly over low heat, stirring until the sugar dissolves and the butter melts. Briefly whisk the eggs and egg yolks together in a bowl. Drizzle the hot lemon mixture into the eggs, whisking all the time, then scrape the contents of the bowl back into the saucepan and cook over low heat, constantly stirring and scraping the bottom of the pan, until the mixture thickens, about 5 minutes. Strain the curd through a fine-mesh sieve and pour, still warm, into the prebaked tart shell. Spread evenly.

To make the blueberry topping, put 1½ cups of the blueberries into a small saucepan with the sugar and water. Cook about 5 minutes over medium heat, stirring and smashing up the berries until they turn into thick jam. Fold the remaining 1½ cups of blueberries into the jam, keeping them whole, and heat for about 30 seconds, just enough to warm them slightly. Spoon the blueberry topping evenly over the lemon curd in the tart shell. Let the tart cool for 30 minutes before slicing.

Makes one 11-inch tart.

BOYSENBERRIES, LOGANBERRIES, OLALLIEBERRIES, AND THEIR RELATIVES

Season: Late spring through midsummer

Wild blackberries grow so abundantly in this country that the early European settlers considered them a weed, and anyone wanting to grow them in her garden would have been considered a little nuts. In time, as American cooks and farmers became better acquainted with them, particular wild berry strains were singled out, and those that performed well were cultivated and commercialized. (Some of the first domesticated berries were probably natural crosses of blackberries and raspberries, which are both members of the genus *Rubus* and both ready hybridizers.) Blackberry cultivation began spreading in the mid-nineteenth century, and growers and plant breeders have continued to develop new, improved berry crosses ever since. Today there are scores of cultivated varieties, and new ones are announced every year.

These cultivated berries have a character distinct from wild blackberries. Most have been selected to bear large berries with small seeds, abundant juice, and firm texture. Their flavor often favors the raspberry side of their lineage. There are varieties that flourish where wild berries will not grow, and there are even thornless varieties.

In the Pacific Northwest and northern California, there are numerous locations where both climate and soil are exceptionally favorable for berry-growing. Among them is the Willamette Valley in Oregon, where millions of pounds of berries are produced annually, more than from any comparable area in the world. It has precisely the climate—rainy springs, warm summer days, and cool summer nights—that predictably produces berries with the proper balance of acidity and sweetness.

Boysenberries may be the best of all the cultivated berries. Rudolf Boysen successfully executed this raspberry-blackberry cross at his southern California ranch in 1923, producing a berry that tastes unlike either parent. Its large, dark red, dusty-looking berries are soft and juicy and have a notably wine-like aroma; when it is ripe, its balance of tart and sweet makes it perfect for cooking or for eating out of hand.

The youngberry is a cross similar to the boysenberry, but shinier-looking and just a little sweeter; it makes especially delicious juice. Youngberries also have hardy vines that are disease- and cold-resistant; they deserve to be more widely grown.

In 1881 a certain Judge Logan discovered vines in his garden bearing what have become known as loganberries, probably an accidental cross of raspberry and blackberry. Light red when ripe, slightly hairy, and distinctly tart in flavor, loganberries are not so good eaten fresh but are wonderful in jam and syrup or frozen into an elegant sherbet.

Marionberries and olallieberries are relatively new varieties of cultivated blackberries, both very popular with Northwest growers. Both bear large, black, shiny, sweet berries with a medium-to-firm texture and more than a hint of wild blackberry flavor. In our local markets we also sometimes find the sweet, black, shiny sylvanberry, a boysenberry-marionberry cross, and occasionally a Scottish variety called the tayberry, a loganberry–black raspberry cross that ripens early in the season and bears dark purple, strongly flavored fruit. In southern markets, look for the Brazos, a large, sweet domesticated blackberry; and in the East, look for Black Satin, a tasty thornless variety.

In most places berry season starts in late spring and lasts through midsummer. Because cultivated blackberries are generally larger, juicier, sweeter, higher in acid, and decidedly less seedy than wild ones, they are better for canning and jam-making. They also make delicious sauces and syrups and are effective in fruit soups; just a few berries mixed with peaches or nectarines transforms a crisp or cobbler both visually and gustatorily.

The cultivated berry varieties are generally firmer and less fragile than wild blackberries, but you should still inspect them carefully before buying. Choose plump, firm berries that have the right color and sheen for their variety. They should not be moldy or overripe and oozing juice. Pick over them when you get home. (You need to do this carefully, looking over every one.) If you're not using them right away, refrigerate them, spread out on paper. If it is necessary to wash them, do so just before using.

Any berries that get too mushy but are otherwise sound should be tossed into a pot with a little water and sugar, and brought to a boil to make a delicious sauce or cooked down for jam.

BOYSENBERRY JAM

4 cups boysenberries
2 cups sugar
Optional: 1 teaspoon lemon juice

Stir the berries and sugar together in a medium-size heavy-bottomed nonreactive saucepan. Let the berries macerate for 15 minutes, until they start yielding their juices. Put a small plate in the freezer to use later to test the consistency of the jam.

Prepare three 8-ounce canning jars and their lids in boiling water, following the manufacturer's instructions.

Cook the berries over high heat, stirring occasionally to make sure there is no sticking (reduce the heat if there is). The mixture will bubble up, rising high up the sides of the pot. Skim off any light-colored foam as it collects on the edges. Soon the jam will subside, forming smaller, thicker bubbles.

At this point, start testing for consistency by putting a small spoonful of jam on the chilled plate. This cools a small amount of jam quickly so you can tell what the finished texture will be like. When the jam has cooked to the thickness you want, stir in the lemon juice, if you think it is needed. Turn off the heat and carefully ladle the jam into the prepared jars, allowing at least ¼ inch of headroom and cleaning any spills on the lip of the jars with a damp, clean towel. Cover with the lids and seal, following the manufacturer's instructions.

Makes 2¼ cups.

Boysenberry Soup with Bitter Almond–Flavored Parfait and Elberta Peaches

This is a simple dessert made with clear berry juices, ice milk, and sliced fresh peaches. It's the perfect ending to a meal on a hot summer night.

4½ cups fresh boysenberries (about 4 half-pint baskets)
2 cups sugar (plus 1 teaspoon, if needed)
1¼ cups water

Optional: ¼ cup dry red wine
1 teaspoon lemon juice
3 Elberta peaches
1 pint bitter almond–flavored parfait (page 215)

Begin preparing this soup the day before you plan to serve it.

Put the berries and 1 cup sugar in a medium-size nonreactive pot and heat slowly for about 3 minutes to release the juices. Break up the fruit with a masher and let the berries macerate for 1 hour off the heat.

Meanwhile, prepare a sugar syrup for the peaches: Melt 1 cup sugar in ½ cup water in a small saucepan over low heat. When the sugar is completely dissolved, chill the syrup overnight.

To strain the berry juice, set up a colander or strainer made of plastic or another nonreactive material over a nonreactive bowl. Line the colander or strainer with 2 large square pieces of cheesecloth, doubled up. Pour the macerating berries into the cheesecloth and tie the ends together to form a pouch. Cover the entire apparatus with plastic wrap and let the berries drain overnight in the refrigerator.

The next day, remove the berries from the refrigerator and squeeze as much liquid as possible out of the cheesecloth pouch. Thin out the juice with ¾ cup water and the wine (if using). Taste for sweetness, adding a tablespoon of sugar or a teaspoon of lemon juice if needed.

Put 6 dessert bowls in the freezer to chill.

With a sharp paring knife, peel the skin off the peaches and cut slices into the chilled sugar syrup. The cold syrup sweetens the peaches and prevents them from oxidizing. Leave the peaches 10 minutes in the syrup, then distribute them among the chilled bowls. Cover the fruit in each bowl with about ¼ cup of the boysenberry soup and top with a generous scoop of bitter almond–flavored parfait.

Serves 6.

Variation: Substitute 2 pints of mulberries for the boysenberries, cooking them with a little less sugar and thinning out the soup with a little more water; serve topped with vanilla parfait (page 215).

DOMED BERRY CAKE

This makes a dramatic summer birthday or wedding cake. Any mixture of berries works. You can add peeled peach or nectarine pieces too.

SOAKING LIQUID
2 tablespoons sugar
5 tablespoons warm water
1 teaspoon lemon juice
2 tablespoons kirsch

FILLING
5 cups berries
¼ cup plus 3 tablespoons sugar

1 teaspoon kirsch
2 cups heavy cream
One 9-inch round piece sponge
  cake (page 300)

COVERING
2 cups heavy cream
3 tablespoons sugar
½ teaspoon vanilla extract

First mix the soaking liquid: Stir the sugar and warm water together until the sugar dissolves. Stir in the lemon juice and kirsch.

To prepare the filling, toss the berries with ¼ cup sugar and 1 teaspoon kirsch and set aside to macerate. Whip the cream into soft peaks with 3 tablespoons sugar. Drain the juice that has come off the berries into the soaking liquid. Fold the berries into the cream.

To assemble the cake, slice the round of sponge cake horizontally into three ⅓-inch-thick layers. Line a 3-quart bowl with plastic wrap, leaving enough hanging over the edge to cover the cake once it fills the bowl. Line the plastic wrap with a layer of sponge cake, cutting the cake as needed to cover the entire inside of the bowl. Use a pastry brush to moisten the layer of sponge cake with soaking liquid.

Pour half of the berry cream filling into the cake-lined bowl and cover the filling with a layer of cake. Moisten this layer with more of the soaking liquid. Spoon in the rest of the berry cream, covering this with the final layer of sponge cake. Moisten with the last of the soaking liquid. Cover the exposed cake with the overhanging plastic wrap and refrigerate overnight.

The next day, just before serving, make the whipped cream covering: Whip the heavy cream, sugar, and vanilla until the cream forms soft peaks. Remove the cake from the refrigerator. Peel back the plastic wrap. Place a large plate over the bowl and invert, turning out the cake onto the plate. With the cake now on the plate, remove the rest of the plastic wrap. Spread the whipped cream evenly over the cake. Slice in wedges. Serve immediately.

Serves 10.

Olallieberry Cobbler

5 cups olallieberries	*6 unbaked 2-inch biscuits*
½ cup sugar	*(page 291)*
3 tablespoons flour	*2 tablespoons heavy cream*

Preheat the oven to 400°F.

Toss the berries with the sugar and flour. Put the berries in a 1½-quart baking dish. Place the dish on a baking sheet to catch any overflowing juices. Brush the biscuits lightly on top with cream and place on top of the berries, spaced evenly apart. Bake for 40 minutes, until the biscuits are cooked through and turning golden. Serve with a cold pitcher of cream.

Serves 6.

CAPE GOOSEBERRIES OR POHA BERRIES 🐝

Season: Late summer through early fall

If you are a gardener, you probably already know about the Cape goose-berry, a rather invasive plant of the potato family, also known as the goldenberry, husk cherry, Peruvian ground cherry, bladder cherry, husk tomato, and strawberry tomato. Although the plant volunteers in back-yards across the country, the fruit is rarely seen in the market. Cape gooseberries are reasonably well known in Pennsylvania Dutch country and parts of the Midwest, but of all the places in the United States where they can be found, they are best known—and most eaten—in Hawaii, where they are called pohas or poha berries. Pohas have established themselves on the mountain slopes of all the Hawaiian islands, where they are commonly gathered from the wild and used in cooking.

Like tomatillos, Cape gooseberries come enclosed in papery husks that protect the fruits from insects and cushion them when harvested. To eat out of hand, you simply peel back the husk, which makes a nice little wing-shaped handle. The fruits themselves look like small yellow cherry tomatoes with beautifully smooth, rather waxy skin; they con-tain many small seeds. The best poha berries are deliciously sweet and juicy and have a mild strawberry-like flavor with tropical fruit and herbaceous overtones. (The first ones I ever ate I spotted in the window of a fancy food shop in England over thirty years ago. With their husks folded back, they had been dipped in sugar syrup and fondant, and they looked ready to take flight.)

Cape gooseberries originally come from South America and have a long history of cultivation in Peru and Chile. Brought back to Europe by the early explorers, they spread to England in the mid-eighteenth century and were eventually planted by settlers on the Cape of Good Hope. When they were introduced to Australia via South Africa, Australians started calling them Cape gooseberries. The plants naturalize easily and have escaped into the wild almost everywhere they have been cultivated, most successfully in tropical and subtropical areas such as Hawaii and Australia.

Cape gooseberries ripen in the late summer and fall. At the restaurant we like to peel back the husks, dip the berries halfway into molten white or dark chocolate, and serve them with coffee as a sweet treat after dessert. Cape gooseberries are smaller and sweeter than tomatillos, but you can use them to make a good sweet salsa. You will also find them surprisingly tasty in salads, especially with spicy and bitter greens such as rocket or chicory, or mixed with apples in a pie. And because Cape gooseberries have a lot of pectin, they make very good preserves.

At the market, open the husks of a few and inspect the berries. They should be well colored, firm, and shiny. The fruit is harvested when it falls to the ground; some growers simply shake them loose, but not all fruit that is harvested this way will be ripe. Cape gooseberries continue to color and ripen after harvesting and should not be eaten until they have turned yellow or orange. Always allow greenish berries to ripen completely. Ripe Cape gooseberries will keep for months in a cool, dry place.

Backyard growers should look for varieties that are identified as *Physalis pruinosa*, such as Goldie. These grow into compact plants with small fruit, suitable for a small garden or for growing in pots. Varieties of *P. peruviana* grow into big, sprawling plants that may reach a diameter of three or four feet.

CHERRIES &

Season: Late spring through early summer

Every May we pray for sunny days because cherries can be a dicey proposition in northern California orchards. Cherries and apricots are the first stone fruits to ripen, and in some years an untimely rain in late May ruins the fruit just as the harvest is about to begin. And sometimes cherry-loving birds launch full-scale attacks a day or two before the fruit is perfectly ripe. (My own backyard cherry tree seems to be a particularly vulnerable target; usually there are only a handful of cherries left for my daughter and me.) But nearby growers—including Al Courchesne in Brentwood, the Van Dykes in the Santa Clara Valley, and John Lagier in Escalon—carry on, and in the good years the results are glorious.

Crisp, dark, sweet cherries are among our most precious culinary treasures. Other than a quick rinse in cold water, the best cherries need no preparation at all and can be eaten at will. Cooked, cherries fill memorable pies, cobblers, tarts, and clafoutis; pickled or braised, they lend a tart-sweet accent to fatty meats like pork and duck. Preserved in Cognac or dried and plumped in grappa, cherries cheer up midwinter desserts with a memory of summer.

The best cherries grow in temperate climates. The trees need a chill winter to induce dormancy, no frosts during their spring bloom period, and warm weather to ripen well. Cherry-growing in the United States is divided rather neatly between east and west. East of the Rocky Mountains, sour cherries, the kind used mostly for cooking and canning, predominate, especially in the orchards of Michigan and New York. In the West are grown mainly sweet cherries, the best for eating out of hand, with major commercial production in Washington, Oregon, Utah, and California.

The season for both sweet and sour cherries is late spring to early summer. Sweet cherries (*Prunus avium*) begin ripening at the end of May. The best early varieties include Black Tartarian, Tulare, and Burlat. They all are dark red and have tender-crisp, sweet flesh. Later comes the Bing, the quality standard by which all other dark sweet cherries are measured. Large, round, and plump, Bings have an unmatched crisp texture, a shiny black-red color, and rich, sweet flavor. Because Bings come from several sweet-cherry-growing areas, their season can extend from early June through mid-July. Similar to Bing but ripening later, Lambert, Van, and Black Republican cherries all have good flavor but a softer texture.

Two white sweet cherries that ripen midseason deserve special mention. Royal Ann is a very pretty, very old French variety, yellow with a red blush. It is delicious fresh, and its balance of sweetness and acidity makes it perfect for canning and pickling, but it is losing favor because its thin skin bruises easily. (My sister and brother-in-law in Michigan have a perfect Royal Ann cherry tree, and one year its fruit ripened in time for their twenty-fifth wedding anniversary party; lucky guests feasted right off the tree.) Growers are replacing Royal Ann with a newer variety, Rainier, which looks very much like Royal Ann but is firmer and less likely to bruise. Rainier is delicious as a fresh cherry, but it does not have sufficient acidity to be interesting cooked or canned.

Maraschino cherries are not a variety at all. They are light cherries, often Royal Anns, that are bleached, dyed, sugared, flavored with bitter almond, and preserved, and don't resemble fresh cherries of any stripe.

The sour or pie cherries (*P. cerasus*) so popular in the Midwest and East include Early Richmond and English Morello, which are both mid- to late-season ripeners. They are used almost exclusively for pies and canning. Montmorency is an old French variety first planted in the United States in 1760. Considered by many to be the best pie cherry (and also good eaten fresh), the bright red Montmorency matures in late June and July. Meteor is a hybrid very similar in quality to Montmorency but ripens a bit later.

All fresh cherries should look bright and plump. They are often sold loose, so take the time to pick through them and toss back any that are bruised, soft, or show signs of mold. The stems should be green and pliable, not brown and dry. Refrigerate cherries as soon as possible in a plastic bag, but do not try to keep them for more than a few days. Pick through them again just before using and wash under cold running water.

Cherry pits impart a subtle bitter-almond flavor, and cherries to be preserved in brandy, pickled, or canned will taste much better with the

pits left in. The French never pit cherries for clafoutis. But unless you are eating cherries fresh out of hand, you will usually want to pit them before using. This job can be more or less of a chore, depending on how you go about it and how patient you are. No system or gadget is totally foolproof. If you are pitting just a few, pry out the pit with the point of a small knife. If you try to squeeze the pit out, you will end up covered with juice. There are little handheld cherry pitters that work rather like a paper punch; one by one, you seat cherries in the tool and punch out their pits. It is also easy to use the loop of an unbent paper clip as a tool to slip out the pit and stem. At Chez Panisse we use a hand-operated plastic contraption that is fitted over a small plastic box. The cherries go into a hopper on top, and with each thrust of the plunger a pitted cherry rolls down a chute into a bowl while the pit falls into the box. It's a speedy gadget, but we still have to check each cherry afterward because a few pits always remain lodged inside.

ROASTED DUCK WITH CHERRIES

1 duck (about 3 to 4 pounds) *3 tablespoons Madeira wine*
Salt and pepper *¼ cup chicken or duck stock*
½ pound cherries, pitted

Remove any fat from the cavity of the duck. Pierce the skin of the legs and breast with the tip of a small sharp knife or the tines of a sharp fork; this helps the fat to render out as the duck roasts. Season well with salt and pepper, inside and out. (This can be done ahead of time.) Let the duck sit at room temperature for ½ hour or more before roasting.

Preheat the oven to 400°F.

Roast the duck for about 45 minutes, turning it from side to side every 10 minutes and finishing with the breast up (the duck should still be a bit too rare). Pour and skim off as much fat as you can from the pan and add the cherries, Madeira, and stock. Roast 15 more minutes. The duck should still be pink next to the bone. When the duck is done, let it rest for 15 minutes.

To carve, remove the legs and slice the breast, reserving all the roasting juices, which should be skimmed again before serving. Taste the juices for salt and serve the duck garnished with the cherries and the pan juices.

Serves 4 to 6.

Cherry Soup à la Maxim's

We got the idea for this lovely soup years ago from Maxim's, the famous Paris Belle Époque restaurant. As for any recipe this simple, all the ingredients must be perfect, but it is absolutely wonderful when you use beautiful ripe cherries.

1 pound ripe, sweet, dark red
cherries, preferably Bings
(about 3⅓ cups)
1 quart chicken or veal stock

1 to 2 teaspoons sugar, to taste
1 to 2 tablespoons kirsch, to taste
Salt and freshly ground black
pepper

Pit about 1½ cups of the cherries, saving the pits. Put the pitted cherries in a food processor and process to a coarse purée. Crush the reserved pits with a sturdy mortar and pestle, or wrap them in cheesecloth and crush them with a hammer on a cutting board.

Skim any fat from the stock and bring to a boil in a small saucepan. Stir in the puréed cherries and crushed pits. Immediately remove from heat, cover, and let steep for 10 minutes.

Pit the remaining cherries, discarding the pits. Strain the soup through a fine strainer. Rinse the saucepan and pour the strained soup back into it. Add the pitted cherries and a teaspoon of sugar and warm over low heat for 2 minutes, but do not allow the soup to come to a simmer. Add the kirsch and season with salt, pepper, and more sugar if needed. Serve hot or cold.

Serves 4.

Brandied Cherries

Cherry season always seems so short, but this is a nice way to keep some for later in the year. Fold them into vanilla ice cream with a little bit of their juice, or spoon a few over crème caramel or panna cotta. They are also good with roasted meats and fowl. And by all means, drink the brandy, which gets better and better as it is flavored by the cherries.

Get the best cherries and the best brandy you can afford, or use kirsch if you like. This method works for either sweet or sour cherries, but do not use soft or overripe fruit. Cherries preserved unpitted and with stems on have the best flavor and are pretty served whole. Cherries to be used for such things as ice cream are better preserved after being stemmed and pitted; save the pits to put in the bottom of the brandy jar for more flavor.

For each pound of cherries, mix 2 cups brandy or kirsch with ½ cup granulated sugar. Add a few tablespoons more sugar per pound of cherries if you have doubts about their sweetness; for sour cherries, use ¾ cup sugar per pound. Rinse the fruit in cold water, drain well, and stem and pit them, if desired. If you leave the stems on, you can trim them quite short. Put the cherries in a quart jar with a tight-fitting lid. Stir the brandy mixture and pour over the fruit. Cover tightly and keep in a cool part of the kitchen or in the cellar at least 1 month before using. For the first week, turn the jar upside down daily to help dissolve the remaining sugar crystals. Refrigerate after a month. The cherries will keep for several months more.

PICKLED CHERRIES

Any cherries can be pickled, but sour ones have the best flavor. They are irresistible as an hors d'oeuvre alongside charcuterie.

2 pounds cherries	*4 cloves*
1½ cups sugar	*6 peppercorns*
4¼ cups white wine vinegar	

Rinse, dry, and pick over the cherries, throwing out (or eating!) any blemished ones and cutting the stems down to about ½ inch.

Prepare eight 1-pint canning jars and self-sealing lids in boiling water, following the manufacturer's instructions.

Stir together the sugar, vinegar, cloves, and peppercorns in a nonreactive saucepan, bring to a boil, and cook for 3 minutes. Pack the cherries into the canning jars. Pour the hot syrup over the cherries, cover, and seal, following the manufacturer's instructions. Let sit for 2 months in a cool, dark place before eating. After opening the jars, the cherries will keep refrigerated for a year.

Makes 8 pints.

CHERRY CLAFOUTIS

Cherries with the pits left in, as in the following recipe, are more flavorful and juicy than pitted cherries would be. Just be sure you place a few small plates around the table for collecting the pits.

This clafoutis is also very nice made with blackberries, blueberries, raspberries, or even a mixture of summer berries. They don't need the preliminary cooking but should be tossed in a big bowl with sugar and lemon zest (no cinnamon) and several tablespoons of flour, then arranged in a generously buttered baking dish.

2 tablespoons unsalted butter	¼ teaspoon grated lemon zest
1 pound sweet or sour cherries, washed and stemmed	2 eggs, separated
	3 tablespoons flour
⅓ cup plus 3 tablespoons granulated sugar (⅓ cup for sweet cherries; ½ cup for sour cherries)	1 teaspoon vanilla extract
	¼ teaspoon almond extract
	⅓ cup heavy cream
	1 pinch salt
⅛ teaspoon ground cinnamon	Powdered sugar for dusting

Melt the butter in a sauté pan over medium heat. When the butter is foaming but hasn't begun to brown, add the cherries, ⅓ or ½ cup sugar, cinnamon, and lemon zest. Cook for 7 to 10 minutes, stirring occasionally, or until the cherries are tender when pierced with the point of a small knife and the juices have begun to thicken. Arrange the cherries in the bottom of a 9-inch baking dish.

Preheat the oven to 375°F.

Beat the egg yolks and 3 tablespoons sugar together for several minutes, until light and creamy. Beat in the flour, vanilla, almond extract, and cream.

In a separate bowl, beat the egg whites with a pinch of salt until they form soft peaks. Fold the whites into the batter just until blended, and pour the batter over the fruit.

Bake in the upper third of the oven for about 20 minutes, until the batter is puffed and well browned. Let the clafoutis cool slightly, dust with powdered sugar, and serve.

Serves 6.

Sour Cherry Pie

The season for tender, translucent, tiny, red sour cherries is only a few weeks long, so we buy as many as we can and make cherry pie as often as we can. We like to top them with lattice crusts so that plenty of steam can escape, allowing the filling to get nice and syrupy. (You can use this recipe to make a Bing cherry pie, but use half as much sugar.)

2½ pounds sour cherries,
  stemmed and pitted
  (about 5 cups)
1 cup sugar
3 tablespoons quick-cooking
  tapioca

1 teaspoon kirsch
Two 9-ounce pieces pie dough
  (page 292)
2 tablespoons heavy cream
1 tablespoon unsalted butter

Preheat the oven to 400°F. and line the oven rack with foil; this pie will boil over a little.

Toss the cherries with the sugar, tapioca, and kirsch. Let the fruit mixture stand for 30 minutes so that the cherries will release their juices, plumping the tapioca and dissolving the sugar. Roll out the first piece of pie dough into a circle ⅛ inch thick. Line a 9-inch pie plate, leaving a ¾-inch-wide overhang around the edges. Roll out the second piece of dough into a 13-inch circle; slide this onto a baking sheet and refrigerate. Pour the cherry mixture into the pie shell.

To make a lattice top, remove the second piece of pie dough from the refrigerator and cut into ½-inch-wide strips. Arrange half the strips on top of the pie, about ½ inch apart. Lay the remaining strips crisscross over the others (or, more prettily but more fussily, weave the strips). Trim all the strips of dough so that their overhang is no more than ¼ inch, and neatly fold the edge of the bottom crust over the strips. Pinch a wavy scalloped edge around the rim of the crust by making indentations with your thumb and fingers.

Brush the top with cream and sprinkle lightly with sugar. Dot the fruit exposed by the lattice with little pieces of cold butter (this keeps the fruit from burning). Bake immediately (to prevent the crust from getting soggy) for about 45 minutes, until the top crust is golden brown and thick juices are bubbling from the holes. Let the pie cool awhile on a rack before serving (it can be reheated in a warm oven for 10 minutes), and don't forget vanilla ice cream (page 301) or sweetened whipped cream.

Makes one 9-inch pie.

CITRON 🐝

Season: Year-round; best in fall

Citrons are such beautiful and fragrant fruits. A perfectly ripe citron can fill a room with its exotic floral aroma, and its fresh rind is the most edible of any citrus: sweet, tender, and only mildly bitter. What a shame most people encounter citrons only as chopped bits in commercially candied peel embedded in bad fruitcakes. It's a sad fate for the very first citrus to have been disseminated and cultivated throughout Europe and Asia.

On the outside, most citrons look like huge, lumpy lemons. The skin is bright yellow. The white rind within is very thick and fleshy, and there is not much juicy pulp. One variety, grown in California mostly as an ornamental, is called Fingered citron or Buddha's Hand. Its fruit is quite astonishing in appearance, being formed of a half dozen or more long, twisting, tapering fingers growing outward from the stem end, within which there may be a tiny bit of pulp. Fingered citron is well known in China and Japan but regularly baffles anyone who hasn't seen it before.

At Chez Panisse we dice fresh citron rind very fine or slice it very thin to use in salads or in vinaigrette sauces for fish. In citrus risotto, mixed with orange and lemon peel, it adds a deep perfumy note.

Most commercially candied citron is harvested green to conform to processors' specifications for color and firmness, so the only way to enjoy the unusual flavor of candied ripe citron is to candy it yourself. The flavor is captivating; soon you will be adding chopped candied citron to all kinds of things—cannoli filling, panettone, panforte, sweet rolls. You might even make your own fruitcake.

The citron, *Citrus medica*, originated in northeastern India. It grows best in subtropical areas and is cultivated in southern Asia and all the warmer parts of the Mediterranean, particularly in Corsica, Sicily, and Crete. A variety known as the Etrog predominates in Israel, where it is used to celebrate the Feast of the Tabernacles. Another variety, the Corsican citron, was probably introduced to California late in the nineteenth century; it and the Etrog are the ones most commonly found here, although Buddha's Hand is popular with backyard growers.

Citrons ripen year-round, but the peak of the supply comes in the fall. Look for large, firm, highly colored fruit with shiny skin. Avoid any with mold, soft spots, or bruises. Be particularly careful examining Buddha's Hands, which are more fragile than the other types: the fingertips start drying out soon after harvest, and mold may lurk in the crevices.

At home, put a few citrons in a bowl and enjoy their aroma. After a week or so they should still be in fine shape to candy. To keep them longer, put them in a loosely covered container in the refrigerator, but use them before they develop soft spots or mold.

Sautéed Scallops with Citron

1½ to 2 pounds scallops	½ cup white wine
1 citron	⅓ cup white wine vinegar
3 shallots (about ¼ cup finely chopped)	½ pound plus 4 tablespoons (2½ sticks) unsalted butter
Salt	Freshly ground pepper
A few peppercorns	Olive oil

Remove and discard the "foot"—the small ligament on the side—from each scallop. Refrigerate the scallops while you make the sauce.

Cut a thick slice off the side of the citron, trimming away any pulp that may be present. Chop this into very fine dice. You will need 2 tablespoons of diced citron rind in all; if necessary, cut off and dice more. Peel all the zest from the rest of the citron and reserve. Plunge the diced rind into rapidly boiling water and cook until tender, about 3 minutes. Drain and set aside.

To make the beurre blanc sauce, finely mince the shallots and put them in a small saucepan with the reserved citron zest, a pinch of salt, the peppercorns, wine, and vinegar. Bring to a boil and reduce over medium-high heat until only 2 or 3 tablespoons remain. Remove from the heat.

Cut the butter into small pieces. Over very low heat, whisk the butter into the sauce bit by bit, waiting until each addition is mostly melted and emulsified into a silky sauce before adding more. Monitor the heat: it should be quite warm, but if it gets too hot, the sauce will break—and it will also break if it is allowed to cool down. When all the butter has been incorporated, taste for salt and adjust as needed. Strain the sauce, pressing the shallots well. Add the blanched citron. Keep the sauce warm, but not hot, until ready to use. You can use the top of a double boiler over warm, not hot, water or a warmed thermos.

Season the scallops with salt and pepper. Heat a sauté pan (preferably nonstick) over high heat and pour in enough olive oil to coat the bottom. When the oil is hot, add the scallops and sear for 2 to 3 minutes on each side. Don't crowd the pan or they will sweat instead of browning. Brown them in as many batches as necessary, keeping the cooked scallops warm while you finish. When the scallops are done, arrange them on plates and spoon the beurre blanc sauce over them.

Serves 6.

Panforte

This dense Italian fruit confection is our primary vehicle for candied citron. We slice it into thin wedges and serve it with vin santo for dessert.

One 9-inch disk edible rice paper
1½ cups almonds
1 cup candied orange peel
(page 192)
1 cup candied citron (page 66)
⅔ cup unbleached
all-purpose flour
⅛ teaspoon salt

½ teaspoon ground cinnamon
¼ teaspoon grated nutmeg
¼ teaspoon ground cloves
¾ cup granulated sugar
½ cup honey
¼ cup light corn syrup
Powdered sugar for dusting

Preheat the oven to 350°F. Brush the sides of a 9-inch round cake pan with melted butter and dust the sides with flour. Fit the bottom with the disk of rice paper.

Spread the almonds evenly on a baking sheet and toast them in the oven for about 10 minutes. Let cool completely. Reduce the heat to 300°F.

Chop the candied orange and citron peel into roughly ⅛-inch pieces. In a large mixing bowl, stir together the chopped peel, almonds, flour, salt, cinnamon, nutmeg, and cloves. Measure the sugar, honey, and corn syrup into a small heavy saucepan. Bring this syrup to a boil over medium heat and cook until it reaches 245°F. At this temperature a small quantity dropped into cold water will form a firm but still pliable ball. Carefully pour the syrup over the nut-and-peel mixture and mix thoroughly. Press the sticky batter into the prepared cake pan, flattening it with a lightly oiled spatula or your moistened fingers.

Bake the cake for 40 minutes at 300°F. It will look bubbly and soft, but it will firm up substantially as it cools. While it is still warm, run an oiled knife around the outside edge so that the cake will release from the pan later. (You may have to stop every few inches to clean the hardening sticky syrup off the knife.) Once the cake is completely cool, remove from the pan. (If the cake sticks to the pan, you may have to warm it up slightly on the stove over low heat before you can free it.) Dust heavily with powdered sugar and store in a cool, dry place, wrapped airtight, for at least 1 month (it will keep for a year). Slice into ½-inch wedges to serve.

Makes one 9-inch cake, about 25 pieces.

Shaved Citron Salad

This was a wintertime favorite of Chez Panisse chef Catherine Brandel.

1 medium citron	*Salt and pepper*
2 small fennel bulbs	*¼ cup extra-virgin olive oil*
6 radishes	*Parsley leaves*
1 stalk celery	*Parmigiano-Reggiano cheese*
2 tablespoons lemon juice	

Wash the citron thoroughly. Cut off the leafy tops and stem ends of the fennel and remove any bruised outer layers. Wash the radishes and cut off the root ends, but leave some of the green stems to hold on to. Clean and trim the celery.

Slice all the elements of the salad quite thin with a Japanese mandoline, but not so thin that they break up when dressed and tossed. Just under ⅛ inch is a good thickness. Start with the citron; you will need about ¼ cup slices. The fingers of a Buddha's Hand citron will make perfect coin-size slices, but if you have another kind of citron, simply cut the slices into smaller pieces. Layer all the slices together on plates and dress with the lemon juice, salt, and a drizzle of extra-virgin olive oil. Garnish the salad with parsley leaves, shavings of Parmesan cheese, a final sprinkle of olive oil, and a grind or two of black pepper.

Serves 6.

CANDIED CITRON

1 citron (about 2 pounds)
5½ cups sugar
2½ cups water

Cut the citron into ½-inch-thick slices, then into ½-inch-wide strips. Cut away and discard the fruit's seedy center, if there is any, and cut the strips into ½-inch cubes. Put the cubes into a medium-size saucepan and cover with cold water. Bring the citron to a boil over low heat, simmer for 10 minutes, and drain. Repeat this process twice, blanching the citron a total of 3 times.

After the final blanching and draining, return the citron to the saucepan and add 5 cups sugar and the water. Stir the mixture over low heat until the sugar is dissolved. Allow the citron to continue cooking slowly in the sugar syrup until it becomes translucent. The temperature of the syrup will reach about 230°F. Turn off the heat and let the fruit sit in the syrup for ½ hour. Drain the citron and arrange the pieces, not touching one another, on a baking sheet lined with parchment paper or on a rack. Let them air-dry overnight. The next day, toss them with ½ cup sugar, place in an airtight container, and refrigerate. The candied citron will keep for 4 months.

Makes 3 cups.

CRANBERRIES ❧

Season: Fall through midwinter

Cranberries are the last red berries of the year, coming to market in September and available until January. Their bright red color and sprightly, sour flavor are welcome both as an accompaniment to meat dishes and in desserts. Eaten out of hand, they have a tartness that can be breathtaking, but combined with savory flavors or balanced with sugar, they provide a particularly American accent to cooking.

Cranberries, *Vaccinium macrocarpon*, are found in the wild in damp, boggy areas from Newfoundland down to the Carolinas and west to the prairies. Native Americans added cranberries and blueberries to pemmican, a sort of preserved meat mixture, and made cranberry sauce sweetened with maple syrup or honey.

The cranberry season peaks in November, in time for the berries to make their traditional appearance at Thanksgiving dinner, but because cranberries keep extremely well, they can be used throughout the winter months. Cranberry sauce or relish marries well with game, especially venison, and with richly flavored poultry, such as goose, duck, squab, and of course turkey. In desserts we usually use fresh cranberries by themselves, but they are also particularly good combined with oranges or apples. Cranberries make beautiful and refreshing ice cream and sherbet, and they are stunning in tarts and as a topping for upside-down cake. Dried cranberries can be used all year in baking, the same ways raisins are.

Cranberries are grown commercially in their native habitats—New Jersey, Massachusetts, and Wisconsin are big producers—and in the West, in Washington and Oregon. Wild cranberries from the United States and Canada are available for a limited time at the height of the season. Smaller than their cultivated relatives and more variably colored, they are charming used whole in a sauce.

Cranberry farmers are relearning the lessons of the past. Cranberries do not produce good crops in competition with other plants, but organic farmers, rather than resorting to the chemical solutions of conventional growers, are again using hand labor to keep the bogs clean of grass, brambles, and other weeds. They also apply sand to the bogs, which stimulates the growth of the bearing parts of the plants and helps control weeds and insects. (This technique, used by cranberry farmers as long ago as the 1800s, was detailed in a 1924 USDA publication.) Organic growers routinely check their plants for the first signs of problem insects and use traps and organic sprays to control them. Careful management of vegetation at the edges of the bogs is also important.

Cranberries are most often packaged in plastic bags, which limits your ability to check quality before buying. Ripe, fresh cranberries are firm, plump, and bright. Their color ranges from light red to almost black, depending on the variety, and some even have an attractive yellow background color that shows through the red. Do not buy cranberries that are soft or shriveled or that have dull skin.

Cranberries store very well. When you get them home from the market, pour them out of the package onto a big plate. Pick over them, discarding any berries that are soft or have brown spots. Put the good berries in a covered container. Fresh cranberries will keep for at least a month in the refrigerator and for many months in the freezer. Just before using, pick through the berries again and wash them in cold water.

To make a quick cranberry sauce, combine 2 cups berries in a saucepan with 1 cup sugar and 1 cup water or orange juice. Bring to a simmer and cook for 10 minutes or so, until the berries pop.

CRANBERRY UPSIDE-DOWN CAKE

When I walk into the Café in the late fall, this is one of the first desserts to catch my eye, its red top glistening like coiled strings of glass beads.

TOPPING
4 tablespoons (½ stick)
    unsalted butter
¾ cup brown sugar, packed
2¾ cups fresh cranberries
¼ cup orange juice

BATTER
1½ cups all-purpose flour

2 teaspoons baking powder
¼ teaspoon salt
¼ pound (1 stick) unsalted
    butter, room temperature
1 cup granulated sugar
1 teaspoon vanilla extract
2 eggs, separated
½ cup whole milk
¼ teaspoon cream of tartar

Use a 9-inch round or an 8-inch square cake pan with 3-inch sides. To make the topping, place the butter and brown sugar in the cake pan. Place the pan on a stovetop burner over low heat and melt, stirring with a wooden spoon. When the mixture starts to caramelize, turning a slightly darker shade of brown, remove from the heat and let cool. Scatter the cranberries evenly in the bottom of the pan and drizzle in the orange juice. Set aside.

Preheat the oven to 350°F.

To make the cake batter, sift the flour, baking powder, and salt into a bowl. In a large mixing bowl, using an electric mixer, cream together the butter and sugar until pale and fluffy. Mix in the vanilla. Add the egg yolks one at a time, scraping down the sides of the bowl after each one to make sure it is thoroughly incorporated. Gradually add the dry ingredients and the milk in stages: mix in about a third of the flour mixture, followed by about half the milk; mix in another third of the flour, then the rest of the milk; finally, add the last third of the dry ingredients.

In another large mixing bowl, whisk together the egg whites and the cream of tartar. Beat the whites until they form firm peaks. Fold the whites into the batter in two batches. Pour the batter over the topping in the prepared pan and bake until the top is slightly brown and the cake pulls away from the sides of the pan, about 50 to 60 minutes. Let the cake cool for 15 minutes. Run a knife around the edge of the pan and invert the cake onto a serving plate. Serve with lightly sweetened whipped cream flavored with a little orange liqueur.

Makes one 9-inch round cake or one 8-inch square cake; serves 8.

Cranberry Walnut Tart

6 tablespoons (¾ stick) unsalted butter	½ teaspoon vanilla extract
	¼ teaspoon salt
1 cup brown sugar, firmly packed	1½ cups walnuts
	1½ cups cranberries
1 egg white	1 prebaked 11-inch pâte sucrée shell (page 296)
1 teaspoon Cognac	

Preheat the oven to 375°F.

Cream together the butter and brown sugar in a mixing bowl. Beat in the egg white, Cognac, vanilla, and salt. Beat until light and creamy. Coarsely chop together the walnuts and cranberries and stir them into the mixture in the bowl. Press the filling into the tart shell and bake for 30 minutes. Let cool completely and serve with lightly whipped cream.

Serves 9.

Raw Cranberry Relish

This is a radically simple, refreshing relish that is delicious with roasted meats. Into a food processor or grinder, put 2 cups cranberries, washed and picked over; 1 orange, peel and all (I usually cut it in quarters and pick out most of the seeds, but sometimes I don't); and ¾ cup sugar. Process to a uniform consistency and let sit for a few hours. Cover and refrigerate if necessary. For a variation, add ⅓ cup walnuts.

Makes about 3 cups.

CURRANTS: RED, WHITE, AND BLACK 🍃

Season: Mid- to late summer

Fresh currants and dried currants, two very different fruits, derive their name from the same source, a reference to the tiny black grapes of Corinth in ancient Greece. Recipes that use dried currants, the tasty little raisins made from Zante grapes, will be found in the grape chapter. The fresh currant is a fruit of another genus altogether, a close relative of the gooseberry. Fresh red currants are popular all over northern Europe, but are only rarely found in our markets. They deserve to be better known. On a hot summer's day they are refreshingly tart, served plain or with sugar and cream. White currants, sweeter and more delicate than red ones, need no service at all: you pull them off their stems and eat them like candy.

The late English writer and scholar of food, Elizabeth David, whose influence on us is very much alive, loved red currants in desserts, especially in combination with raspberries. She put them in mousses and jams and fruit salads, and she insisted that they were obligatory in a proper summer pudding. Red currants are also prized for the tart flavor and vivid color they add to savory dishes; without them you cannot make a Cumberland sauce, for example. They are used in northern Europe to add an acid tartness to savory foods, much in the way pomegranates are used in the Middle East and around the Mediterranean.

Preserved red and white currants are a famous specialty of the French city of Bar-le-Duc, in Lorraine, where purists still follow a fourteenth-century recipe, using goose quills to poke the seeds out of each tiny currant before the berries are given a brief cooking in sugar syrup. Currant preserves are traditionally served with scones and fresh cheese.

Black currants are seldom eaten as fresh fruit. They have a very strong, almost resinous character, which is tamed and altered somewhat by cooking. Black currants are extensively grown in Burgundy, where they go into the making of crème de cassis, the essential cordial of kir, the cassis-flavored white wine apéritif. Black currants can be cooked down for jam or strained to make a purée, and they are delicious for syrups and superb in sherbet and ice cream.

All three currants are members of the botanical genus *Ribes*, the same genus as gooseberries. As early as the seventeenth century, English colonists had transplanted cultivated varieties of currants to New England, where they flourished, but from the 1920s until the mid-1960s, growing currants and gooseberries was banned by the federal government in some areas because they can be a host to a serious disease, white pine blister rust. With the bans long since lifted and more new rust-resistant varieties available, we hope currants make a strong comeback in North American markets.

Red and white currants are extraordinarily beautiful, with a translucent skin that almost glows. They grow on bushes in loose, gracefully drooping clusters called strigs and ripen from mid- to late summer. At harvest the strigs are picked and packed in flat berry baskets. Currants are produced commercially in the cooler parts of the Northeast and Northwest and do not do well where it is hot and dry.

When you find fresh currants in the market, if they are local and organically grown, plump, bright, and mold-free, by all means buy them. Beware of packaged currants; they may look enticing, but they may have been picked unripe and shipped a long way. Very fresh currants can be refrigerated for several days. If you grow your own, remember that ripe currants hold up very well if they are left on the plants; you can pick them over a period of several weeks at your leisure. Wash them just before using. Elizabeth David wrote that when she made jelly or juice she never bothered stemming currants, let alone seeding them. Nevertheless, you may want to get rid of at least some of the stems, in which case a table fork can be a helpful tool.

CUMBERLAND SAUCE

Cumberland sauce is a simple fruit sauce for meat that became hugely popular a hundred years ago in England and elsewhere. Its history is recounted with great authority by Elizabeth David in her *Spices, Salt and Aromatics in the English Kitchen*; her recipe, reprinted below, is the one we use at Chez Panisse. It is adapted from the great Victorian chef Alexis Soyer's 1853 version, and it is—there is no other word—delicious. We would add only that you should use bitter Seville-type oranges for this, if you can find them.

This best of all sauces for cold meat—ham, tongue, pressed beef, venison, boar's head or pork brawn—can be made in small quantities and in a quick and economical way as follows:

With a potato parer cut the rind, very thinly, from two large oranges. Slice this into matchstick strips. Plunge them into boiling water and let them boil 5 minutes. Strain them.

Put them in a bowl with 4 tablespoons of redcurrant jelly, a heaped teaspoon of yellow Dijon mustard, a little freshly milled pepper, a pinch of salt and optionally a sprinkling of ground ginger.

Place this bowl over a saucepan of water, and heat, stirring all the time, until the jelly is melted and the mustard smooth. It may be necessary at this stage to sieve the jelly in order to smooth out the globules which will not dissolve. Return the sieved jelly to the bowl standing over its pan of hot water.

Now add 7 to 8 tablespoons (2½ oz.) of medium tawny port. Stir and cook for another 5 minutes. Serve cold. There will be enough for four people.

Made in double or triple quantities this sauce can be stored in covered jars and will keep for several weeks.

N.B. On no account should cornflour, gelatine or any other stiffening be added to Cumberland sauce. The mixture thickens as it cools, and the sauce is invariably served cold, even with a hot ham or tongue.

Pickled Currants

4 cups red currants   1 allspice berry
3 cups white or red wine vinegar   2 cloves
¼ cup sugar

Strip the currants off their stems—or leave them be: unstemmed, they make a pretty garnish as little branches of fruit. Bring the vinegar, sugar, allspice, and cloves to a boil and simmer for 5 minutes. Let cool. Pack the fruit into canning jars with self-sealing lids prepared according to the manufacturer's instructions. Pour the cooled vinegar over the fruit and seal. Let sit in a cool, dark place for 6 weeks before serving.

Makes 4 cups.

Note: The currant-flavored vinegar is a worthwhile addition to vinaigrettes and meat sauces.

Squab Salad with Pickled Currants and Watercress

This is a wonderful salad, particularly in the winter: watercress is at its best, and the pickled currants will bring back memories of summer. Toss watercress in a vinaigrette made with some of the pickled currant liquid (preceding recipe) and a touch of Dijon mustard. Arrange grilled and carved squab over the salad (being sure to pour the carving juices over as well) and garnish with pickled currants. The watercress can be mixed with other hearty salad greens, such as escarole or curly endive.

CURRANT JELLY

It's difficult to get enough currants every season to make even a few months' supply of jelly, but even if you only have a few handfuls, it's worth making. It's easy, because currants have lots of natural pectin, and the jelly that tastes brightest and has the clearest color is best made in small batches anyway. Our favorite thing to do with currant jelly is to spread it between the layers of an almond torte. We also use it as a glaze for raspberry tarts.

4 cups (about 3 pint baskets) red, black, or white currants
1½ to 2 cups sugar

Pick the currants off their stems, discarding any mushy or moldy ones. Rinse the currants in cold water and put them in a large heavy-bottomed nonreactive saucepan. Cover with water to a depth of ½ inch or so. Cook the currants over medium heat until they have released their juices, about 5 minutes, crushing them with a potato masher or the end of a wooden mallet until all the berries appear to have popped.

Drain the mixture (the "mash") through a jelly bag or very fine strainer into a clean glass bowl. If you want the jelly to be perfectly clear, let the mash just sit in the strainer so that the juice drips out on its own, without being forced through; it is okay to let it drain overnight if necessary. If you don't care whether or not the jelly is a bit cloudy, go ahead and push the juice through the strainer with the back of a spoon. Once you have extracted as much juice as you can, discard the mash.

Measure the juice and return it to the jelly pot. For every cup of juice you have, add ¾ cup of sugar. Over high heat, bring the mixture to a boil and skim off any white foam. Keep boiling the mixture until it becomes syrupy. If you monitor the temperature with a candy thermometer, when it reaches 220°F., it's definitely done. If you don't have a thermometer, use the cold-plate test: put a teaspoonful on a refrigerated or frozen plate and put it back in the refrigerator for a minute; the texture should be like very thick syrup. (It is better to err on the loose side with jelly because it can easily get rubbery. If it's really too thin, you can always cook it a little more the next day.)

While the jelly is boiling, prepare two 8-ounce canning jars and self-sealing lids in boiling water, following the manufacturer's instructions.

When you have determined that the jelly is the right consistency, carefully ladle the hot liquid into the prepared canning jars, allowing at least ¼ inch of headroom. Cover and seal, following the manufacturer's instructions. The jelly will keep for about a year.

Makes 2 cups.

Black Currant Ice Cream

We use a commercial brand of black currant syrup to make fruit sodas in the Café. We have found that it makes a delicious ice cream as well.

6 egg yolks	*⅔ cup black currant syrup*
1 cup half-and-half	*2 teaspoons lemon juice*
1 cup sugar	*Optional: 2 teaspoons kirsch*
2 cups heavy cream, chilled	

In a large bowl, whisk the egg yolks just enough to break them up. Gently heat the half-and-half and sugar in a nonreactive saucepan, stirring slowly over low heat until the half-and-half is steaming and the sugar is dissolved. Drizzle the warm cream into the egg yolks, whisking constantly as you pour. (This is called tempering the egg yolks.)

Pour the mixture back into the saucepan. Measure the heavy cream into the mixing bowl. Cook the mixture over low heat, stirring slowly and scraping the bottom of the pan with a wooden spoon or heat-resistant rubber spatula, until it thickens enough to coat the spoon. Immediately remove from the heat and strain through a fine-mesh sieve into the bowl with the heavy cream. Whisk together to cool the mixture, cover, and chill thoroughly.

Stir the black currant syrup, lemon juice, and kirsch, if using, into the chilled ice cream mixture. Freeze, following the instructions for your ice cream maker.

Makes about 1 quart.

FROSTED RED CURRANTS

At Chez Panisse sugar-frosted currant clusters sparkle fancifully atop summer puddings and on candy plates.

2 cups red currants
1 egg white
1 tablespoon water
Sugar for sprinkling

Rinse the currants in a basin of water. Trim away and discard any extra stems and branches and bruised berries. Divide the currants into bunches of 10 to 12 berries each. Pat them dry.

In a small bowl, lightly stir together the egg white and water with a fork, enough to break up the white but not enough to make it frothy. With a small pastry brush, carefully paint a thin layer of egg white on the currant clusters. Sprinkle with sugar and let dry on a rack until crisp. Serve the same day.

Makes 2 cups.

SUMMER PUDDING

At the zenith of berry-picking, when there is a plethora of summer berries, our summer puddings are enhanced by the tartness of red currants and the perfume of black raspberries. The other essential component of summer pudding is good, homemade, densely textured white bread of the type baked in loaf pans—what the French call pain de mie.

Start by removing the crusts and slicing the bread ¼ inch thick. Toss together red currants, black raspberries, raspberries, boysenberries, olallieberries—in any proportions. (For 1 loaf of bread you will need at least 5 cups of berries.) Lightly sugar the berries and warm them gently in a nonreactive saucepan until juicy. Layer the berries and bread slices in a nonreactive container or bowl, starting and finishing with berries and making about 4 or 5 layers of bread. Cover with plastic wrap and weight down the pudding by nesting a similarly shaped container on top of it. Let the pudding sit overnight. Cut into 3-inch-square pieces, scoop them out, and serve with lightly sweetened, vanilla-scented, softly whipped cream—and a drizzle of berry coulis (page 271).

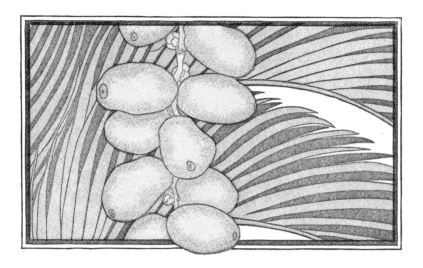

DATES 🌰

Season: Fresh, late summer through winter; dried, year-round

Eating a fresh ripe date is a civilized pleasure, one that people in North Africa and the Middle East have enjoyed for thousands of years. As fresh dates become easier to find in specialty produce stores, this pleasure is increasingly available in North America. If you've eaten only the dried Deglet Noor dates sold at the supermarket in little cardboard boxes with a camel on the front, your first fresh date may seem like a different fruit altogether. The best fresh dates have smooth brown skins containing soft yielding flesh with a mildly sweet, rich flavor entirely different from that of the hard, wrinkled, and cloyingly sweet dates in the package.

Plain dates are delicious eaten out of hand as a sweet snack, but they can be consumed in many other ways as well: on cereal, in breads and cakes, in cookies and ice cream, in salads, and with meats. They are luscious stuffed with nuts or cheese. At the restaurant we sometimes offer a bowl of sweet fresh dates and tart tangerines after a rich winter dinner, a refreshing and satisfying combination. Dates find their place on the savory side of the kitchen too, as they do in North Africa, steamed with couscous or cooked in a tagine with lamb or chicken. We sometimes make Paula Wolfert's lovely recipe for a Moroccan salad of oranges, dates, and almonds (found in her book *Mediterranean Cooking*).

Date varieties are described as soft, dry, and semidry, according to the appearance and texture of the ripe fruit. Soft dates have a high moisture content and are relatively low in sugar. After they are harvested, they are dried to increase the sugar concentration and retard spoilage. They must be harvested, packed, and transported with care and stored under refrigeration. Dry dates have less moisture than soft dates and a higher concentration of sugar. Because the flesh is dry and firm, the fruit travels and keeps very well without refrigeration. Dry dates are also known as bread dates—the staple food of desert nomads. Semidry dates have sugar and moisture characteristics that fall somewhere between the extremes of soft and dry.

There are about 1,500 known varieties of dates. Around a hundred are grown in California, and a few of these are standouts. Our favorite is the Black Sphinx, a soft date variety that traces its origins to a seedling in Phoenix, Arizona; it has one organic producer, the Arizona Date Gardens. Its fruits have fragile, black-brown skins and rich, sweet, flavorful flesh. The Medjool date is the soft fruit of trees descended from the date palms imported to California in 1927, offshoots of the date palms at the Bou Denib oases in Morocco. Easier to find than Black Sphinx, Medjools are big plump dates over two inches long, moist and meaty and firm, with lovely dark brown, tender skin. They are so popular in the Middle East that significant quantities are shipped there from California.

Barhi dates are a special treat. The medium-size round fruits are harvested at two distinct stages of development: before and after ripening. Before they have ripened completely, at a point called *khalal*, the dates are yellow and have a sweet-tart flavor and the crispness of an apple. Highly perishable, they are rushed to the market still on the branch. The season for these is short, in August and September. Later in the year, after they have ripened on the tree, the fruits are picked as soft dates. These Barhi dates are brown-skinned and have a sweet, meaty flavor.

Deglet Noor is the variety that dominates date production in California (as it does in Algeria and Tunisia) and the one most often dried and packaged. As a fresh date, it is considered semidry; it has a mild flavor, firm texture, and a color that may range from amber to reddish brown.

Other varieties we have liked include the Halawy, a small golden-brown, wrinkled semidry date with a very sweet, concentrated flavor. The Khadrawy is a medium-size, reddish-brown soft date with firm flesh, a thickish skin, and a lovely, distinctive flavor. Khadrawys are sold both fresh and dried. Zahidi dates are semidry and have soft fibrous flesh that becomes somewhat crunchy when dried. This date is very easy to dice, which makes it useful in baking.

The date palm, *Phoenix dactylifera*, grows best in hot, dry areas where there is a good water supply for the trees' roots. Just as in Orientalist fantasies, desert oases are indeed crowded with date palms: nomads planted them on their journeys across the desert. But most dates are cultivated in orchards called, romantically, date gardens. Enormous quantities of dates are produced in North Africa and the Middle East. Egypt, Iraq, Iran, Pakistan, Saudi Arabia, Algeria, Morocco, and Tunisia are the biggest producers.

Dates were first brought to California as seedlings by Spanish missionaries in 1769, but most varieties cultivated today came from Egypt, Algeria, and the Middle East around 1900. Date production in the United States is limited to the deserts of southern California and southern Arizona, where the total number of bearing trees is about 250,000, puny compared to the 22 million date palms growing in Iraq, for example.

Date palms can grow as high as 100 feet, with straight trunks that taper very little from bottom to top. The feathery leaves, which may be up to twenty feet long, grow out of the top of the trunk, as do the flowers and fruit. Dates flower in late winter and spring, each tree producing either male or female blossoms; the male flowers release pollen, and the female flowers develop into the fruit. Most dates ripen between August and December. A full-grown date palm can yield as many as 200 pounds of dates in a season. Date sugar, which is used in Middle Eastern and Indian cooking, is made by boiling the sap from the trees.

Organic date farmers don't use synthetic chemicals for insect control or for fertilizer. Grasses are planted in the date gardens as cover crops to be tilled under to improve the soil, and chicken or other animal manure is used for fertilizer. The developing fruit clusters are covered with brown paper or nylon mesh bags for protection from insects and birds, as well as from the sun and the occasional raindrop. Organic dates are not fumigated after harvest, as many conventional dates are, to prevent mold and other spoilage; instead, they are treated with heat or cold.

At the market fresh soft dates should look shiny and plump. Dry and semidry dates may be wrinkled. If they are sold in bulk, choose whole, unblemished fruit that hasn't been squashed out of shape. Check carefully for mold, which usually starts to form at the stem end or around cuts and bruises, but be aware that as dates lose moisture, the skin develops a powdery coating of sugar, and sometimes sugar crystals will form under the skin as well. This is not a quality problem. When you get the dates home, you can dissolve the sugar by steaming the dates for ten minutes or by heating them on a baking sheet, covered with a damp towel, for fifteen minutes in a 300°F. oven. Most fresh dates will keep for weeks covered in the refrigerator. Store dried dates wrapped airtight, either refrigerated or at room temperature.

Dates are easily pitted by cutting a slit along the side and prying out the seed. Dates for baking can be snipped into pieces of the proper size with a pair of kitchen scissors.

MOROCCAN CHICKEN WITH DATES

The best dates to use in this dish are the harder, smaller, lighter colored varieties, such as Zahidi, because they aren't as sweet as the softer, darker varieties, such as Medjool and Black Sphinx.

1 chicken (3 to 4 pounds),	*½ teaspoon ground cinnamon*
quartered	*2 teaspoons grated fresh ginger*
Salt and pepper	*½ cup chopped cilantro*
2 onions	*½ pound Zahidi or Halawy*
2 tablespoons unsalted butter	*dates (about 24)*
¼ teaspoon saffron threads	*A few sprigs cilantro*

Season the chicken well with salt and pepper. Peel and grate the onions. Melt the butter in a large heavy-bottomed pot. Add the onions, saffron, cinnamon, ginger, and chopped cilantro; season with salt and stir over high heat for 2 or 3 minutes. Add the chicken and cook another few minutes before pouring in enough water to just cover the chicken pieces. Bring to a boil, reduce the heat, and simmer until the chicken is tender, about 45 minutes, stirring occasionally to make sure nothing is sticking. Add water if necessary.

When the chicken is done, remove it from the pan and set aside while you finish the sauce. Skim the fat from the liquid left in the pan; taste for salt and adjust as needed. Add the dates and simmer for 15 minutes over medium heat. Stir occasionally, but be careful not to break up or smash the dates. Return the chicken to the sauce. After 5 minutes or so, when the chicken is hot again, arrange the pieces on a platter (over a bed of couscous, perhaps) and pour the sauce over the meat. Garnish with sprigs of cilantro and serve.

Serves 4 to 6.

STUFFED DATES

Once pitted, dates can be stuffed with cheese (we use Parmesan, pecorino, or mascarpone) and with nuts. The first walnuts of the season are a favorite, lightly toasted before insertion; when almonds come into season, we use them too.

For another nice filling, knead grated orange zest and a few drops of orange liqueur into almond paste. Fill the cavity of each date with the paste, smoothing over the exposed bit with your finger.

FIGS 🐌

Season: Early summer and late summer into fall

Figs have been growing around the Mediterranean for millennia. Their flavor combines flawlessly with the other ingredients that define the cuisines of southern Europe that inspire us. Even if they weren't so delectable, they would still be an important part of our cooking at Chez Panisse. Their soft, honeyed character tames the aggressiveness of hot peppers, garlic, and onions; stands up to the assertiveness of anchovies; and is beautifully complemented by the herbaceous flavors of thyme, mint, and lavender. The classic Italian combination of figs and prosciutto has led us to explore other combinations of figs with salty or smoky pork and poultry.

As dessert at Chez Panisse, figs bring a completely satisfying end to a meal, served just as they come, ripe from the tree, sweet but not cloying—or perhaps just lightly sugared and sauced with plain cream. (Lightly whipped cream flavored with a little raspberry purée is good too.) Or we may bake a fig galette and drizzle it with lavender honey or serve it with honey cream.

Figs make excellent preserves, both sweet and savory, extending the season. Dried figs poached in red wine or baked in cakes and cookies can instantly awaken memories of summer at a midwinter table.

Besides giving us their fruit, fig trees contribute to our cooking in other important ways: Fish are wrapped in fig leaves and grilled or baked, which imparts a subtle flavor of fig and coconut. Disks of goat cheese that have been marinated in olive oil can also be wrapped and grilled in fig leaves, and meats grilled over fig prunings take on an extra dimension of flavor.

Fig trees thrive in the hot, dry climate of central and southern California, but they are also grown in other warm areas, from the Carolinas south and west to Texas. In the East growers must watch out for high humidity and summer rain, which pose problems for the ripening fruit.

Many fig trees produce two crops a year. The first crop, called *breba*, is borne on twigs grown the previous year. These fruits, which ripen in early summer, are large and juicy and are almost always marketed as fresh fruit. They are bigger than the second crop, which develops on the new growth of the current season and ripens from late summer into fall.

Figs were planted early at the Spanish missions in California. The variety known, not surprisingly, as the Mission (or Black Mission) fig originally came from the islands off the southern coast of Spain; it is still widely grown in California and elsewhere. Its purple-black delicate skin contains flesh that ranges from pale to dark pink and has good flavor; even the first crop yields tasty, luscious fruit. The second-crop figs are smaller and sweeter and concentrated with flavor. They start to ripen in August and continue until cold and rainy weather halts the growth of the trees, sometimes not until November. Picked when they are just about to fall from the tree, Mission figs will sun-dry in a matter of days.

Mission was the only fig variety grown in California until the mid-nineteenth century, when other varieties were brought from the East Coast and Europe. Brown Turkey, one of the later introductions, is a large fig with shades of copper and brown mixed with purple on the skin. Its flesh is paler in color than that of the Mission, no more than a pinkish amber, and its flavor is milder. Brown Turkey has a small early crop but produces a large second crop, which is always sold fresh, never dried. California Brown Turkeys are similar to the variety of the same name grown in the Southeast and in Hawaii.

The fruit of Adriatic figs is stunningly beautiful. When cut into, the thin green skin reveals brilliant red flesh that has a rich, slightly raspberry character. Early-crop Adriatic figs are good quality but few in number; sometimes there are no early figs at all. Adriatics are too fragile to ship well, so many are dried or processed for baking.

Calimyrna, the variety most commonly grown in California and the one most widely available throughout the United States, became established only after growers learned enough about the ecology of its antecedents. Smyrna fig trees had been imported from Turkey, planted in California, and tended for twenty years without ever bearing fruit. This was because Smyrna figs must be pollinated by tiny wasps that spend part of their life in a wild fig, the caprifig. Only when growers were able to establish caprifigs and their associated wasps did abundant harvests begin. Fresh Calimyrna figs have greenish-yellow to golden skin; their flesh is amber to pale red, and their rich flavor is accentuated by the nutty quality of the seeds. You are most likely to encounter Calimyrnas and imported Smyrnas as whole dried figs.

Celeste is the fig variety most commonly planted in the eastern United States. It can tolerate winter temperatures as low as 0°F. but grows best in the cooler parts of the Southeast. The medium-size fruits have beautiful bronzy-violet skin and juicy sweet flesh that ranges in color from amber to rose. Celeste figs dry easily without spoiling.

Fresh figs must be harvested and handled carefully. To be divine, they must be allowed to fully ripen on the tree; once picked, they are extremely perishable. If you live in a fig-growing area, buy them at a farmers' market or at a roadside stand. We are very fortunate to be able to buy figs from Rick Knoll's family farm in Brentwood, where the figs are never, ever picked unripe. Ripe figs give to gentle pressure and often have small cracks in the skin. A distinct bend in the stem is also a good sign. Don't buy figs that have traces of milky latex sap at the stems; they will not be ripe.

Slightly underripe, firm figs will soften and improve in flavor if kept at room temperature for a day or two. Just lay the fruit out on a paper-lined baking sheet and keep checking until they soften. Figs for shipping are always picked underripe and are refrigerated for transport; they may improve for a day at room temperature, but don't try to keep them longer. Mold is a fig's worst enemy. Keep an eagle eye out. Discard any moldy figs you find and immediately use up the rest of the bunch. Point out moldy figs to your storekeeper.

To prepare figs for eating or cooking, rinse quickly under running water and snip off the tough end of the stem. Figs are easy to peel, but at the restaurant we peel them only if the skin is especially tough. Sound, ripe figs are easy to dry; they take less than a week in a warm, dry, sunny spot, or about twelve hours in a dehydrator.

ANCHOÏADE WITH FIGS

The simplest anchoïade is nothing more than pounded anchovies, garlic, and olive oil; this refinement is adapted from the recipe of Austin de Croze, the early-twentieth-century French gastronomic chronicler. It is delicious served with grilled fish or grilled vegetables or spread on bread and grilled over the dying embers of a wood fire.

8 salt-packed anchovies	Salt and pepper
2 cloves garlic	¼ cup walnuts
4 dried figs	3 or 4 tablespoons extra-virgin
2 small branches savory	olive oil
2 small branches wild fennel	Splash of Cognac

Rinse the anchovies of any extra salt and then soak them in cool water for about 10 minutes. Carefully fillet them with your thumb and fingers, removing the fins, tails, and most of the innards. Don't worry about the tiny bones; they are very soft and will disappear in pounding. Rinse the fillets well and dry on a towel.

Peel the garlic. Cut off and discard the woody part of the fig stems. Finely chop the figs. Strip off the leaves from the savory and fennel stems. Finely chop the herb leaves.

Pound the garlic, savory, and fennel to a fine paste in a mortar with a bit of salt. Add the walnuts and pound to a paste. Next add the figs, pounding enthusiastically. When the figs have been incorporated in the paste, pound in the anchovy fillets, along with a drizzle of olive oil, the Cognac, and a good grinding of black pepper. Keep pounding and adding olive oil until the mixture is smooth and quite spreadable but still thick.

Makes ½ cup.

Note: Fresh figs may be used to make this dish as well. Trim and chop 5 or 6 fresh figs. Dice 1 shallot and brown it in a little olive oil in a heavy-bottomed pan over medium heat. Add the figs, season with salt and pepper, and add the chopped savory and wild fennel. Cook down to a thick paste and add this to the mortar instead of the dried figs.

Fig and Grape Salad with Pancetta Crostini

Of course, this tastes best made with an authentic, costly, artisanally made balsamic vinegar (the kind labeled "aceto balsamico tradizionale di Modena" and bearing the seal of the producers' consortium), but it can be approximated by using instead a reduction of good commercial balsamic vinegar.

3 tablespoons artisanally made
  balsamic vinegar, aged
  12 years or more, or ½ cup
  good-quality commercial
  balsamic vinegar plus
  1 teaspoon brown sugar
6 thick slices country-style bread
Extra-virgin olive oil

12 thin slices pancetta
  (about ¼ pound)
9 ripe figs
1 cup grapes, stemmed
  (wine grapes, if available)
6 small handfuls rocket
  (arugula)
Salt and pepper

If substituting commercial balsamic vinegar, put it in a small saucepan with the brown sugar and reduce by a little more than half, until the vinegar is thick and syrupy.

Preheat the oven to 375°F.

Trim the crusts off the bread and cut the slices in half lengthwise, making 12 long, thin crostini. Brush them lightly with olive oil and wrap with slices of pancetta—spirally, like candy canes. Place them on a baking sheet and bake until the pancetta begins to crisp, about 10 minutes.

While the pancetta-wrapped crostini are baking, quarter the figs, cut the grapes in half, and thoroughly wash and dry the rocket. When the pancetta crostini are almost ready, gently toss the rocket and fruit with a pinch of salt, a few grinds of the peppermill, and about 3 tablespoons olive oil. Arrange the salad on plates and drizzle with the balsamic vinegar. Garnish with the crostini.

Serves 6.

Quail Salad with Roasted Fig Vinaigrette

6 quail
Salt and pepper
16 figs
1 teaspoon plus 1 tablespoon
  red wine vinegar
1 teaspoon plus 1 tablespoon
  sherry vinegar
1 tablespoon plus
  ¼ cup red wine

Optional: 1 tablespoon port or
  other sweet wine
1 tablespoon plus ½ cup
  extra-virgin olive oil
2 to 3 heads curly endive (frisée),
  with tender white centers
1 large or 2 medium shallots

Season the quail generously with salt and pepper. This can be done a few hours in advance.

Preheat the oven to 375°F.

Cut the stems from the figs and cut the figs in half lengthwise. Arrange in a shallow baking dish, cut side up. Sprinkle with 1 teaspoon red wine vinegar, 1 teaspoon sherry vinegar, 1 tablespoon red wine, the port (if using), 1 tablespoon olive oil, and salt and pepper. Bake until soft and juicy, about 25 minutes.

Remove the tough green leaves from the curly endive. Cut the root ends off and separate the leaves. Wash and dry well.

Heat a cast-iron pan over medium-high heat. When the pan is hot, pour in enough olive oil to cover the bottom of the pan. Add the quail, starting them breast side down. (Do this in batches, if necessary, to avoid crowding the pan.) Brown the quail well on both sides of the breast before turning. Turn and brown the other side. This will take 10 to 12 minutes. When done, the breast should be springy to the touch and the juices should run clear when a thigh is pierced with a sharp knife. Let the quail rest for 7 minutes or so in a warm place.

Meanwhile, let the pan cool a bit and add the shallots. Cook a minute or two and add ¼ cup red wine; bring to a boil and reduce by half. Turn off the heat and add 1 tablespoon of each vinegar, scraping up all the brown bits. Pour into a salad bowl, add 8 of the roasted fig halves and any roasting juices, and mash with a whisk. Whisk in ½ cup olive oil. Taste and adjust with salt and vinegar as needed. Reserve a third of the vinaigrette to use as garnish later.

Divide the quail into quarters with a sharp knife: cut each in half down the back and separate the legs from the breast. Toss the curly endive in the vinaigrette and arrange on a platter. Place the warm quail pieces on top of the salad and garnish with the warm roasted figs. Drizzle over the remaining vinaigrette. Serve immediately.

Serves 6.

GRILLED BACON-WRAPPED FIGS

As a hot hors d'oeuvre or alongside a salad and a slice of grilled meat, a ripe fig that has been wrapped in good bacon and perfectly grilled is a very fine thing. Choose figs that are ripe but not overly soft. Cut off the stems and scantily wrap the figs in thin slices of bacon; secure with toothpicks. Grill, turning frequently, over medium-hot coals until the fat is rendered and the bacon is browned but not too crisp, about 6 minutes. Be careful of the dripping bacon fat and keep moving the figs around the grill to avoid flare-ups. Drain on paper towels and season with freshly ground pepper. If you don't have a charcoal- or wood-fired grill, use a broiler, turning the figs once and cooking 3 to 4 minutes on each side. (Grilled prune plums are equally delicious: Cut the plums in half, remove the pits, wrap the halves with bacon as above, and grill or broil the same way.)

DRIED FIGS POACHED IN RED WINE

Put the figs in a saucepan with a splash of water and cover with red wine. Drizzle in some honey (about ¼ cup for each cup of wine) and add a cinnamon stick, a strip of orange peel, the juice of an orange, and a small piece of vanilla bean. Simmer slowly over low heat until the figs are very tender. Remove from the heat and let them cool off and plump up a little in their liquid. Our favorite way to serve them is warm or cold with coffee ice cream. They also complement roast pork if poached with a little less honey and no orange juice and no other flavoring than a branch of thyme. The poaching liquid can be strained and reduced to a sauce.

Fig Cookies

This recipe is adapted from one given to us by the Downtown Bakery and Creamery in Healdsburg, California, which was founded by Chez Panisse's founding pastry chef, Lindsey Shere. These jam-filled bars are our favorite use for fresh fig jam. You can make them as the bakery does, with dried figs, but you will need a little more water to make the fig jam filling.

FIG JAM (MAKES 3 CUPS)
1¾ pounds ripe figs (about
    6 cups quartered)
¾ cup granulated sugar
1 tablespoon grated lemon zest
¼ teaspoon salt
½ cup water

DOUGH
6 tablespoons (¾ stick)
    unsalted butter

1 tablespoon heavy cream
⅔ cup brown sugar, firmly
    packed
2 eggs
2½ cups unbleached
    all-purpose flour
1 teaspoon baking powder
½ teaspoon baking soda
½ teaspoon salt
¼ teaspoon ground cinnamon

To make the fig jam, cut the tough ends off the stems of the figs. Cut the figs in quarters and put them in a medium-size saucepan with the granulated sugar, lemon zest, salt, and water. Simmer 10 minutes, until the figs are soft and translucent. Purée the mixture by passing it through a food mill and return it to the saucepan. Cook over low heat until it is a very thick paste, about 15 minutes.

To make the dough, in a medium-size mixing bowl, beat together the butter, cream, and brown sugar. Add the eggs one at a time, completely incorporating them. Sift together the flour, baking powder, baking soda, salt, and cinnamon; add to the butter mixture, mixing just until combined. Divide the dough into 2 equal balls. Wrap tightly with plastic wrap and refrigerate for at least 30 minutes.

Preheat the oven to 350°F.

On top of 2 lightly floured pieces of parchment paper, roll out each ball of dough into a ⅛-inch-thick rectangle about 6 inches wide and 15 inches long. Spread half the jam in a 3-inch-wide band lengthwise down the center of each rectangle. Using the parchment paper, not your fingers, to manipulate the dough, encase the filling by folding one long side of the dough over it so that it covers a little more than half the jam.

Fold the other side over to cover the rest of the jam, the edges of the two sides overlapping in the middle by about ¼ inch. Pinch the dough together at each end to completely seal in the filling. Brush off any excess flour. Lifting from underneath the paper again, roll the entire log over so that the seam is on the bottom. Brush off any excess flour from this side and transfer each log, still on its parchment, to a baking sheet.

Bake for 20 minutes, just until golden. While the logs are still warm, cut at a slight angle into ¾-inch-thick bars. Let cool completely. Store in an airtight container.

Makes 36 cookies.

BAKED BLACK MISSION FIGS WITH LAVENDER HONEY ICE CREAM

Cut the figs in half vertically and arrange them, cut side facing up, in a buttered ceramic baking dish just large enough to hold them. Sprinkle with a sweet Muscat wine, such as Beaumes-de-Venise. Sprinkle sugar over lightly and bake in a 400°F. oven for 15 minutes, until tender. Serve warm, with honey ice cream infused with lavender flowers, using the drippings in the baking dish as a sauce.

To make lavender honey ice cream, follow the vanilla ice cream recipe on page 301 but use half-and-half instead of milk, and when heating, omit the sugar and add a tablespoon of dried lavender flowers. After adding the heavy cream and before chilling and freezing the mixture, whisk in ¾ cup honey.

FIG AND RASPBERRY GALETTE WITH CHARTREUSE

This galette is enhanced by the unique flavor of green Chartreuse, the herbal liqueur still distilled by French monks according to a centuries-old secret formula.

*10 ounces galette dough
 (page 290), rolled into a
 14-inch circle and chilled*
6 tablespoons sugar
1 tablespoon flour
2 tablespoons ground almonds
15 ripe Black Mission figs
*1 tablespoon unsalted butter,
 melted*

*1 basket (½ pint) fresh
 raspberries*

CHARTREUSE GLAZE
5 ripe Black Mission figs
1 cup water
¼ cup sugar
*1 teaspoon green Chartreuse,
 or to taste*

Preheat the oven to 400°F. Place a pizza stone, if you have one, on the center rack.

Remove the rolled-out dough from the refrigerator or freezer and place on a buttered or parchment-lined baking sheet. Mix 1 tablespoon sugar with the flour and almonds and sprinkle evenly on the dough, leaving a 1½-inch border unsprinkled. Cut the tips of the stems off 15 figs. Cut the figs in quarters and arrange them in concentric circles on top of the almond mixture, cut side up. Tilt the stems slightly upward so they will caramelize nicely in the oven. Evenly sprinkle 3 tablespoons sugar over the fruit.

While rotating the tart, fold the border of exposed dough up and over itself at regular intervals, crimping and pushing it up against the outer circle of fruit, creating a containing rim that resembles a length of rope. Pinch off any excess dough. Brush the border gently with 1 tablespoon melted butter and sprinkle it with 2 tablespoons sugar.

Bake in the center of the oven, preferably on a pizza stone, for 20 minutes. Rotate and bake 20 more minutes. Toss the raspberries with a little sugar and scatter them in between the figs. Continue baking for another 10 to 20 minutes, until the crust and figs are browned and caramelized. Remove the tart and slide it off the parchment directly onto a cooling rack.

While the tart is baking, make the Chartreuse glaze: Trim and quarter the figs and cook them with the water in a small saucepan for 5 minutes over high heat. Break up the figs with a potato masher, then reduce the heat and simmer another 5 minutes. Pass the fruit through a fine-mesh sieve, returning the juices to the saucepan. Add the sugar and boil over medium-high heat and reduce until you have a thick syrup, about 5 minutes. Allow to cool, then add the Chartreuse. When you are ready to serve the tart, brush the fruit with the Chartreuse glaze.

Makes one 12-inch tart; serves 8.

CHEZ PANISSE

GRAPES &

Season: Midsummer through fall

The grape is a uniquely important food plant; its contribution to culture is incalculable. Humankind discovered early on that ripe grapes not only were delicious to eat off the vine at the end of summer but could also be made into wine or preserved for the rest of the year by drying into raisins. Unripe grapes, too, could be harvested and pressed and their acidic verjuice used as a seasoning.

The grapevine keeps on giving. The prunings (the French call them *sarments*) can be tossed over coals to flavor grilled food, and the heavier trunks and branches of vines that are no longer producing make excellent firewood. The tender young leaves of early summer can be minced and mixed with olive oil for a simple tart sauce for fish or used as they are in the Middle East, as edible wrappings for meat and vegetable mixtures. Even grape seeds can be pressed and used for cooking oil and vinaigrettes.

At Chez Panisse organically grown grapes and raisins form part of a large repertory of savory dishes inspired by traditional Mediterranean cooking, sweetening the pickled onion sauce for Venetian *sa'or*, accenting the bread-crumb stuffing for Sicilian-style swordfish, and embellishing many a Moroccan-style couscous or tagine. And you can't make sole à la Véronique without fresh grapes. For dessert, grapes make unusual and refreshing sherbets and granitas that are welcome in the late summer heat. Youngsters and the abstemious appreciate the Gewürztraminer juice we serve in the café, made by the folks at Navarro Winery. Sometimes we make our own fresh grape juice and experiment with different varietals.

There are many species of grape native to America, most of them found east of the Rockies. Most of the cultivated varieties grown in the East are hybrids of the native *Vitis labrusca* and ripen in late summer and fall. They have skins that slip easily from the pulp, but seeds that stick resolutely to the soft flesh. Widely used to make juice, they are also sold as table grapes and used in wine-making. New York, Michigan, Pennsylvania, and Ohio are the leading producers.

The best-known American grape is the Concord, which has a flavor that more or less defines processed purple grape juice. Concords are beautiful round grapes with a purple-black skin covered by a silvery bloom. Their flavor epitomizes the so-called foxy flavor characteristic of this species. Niagara, also called White Concord, has a similar flavor but, of course, pale green skin.

One of the best labrusca types is Bronx Seedless; late every summer we look for the ones that John Lagier brings to our local farmers' market. Bronx is an old variety from New York that thrives on John's organic farm in the hot Central Valley of California. The long clusters of deliciously sweet red fruit have a milder flavor than Concord and are very juicy.

West of the Rockies most cultivated grapes are offspring of varieties of *V. vinifera*, the European wine grapes brought to California and other parts of the West by European immigrants. These varieties form the base of California's enormous grape production, which accounts for about ninety percent of the national total. Washington, Oregon, and Arizona also produce significant amounts of European grapes. Western-grown grapes are used for wine, raisins, and table grapes; only a few are canned or processed for juice. In contrast to native American grapes, vinifera fruit has skin that adheres tightly to the pulp, and seeds that separate easily from the crisp flesh.

The most common grape in California is the Thompson Seedless, a variety developed in the Central Valley. The huge production of crisp, juicy, rather characterless fruit is pumped up by many growers who treat their vines with synthetic growth hormones. The grapes that result are bigger, and there are many more of them, but they lack the concentrated sweetness and flavor that this variety can have. Organically grown Thompsons develop and ripen naturally into small, roundish, translucent golden fruit with an unexpected richness of flavor.

Flame Seedless, a red grape similar in flavor to Thompson Seedless, is similarly delicious when carefully grown, as is Black Monukka, a variety that forms graceful long clusters of high-quality, sweet, reddish-purple grapes. The latter is mostly seedless, but the occasional seed shouldn't discourage you from trying it.

One of the most flavorful European grapes is Muscat of Alexandria, whose evocative name is usually shortened to Muscat. These large golden-green grapes have a flavor unlike any other—rich, spicy, and musky. (Muscat Hamburg is a black-skinned cousin.) When Muscats are perfectly ripe and sweet, they are utterly satisfying served as a dessert all by themselves; they also have enough character to be paired successfully with cheese. Muscats are also used to make richly flavored, unforgettable dessert wines such as Beaumes-de-Venise.

Black Corinth grapes are called black currants when they are dried, but they have begun to be marketed as a fresh grape as well. Tiny grapes with a sprightly flavor, they are irresistible when frosted with sugar. They are sometimes marketed as Champagne grapes.

It is almost impossible to find a dark-skinned raisin that has not been made from a Thompson Seedless grape—even the light-skinned sultana raisins are Thompsons bleached with sulfur during the drying process. Try Flame Seedless raisins if you find them and if you don't mind crunching on a few seeds, Muscat raisins are a special treat.

In wine-making regions, wine grape varieties make a brief appearance at farmers' markets and produce stores in the fall. They typically have smaller, sweeter fruit than the table varieties. European types that we see locally include Zinfandel, Pinot Noir, Chardonnay, Riesling, and Gewürztraminer; east of the Rockies, look for labrusca wine grapes or the French hybrids of labrusca and vinifera.

At the market, choose organically grown grapes that are plump and highly colored for their variety. The sweetest, ripest white grapes will have an amber glow to them. Don't worry if some have become detached from the stem; that happens when grapes are ripe. But don't buy bunches that have soft, moldy, or discolored grapes.

To serve grapes at the table, cut the bunches into convenient sizes with scissors or kitchen shears and rinse in a basin of cold water. To serve them cold, just put the clusters into a bowl of ice water. Grapes with seeds should be halved and seeded before being used for cooking, but only the most fastidious will want to peel them.

Frosted grapes are fun and easy to do: Cut grape bunches into clusters of half a dozen or so. Mix an egg white with a teaspoon of water and paint this mixture on the grapes. Dust with granulated sugar and allow to dry on a rack before serving.

Zinfandel Grape Schiacciata

This focaccia-like bread is baked in the wine-growing regions of Italy at harvest time, when you see them in every bakery, bar, or café. The word *schiacciata* means "flattened out."

1½ teaspoons yeast
2 cups warm water
5½ cups unbleached all-purpose
   flour
½ teaspoon salt

2 pounds Zinfandel grapes
5 tablespoons olive oil
4 sprigs rosemary
¼ cup sugar or ⅓ cup honey

In the bowl of an electric mixer, stir the yeast into the water until it dissolves. Mix the flour and salt together in another bowl. Fit the electric mixer with a dough hook and, mixing at the lowest speed, gradually add the flour to the dissolved yeast. Keep mixing for 14 minutes. The dough should be soft and moist, just forming a loose ball that comes away from the sides of the bowl without completely lifting off the bottom. Add a little more flour if the dough seems too wet, a little more water if it seems too dry. (If mixing by hand, stir the flour and salt into the dissolved yeast and knead in the bowl for 5 minutes. The dough should be quite moist and slightly sticky. Let rest 12 minutes and then knead another 5 minutes.) Cover the bowl and let rise for 2 hours, or until the dough is doubled in size.

While the dough is rising, stem the grapes, rinse, and dry well. Heat the olive oil and gently fry the rosemary over medium heat just until crisp, about 2 or 3 minutes. Don't let it burn. Set aside to cool.

Preheat the oven to 450°F. Place a pizza stone, if you have one, on a lower rack.

Oil a 12- by 20-inch baking sheet with sides. When the dough has risen, gently stretch and press it with your fingers until it fills the pan. Let the dough rest for about 15 minutes. Dimple the surface with your fingertips, spread the grapes evenly over the surface, and sprinkle with sugar or drizzle with honey. Remove the rosemary sprigs from the oil, strip off the leaves, and scatter them over the dough. Pour the oil all over the schiacciata and bake in the lower third of the oven, preferably on a pizza stone, until the bottom and sides are golden, from 30 to 40 minutes. Halfway through the baking time, use a pastry brush to spread the liquids collecting in the middle over all the schiacciata.

Makes 1 schiacciata, about 12 by 20 inches; serves 8 to 10.

Note: The dough can be made a day ahead and kept in the refrigerator overnight. Take it out the next day, put it in a bowl, and let it rise until it is doubled in size, then proceed as above. This yields a tastier dough.

VERJUICE

Verjuice (literally "green juice") is the sour juice of green, unripe wine grapes. Called *verjus* in France, it was widely employed in European cooking as a souring ingredient as long ago as medieval times and as recently as the twentieth century, when its use mostly disappeared, perhaps because of the availability and convenience of cheap lemons. The common use of verjuice has survived in southwestern France, however, where it can still be found at farmers' markets and, more surprisingly, at pharmacies, where it is sold for its medicinal properties. For centuries certain grape varieties were grown for verjuice alone, but these have disappeared, and nowadays verjuice is made from various kinds of wine grapes. Grapes for verjuice should be green but not *too* tiny and immature, picked about halfway through the ripening process. Unless verjuice is pasteurized, it does not keep well because it ferments quickly.

If you have access to unripe grapes, you can make your own verjuice. To help retard fermentation, plunge bunches of the grapes into boiling water and immediately refresh them in cold water. Drain and dry well. Pluck the grapes off their stems and crush them with a pestle or process them briefly in a mixer with a paddle attachment. Strain the crushed grapes through a strainer lined with cheesecloth, pressing down on the skins to extract as much juice as possible. Use all the verjuice over the next few days; it won't keep long.

Verjuice is a delightful flavoring and acidifying agent in the kitchen. It has a little less acidity than lemon juice and vinegar and a little more subtle sweetness. When ordinarily you would squeeze a lemon or sprinkle a few drops of vinegar over a dish, try reaching instead for verjuice. It is delicious with poultry, foie gras, fish, and all kinds of salads, particularly those with fruit.

Sardine Pasta with Fennel and Raisins

This dish, *pasta con le sarde*, is among those that reflect the strong Moorish influence on Sicilian cuisine. It is best made with wild fennel, which has a deeper, more pungent anise flavor than the cultivated strains. Fennel is a common weed in northern California, easily found; spring is the best time to forage for it, when it has lots of tender new growth. If wild fennel is unavailable, use sweet fennel, but be sure to use the stalks and feathery leaves as well as the bulb.

1¼ pounds whole fresh sardines, or ¾ pound fresh sardine fillets	*1 onion, diced*
	⅓ cup dried currants or sultana raisins
1 pound wild fennel stalks and leaves, or 2 small bulbs sweet fennel plus 1 cup chopped stalks and leaves	*⅓ cup pine nuts*
	2 pinches saffron threads steeped in 2 tablespoons warm water
Salt and pepper	*1½ pounds pasta (bucatini or perciatelli)*
Olive oil	
4 salt-packed anchovies	*1 cup bread crumbs, toasted*

Fillet the sardines, taking care to remove all the scales and large bones; the small bones are too fine to worry about. Boil the fennel in salted water until tender, about 10 to 15 minutes. Drain well, reserving the water; allow to cool, squeeze out the excess moisture, and chop.

Take half the sardine fillets, season with salt and pepper, and fry them in a little olive oil on both sides until golden, 2 to 3 minutes per side. Remove and set aside. In the same pan, sauté the chopped fennel for a few minutes. Soak the anchovies for 5 minutes and then fillet.

Heat about ¼ cup olive oil in a large heavy-bottomed pan over medium-high heat. Sauté the onion until golden. Add the currants and pine nuts and cook for another few minutes. Add the other half of the sardine fillets, the anchovies, and the saffron and water and season generously with salt and pepper. Continue to cook, mashing the sardines and anchovies with a wooden spoon until the fish has been reduced to a paste, 7 minutes or more. Add the fennel and some of its cooking liquid and cook another few minutes. Taste for seasoning.

Cook the pasta in the fennel water (topped up with as much more water as needed). When done, drain, reserving 1 cup of the liquid. Toss the noodles with the sauce in the pan, adding liquid if the pasta appears too dry. Let the dish sit for 5 to 10 minutes in the warm pan before serving to allow the flavors to intermingle. Serve garnished with the fried sardine fillets and toasted bread crumbs. In Sicily the dish is served both warm and cold.

Serves 6.

GRAPES ROASTED IN A WOOD OVEN

Roasted grapes are an absurdly simple and unexpectedly tasty accompaniment to roasted meat. When the wine harvest is in full swing and delicious wine grapes are available, use those, but even prosaic table grape varieties—seedless Red Flame grapes, for example—gain considerable gustatory interest prepared this way. Start with beautiful bunches of grapes; with a sharp pair of scissors, cut the bunches into smallish pretty clusters. Lay them in a single layer in a baking dish or on a sheet pan and drizzle with olive oil. Roast them in a very hot oven, preferably an aromatic wood-fired one, for about 10 minutes, until they are very hot all the way through and just beginning to pucker and collapse. Serve immediately.

FRESH GRAPE JUICE

Use fresh, ripe organic grapes. Not surprisingly, wine grapes make good juice. First crush the grapes in a barrel with your feet—just kidding!—in an electric mixer with the paddle attachment or in a bowl with a potato masher or a whisk. Let the resulting mush sit for a few hours to allow the skins to give flavor and color to the juice. Strain through a sieve, pushing down hard on the fruit to extract as much juice as possible. If you think it needs it, sweeten the juice to taste with honey or sugar. Drink chilled, either straight or diluted with a little water.

Sicilian-Style Swordfish Stuffed with Currants and Pine Nuts

The exact dimensions of the swordfish are not so important, but the slices must be very thin in order to be flexible enough to roll up. Your fishmonger may be able to slice the swordfish for you.

This stuffing is also notably delicious rolled up inside boned fresh sardines.

1 cup fresh bread crumbs
Extra-virgin olive oil
1 small onion
1 pinch saffron threads
3 salt-packed anchovies
2 oranges
¼ cup dried currants or
*   sultana raisins*

¼ cup pine nuts
3 tablespoons chopped parsley
1 teaspoon chopped oregano
Salt and pepper
2 pounds swordfish, cut into
*   twelve ⅛-inch-thick slices,*
*   about 4 by 6 inches*
Bay leaves

Preheat the oven to 375°F.

Toss the bread crumbs with 2 tablespoons olive oil, spread them out on a baking sheet, and toast in the oven, stirring occasionally, for 10 to 15 minutes, until golden. Dice the onion and gently sauté with the saffron in 2 tablespoons olive oil until soft, about 12 minutes. Rinse and fillet the anchovies and chop coarsely. Squeeze ¼ cup juice from one of the oranges and pour it over the currants or raisins to plump them. Toast the pine nuts just until golden, about 7 minutes.

In a mixing bowl, stir together the bread crumbs, onion, anchovies, currants (with their orange juice), pine nuts, parsley, and oregano. Season generously with salt and pepper.

Lay out the swordfish slices and season with salt and pepper. Spoon about 2 tablespoons stuffing onto each slice and roll up. Arrange each roll, flap side down, in an oiled baking dish just big enough to hold them all snugly.

Cut the remaining orange in half vertically through the stem and cut each half into ¼-inch-thick half-moon slices. Wedge the orange slices and bay leaves between the swordfish rolls, drizzle olive oil over, and bake for 15 minutes, until the rolls are opaque and just firm to the touch.

Serves 6.

Raisin Shortbread Cookies

For a more delicate cookie, chop the raisins instead of adding them whole (most easily done with an oiled knife).

*½ pound (2 sticks) unsalted
    butter, room temperature*
½ teaspoon salt
1 teaspoon vanilla extract
1 cup powdered sugar

*2½ cups unbleached
    all-purpose flour*
2 cups raisins
1 egg

Preheat the oven to 350°F.

Beat together the butter, salt, and vanilla until creamy. Add the powdered sugar and continue beating until light and fluffy. Stir in the flour to make a thick dough. With your hands, gather the dough into 2 balls, one a little larger than the other. Flatten the smaller ball of dough into a thin, even layer on the bottom of a 9- by 13-inch baking dish, as you would a tart shell. (Or use a larger baking sheet with low sides and press the dough into a 9- by 13-inch rectangle.) Spread the raisins evenly over the dough and gently press to embed them. Break the other ball of dough into pieces and distribute them over the raisins. Pressing gently, spread and flatten them to cover all the raisins evenly with a layer of dough. (If the baking dish is shallow enough, you can finish the top with a rolling pin.)

Beat the egg and use a pastry brush to coat the top of the dough evenly with egg. Slowly drag a fork back and forth across the dough to make a decorative pattern, using the back of the tines. Crisscrossed diagonal lines look quite nice. Bake about 40 minutes, until light golden brown. Cool and cut into 1- by 3-inch rectangular bars.

Makes about 3 dozen cookies.

Concord Grape Sherbet

Sherbet brings out the bright candy flavor of dark, seedy Concord grapes. Wine grapes can make good sherbet too. Taste the grapes critically: grape sherbet is only as good as the grapes themselves.

Wash and stem the grapes. Put them in a saucepan with ¼ inch of water in the bottom of the pan. Cook the grapes over medium-high heat for about 15 minutes, stirring and mashing them to release the juice. Pass the cooked grape mash first through a food mill and then through a fine-mesh sieve to remove all the seeds and skin.

Measure the strained juice. For every cup of juice, stir in 1 tablespoon sugar and 2 tablespoons light corn syrup. Heat the mixture gently if necessary, but if the juice is still warm, the sugar should dissolve. Chill the sherbet base and freeze according to the instructions for your ice cream maker.

GRAPEFRUIT, PUMMELOS, AND THEIR RELATIVES ❧

Season: Grapefruit, year-round; pummelos, midwinter through spring

Fruit experts disagree about the origins of grapefruit, how it was named, and even what species it is, but there is little debate about how delicious grapefruit are and how they perk up tired taste buds. Grapefruit are as common at the breakfast table as the morning newspaper and cup of coffee, usually served cut in half with the segments cut free from the rind and from each other for easy spooning.

It's been years since Chez Panisse offered breakfast, so our delectation of grapefruit is limited to lunch and dinner. In the spring and summer we make salads with wedges of rich, pale green avocado and segments of pink or champagne-colored organic grapefruit. In the fall we sometimes serve a risotto with grapefruit and other citrus fruit. In the winter, when fresh fruit can be scarce, grapefruit are made into sherbet or mixed in compotes and macédoines with other tropical and subtropical fruits. And delicious candied grapefruit peel is used all year round.

Grapefruit seems to have a particular affinity for sparkling wines; we like to add Prosecco to our grapefruit sherbet before freezing, and sometimes we serve a tiny scoop of grapefruit sherbet in a glass of Champagne as an apéritif.

When is grapefruit season? Always, because the fruit is grown in parts of the country where it ripens at different times of the year. Depending on how hot the growing season, grapefruit take anywhere from seven to fourteen months to mature after the trees bloom in spring. Grapefruit from Florida and Texas come to market from October through June, while Arizona grapefruit ripen from January through September and California grapefruit from February through November.

Although well known in their native regions of Southeast Asia, where they are associated with New Year's celebrations, pummelos are not yet commonly seen in the United States, although their distribution is expanding. A measure of their rarity is the confusion over their name: "pomelo" and "pumelo" are both commonly encountered spelling variants, and the fruit has also been known in English as the "pompelmous" and as the "shaddock" (after a seventeenth-century seafaring Captain Shaddock, perhaps a progenitor of the nineteenth-century Mr. Shattuck for whom our Berkeley street is named). Pummelos resemble grapefruit but are larger; they may be round or slightly pear-shaped. Because they are the largest citrus fruit (weighing as much as twenty pounds apiece), botanists have given pummelos the name *Citrus maxima*. There are many varieties, ranging in flavor from subacid to very acid, with the most interesting ones somewhere in between. Pummelos ripen from midwinter into spring.

Grapefruit were first identified as a fruit separate from the pummelo in the mid-eighteenth century in Barbados and Jamaica, where pummelos had been introduced at the end of the previous century. For a long time botanists felt that they had developed as a result of a pummelo mutation. Current thinking is that they are a natural hybrid of a pummelo and an orange, not a separate species; this situation is indicated by grapefruit's Latin name, *Citrus x paradisi*. The common name probably comes from the tendency of grapefruit to grow in clusters on the trees.

The most widely grown grapefruit is Marsh, a nearly seedless, medium-size variety with smooth yellow skin, pale beige pulp, and very juicy tender flesh. Another common variety is Redblush, a pink-fleshed grapefruit often called Ruby Red or just Ruby; it has yellow skin tinged with red and flesh that is pale to light pink. (The hotter the climate, the more intense the color.)

Rio Red and Star Ruby are the most common red grapefruit varieties. They both have distinctly reddish skin and deep red flesh that is firmer and smoother than that of Redblush. They also have slightly higher levels of acidity and sugar. Rio Red and Star Ruby grapefruit from Texas are marketed under a broad-brush trademark, Rio Star.

Two varieties of pummelo that were developed in California can often be found in Asian markets. The large, round Chandler pummelo has yellow skin and pink flesh. The even larger, pear-shaped Reinking is white-fleshed. The flesh of both is noticeably firmer and less juicy than that of grapefruit and is well balanced between sweet and sour.

Pummelos and grapefruit have been hybridized to combine the characteristics of their parents in specific ways. One hybrid we like, called Oroblanco, is mild and sweet and has juicy, tender white flesh and none of the bitterness of grapefruit. It is available from early winter into spring and makes delicious sweet juice.

At the market, look for grapefruit with smooth, glossy skins that are heavy for their size: they will be juiciest. Don't buy fruits that look puffy or rough. A grapefruit can be round or slightly flattened but should not look pushed out of shape. The color of its skin or the presence of slight blemishes provides no clue to how good it will taste. Pummelos have thicker skin with very fine hairs and will feel lighter than grapefruit of equivalent size, but the same rules apply for choosing good-quality fruit.

Pummelos and grapefruit keep well for up to a week at room temperature and two to three weeks when refrigerated.

Grapefruit and pummelos are easiest to eat and look their best when peeled and segmented. Use a small, thin-bladed utility knife to slice off both ends of the fruit. Keep shaving off slices of peel until you see the flesh. (The scraps of peel may be trimmed and candied, but it is easier to candy bigger pieces cut from juiced grapefruit or pummelo halves.) Stand the fruit on end and cut away the peel from the sides, going just deep enough to reveal the flesh while retaining a roughly spherical shape. Go back over the fruit to make sure you have removed all bits of the pith, or white part of the peel, which is also called the albedo. Holding the fruit in your hand over a bowl, carefully cut along the membrane on either side of a segment, going toward the center of the fruit. The segment will drop into the bowl when freed from its membrane. Continue around the fruit, removing all the segments. Squeeze the remains of the membrane over the bowl to extract any remaining juice. Taste a segment and season the rest with sugar if you like. Large segments of pummelo may need to be cut into smaller pieces for serving.

Vin de Pamplemousse

This invigorating but light apéritif was popularized at Chez Panisse by one of the Café cooks, who started making it at home in nearly commercial quantities to meet the demand from her colleagues.

2 white grapefruit
4 Ruby Red grapefruit
3 Meyer lemons, or 2 sweet
oranges
One 2-inch piece vanilla bean,
split lengthwise

4.5 liters (six 750-ml bottles)
crisp white wine
(such as Sauvignon Blanc)
¾ liter (about 3 cups) 80-proof
vodka
1¾ cups sugar

Select grapefruit that smell fragrant and floral when the skin is lightly scratched. Wash all the fruit and then slice into ½-inch-thick rounds. Combine all the ingredients in a nonreactive container and stir well to dissolve the sugar. Cover the container and store in a cool, dark place or the refrigerator for 1 month. Check the vin de pamplemousse once a week, stirring and tasting. Adjust the mixture to your taste, adding more sugar if it seems too bitter or adding more fruit and wine if it seems too sweet.

After 1 month, strain out and discard the solids and let the apéritif sit covered and undisturbed for a couple of days so that the cloudy bits settle. Carefully strain the liquid through several layers of cheesecloth, but stop pouring when you get to the cloudy part at the bottom. This process can be repeated until the vin de pamplemousse is crystal clear—or not, depending on how fussy you are.

Bottle the apéritif in clean wine bottles and cork tightly. Vin de pamplemousse will keep for several months at cellar temperature, longer if refrigerated.

Makes 5 liters (about 5 quarts).

GRILLED SALMON WITH CITRUS SAUCE

Our longtime downstairs chef, Jean-Pierre Moullé, came up with this amazing sauce for salmon. It uses the bounty of citrus in the early spring when the first-of-the-season salmon tastes light and delicate. Serve this on a mound of potato purée, with some wilted spinach on the side.

1 tangerine	*2 cups fish stock*
1 lemon	*¼ cup extra-virgin olive oil*
1 orange	*Salt and pepper*
1 lime	*Six 6-ounce pieces wild salmon*
1 grapefruit	

With a sharp vegetable peeler, carefully peel all the zest from the tangerine, lemon, orange, and lime, and half of the grapefruit zest. Be sure to take only the colored peel and none of the bitter white pith. If you do end up with some pith on the strips of zest, remove it with a sharp paring knife. Bring a small pot of water to a boil and parboil the citrus zest for 3 minutes. Drain well and cut the strips into a thin julienne. Squeeze the juice of ½ of each fruit and mix together.

Bring the fish stock to a boil and reduce to ⅓ cup. While the stock is still hot, mix it with ⅓ cup of the fruit juice and whisk in the olive oil. Season with salt and pepper and add 3 tablespoons of the julienned zest. Keep warm but not hot, lest the fruit juices lose their fresh flavor.

Make a fire in the grill and let it burn down to a bed of hot coals. Season the salmon with salt and pepper. Clean the grill well with a wire brush and then oil it with a clean rag and olive oil. Oil the fish well and grill from 3 to 4 minutes on each side, depending on the thickness of the fillets. The salmon should be just set but still a little translucent at its center. Arrange on a plate and spoon the sauce over, distributing the zest evenly around.

Serves 6.

CITRUS RISOTTO ALLA REGALEALI

We adapted this recipe from the version in Anna Tasca Lanza's lovely Sicilian cookbook, *The Heart of Sicily*. It makes an admirable accompaniment to grilled salmon or roast chicken.

1 Meyer lemon	*3 tablespoons unsalted butter*
1 tangerine	*2 cups Carnaroli, Baldo, or*
1 lime	*Arborio rice*
1 blood or Valencia orange	*1 cup white wine*
1 Ruby grapefruit	*1 teaspoon salt*
6 cups chicken stock	*⅓ cup grated Parmigiano-*
1 onion	*Reggiano cheese*

With a swivel-bladed vegetable peeler, remove about half the zest of the lemon, tangerine, lime, and orange and about a quarter of the grapefruit zest, taking care to peel only the thin outer colored part and none of the bitter white pith below. Plunge the strips of zest in boiling water for 3 minutes. Drain them, and when they are cool enough to handle, cut them crosswise into a tiny julienne. You should have about 2 tablespoons. Cut away all the remaining rind from the citrus fruits then cut the sections free, carefully slicing along the partitioning membranes. Set aside about a quarter of the grapefruit sections and about half of the other citrus sections to add to the risotto later and to garnish it. Refrigerate the rest for another use.

Heat the chicken stock to a bare simmer. Dice the onion and sauté it in a heavy-bottomed pan in 2 tablespoons of the butter. When the onion is soft, after 7 to 10 minutes, add the rice. Cook the rice in the butter for 3 to 4 minutes, until the grains begin to turn translucent. Then add the white wine, stir well, and when the rice has absorbed most of the wine, begin adding the stock, a ladleful or two at a time. Cook the risotto at a simmer, stirring frequently and adding more stock as each addition is absorbed by the rice. Do not flood the rice with stock; each addition of liquid should just cover the rice. Keep stirring to prevent sticking and to develop the creamy starch. Add the salt with the second addition of stock. After 10 minutes, add half of the julienned zest and half of the reserved fruit sections. When the rice is almost done but still a little too al dente, turn off the heat and stir in the remaining tablespoon of butter, the grated cheese, and the rest of the zest and fruit sections. Stir well and let sit for 3 to 4 minutes. Check the seasoning and the consistency one last time, adjusting with more salt and stock, as needed, and serve immediately.

Serves 6.

Ruby Grapefruit, Avocado, and Spring Onion Salad

2 large or 3 medium	5 tablespoons extra-virgin
Ruby grapefruit	olive oil
2 teaspoons Champagne	3 handfuls rocket (arugula)
vinegar	1 medium spring onion
Salt and pepper	2 ripe avocados

With a sharp knife, cut the top and bottom off each grapefruit. Cutting strips from top to bottom, cut away the rind and membrane, cutting all the way down to the flesh. Once the grapefruit are peeled, cut the sections free, carefully slicing along the partitioning membranes. Put the grapefruit sections in a bowl and squeeze in the juice from the remaining membrane and pith. Measure out 2 tablespoons grapefruit juice from the bowl and mix with the vinegar. Season with salt and a generous grind of pepper and whisk in the olive oil. Taste and adjust the salt and acid as needed.

Wash the rocket and dry well. Cut off the root end from the onion and trim away the tough dark green part of the stalk. Cut the onion in half lengthwise and remove any dirty outer layers. Cut the onion into thin half-moons, and marinate them in a small bowl, tossed with 1 tablespoon of the dressing. Cut the avocados in half, remove the pits, and gently scoop out the flesh with a large spoon. Place the halves, cut side down, on a cutting board and cut lengthwise into ¼-inch-thick slices. Toss the rocket with 1 tablespoon of the dressing. Make a nest of rocket on a serving platter, arrange the avocado slices and grapefruit segments on it, and spoon over the remaining dressing. Garnish with the marinated onion and serve.

Serves 6.

CANDIED GRAPEFRUIT PEEL

Although grapefruit peel is quite bitter and requires multiple blanchings in fresh water before it can be candied successfully, the results are positively delicious. The famous Parisian *pâtissier* Gaston Lenôtre taught us to blanch the peel five times, although we get away with just four.

3 grapefruit
4½ cups sugar
2 cups water

Wash the grapefruit. Cut them in half and juice them. Drink the juice or save it and make sherbet. Cut the halves in half. Transfer the quarters into a large saucepan and cover with cold water. Bring to a boil over low heat and simmer for 10 minutes. Drain the peel, return it to the pot, cover with cold water, bring to a boil, and again simmer for 10 minutes. Repeat this process twice more, for a total of 4 blanchings in all. After the final blanching, make sure the peel is completely tender: the point of a knife should slide in easily; if it doesn't, continue cooking. Drain the soggy peel and let it cool off. Scrape away the remaining inside membrane and flesh from the peel with a sharp-edged spoon. Slice the peel into long ¼-inch-thick strips.

The grapefruit peel is now ready to be candied. Return it to the saucepan and add 4 cups sugar and the water. Stir the mixture together over low heat until the sugar dissolves. Then slowly cook the peel in its sugar syrup until it has become translucent and the syrup boils with a rapid upsurge of small bubbles. The syrup's temperature should reach 230°F. Turn off the heat and let the peel soak in the syrup for ½ hour. Drain the peel and arrange the strips, not touching one another, on a rack or parchment paper–lined baking sheet and let them air-dry overnight. The next day toss them with ½ cup sugar; store in an airtight container, refrigerated, for up to 6 months.

Makes about 4 cups.

HUCKLEBERRIES 🐛

Season: Late summer through fall

There seems to be some confusion about the difference between huckleberries and blueberries because the two names are used interchangeably for some wild blueberries. Most people can quickly distinguish cultivated blueberries from their wild cousins: the cultivated ones are larger and juicier. But what do you call the small, thick-skinned, tangy, blue-colored wild berries?

Botanists, of course, make a specific differentiation between huckleberries and blueberries. The botanists' huckleberry, *Gaylusaccia*, grows mostly east of the Rockies; its defining characteristic is the ten hard, bony seeds each berry contains, seeds that crunch hard when you bite down on them. There are more than forty native species of true huckleberries; the most commonly found is the black huckleberry, *G. baccata*, which grows from the Atlantic Coast west to Wisconsin, north into Canada, and as far south as Louisiana. Black huckleberries have been found growing wild around Chicago. They also sometimes grow in the same areas as wild blueberries, where they are considered weeds when their large-seeded fruit gets harvested along with the small-seeded blueberries. Black huckleberry bushes grow about three feet tall and have many delicate branches bearing dotted leaves, slender reddish flowers, and shiny black fruit. Black huckleberries ripen in late spring and early summer, as do most other species of wild huckleberries.

Very few true huckleberries are found west of the Mississippi. Most western "huckleberries" are members of the genus *Vaccinium,* which also includes blueberries and cranberries, as well as the English whortleberry, the Danish bilberry, the French myrtille, and the Scandinavian lingonberry. Twelve species of *Vaccinium* can be found in Washington and Oregon, and their fruit can be red, blue, or black. The berries can be variously produced, either in clusters or along the branches one by one. The best of these wild berries is the thin-leafed huckleberry, *V. membranaceum,* which bears small, sweet, aromatic berries singly on its branches. Another choice species is the Cascade huckleberry, *V. deliciosum.*

Very few huckleberries are cultivated; almost all are gathered from the wild. They produce their most abundant crops in sunny forest clearings, burned areas, or at the edges of woods. The huckleberries we use at Chez Panisse are both wild and truly organic, foraged from the slopes of the Cascade Mountains in Washington and Oregon between mid-August and early October.

Individuals who pick berries on public lands in the Cascades and elsewhere are subject to a limit of three gallons of huckleberries per year in certain areas. I doubt if the casual picker ever accumulates much more than a quart, since huckleberries are very tiny and only hand-picking is allowed. Pickers who sell wild berries must obtain a Special Forest Product permit.

Some wild varieties are available for home planting from nurseries that specialize in berries. And some states allow starts of the black huckleberry, *G. baccata,* to be transplanted from the wild. Whether you harvest all your homegrown huckleberries or not, *G. baccata* bushes are very attractive as landscape plants and provide food for birds and other wildlife.

Wild huckleberries are sometimes found in specialty produce markets in the early fall. Look for whole, plump berries that have not started to ooze juice. Their color may vary from red to purple to black, depending on the variety. When you get them home, lay them out on a sheet of parchment paper or some other clean, disposable surface and pick over them, sorting out and discarding any tiny stems and extraneous leaves, twigs, and such. Huckleberries keep very well in the refrigerator, but if you won't be using them within a couple of days, it is a good idea to freeze them. They can be taken directly from the freezer and used as you would fresh berries.

Because of their tart flavor and tough skin (and the large seeds of true huckleberries), huckleberries of all kinds are better eaten cooked than raw. A cupful of wild huckleberries is enough to strongly flavor an apple or pear crisp, and huckleberry preserves and syrups have an intense unusual wild flavor. The bony seeds of true huckleberries are easily strained out once the berries are puréed. Huckleberry purée also makes ice cream and sherbet with concentrated flavor and a pleasing tartness. And a few huckleberries can always be folded into muffin or pancake batter. The affinity of huckleberries for wild game has been observed for a long time: the first European explorers of Wisconsin described Native Americans using huckleberries to thicken and flavor game stews.

APPLE HUCKLEBERRY CRISP

2½ pounds apples (we use
   a combination of Golden
   Delicious and Pippin)
¾ cup huckleberries

1 tablespoon flour
¼ cup sugar
3 cups crisp topping (page 289)

Preheat the oven to 375°F.

Peel and core the apples and slice them into ¼-inch wedges. Toss the apples, huckleberries, flour, and sugar in a large mixing bowl. Transfer the fruit to an ovenproof earthenware dish large enough to hold the mixture, slightly mounded at the center. Spoon the topping evenly over the mixture, pressing down lightly to form a crust and leaving no fruit exposed. Put the dish on a baking sheet to catch any overflowing juices, or wrap the bottom of the baking dish with aluminum foil, folding the sides up and around the rim to catch the drips.

Bake on the center rack of the oven for 45 to 55 minutes, until the topping is dark golden brown and the juices have thickened slightly. Serve warm with lightly sweetened cream or ice cream.

Serves 6.

Variations: Other fruits may be substituted in the same general proportions, but some fruits may require more or less sugar and flour, depending on their natural sweetness and juiciness. Peaches, for example, require more flour and less sugar.

GRILLED SQUAB WITH HUCKLEBERRY SAUCE

6 fresh whole squab	*1 clove*
Olive oil	*2 allspice berries*
1 carrot, peeled and roughly	*1 branch thyme*
* chopped*	*5 cups chicken stock*
1 onion, peeled and roughly	*Salt and pepper*
* chopped*	*3 tablespoons sweet wine*
1 stalk celery, sliced	*¼ cup white wine*
1 cup red wine	*2 cups huckleberries*
¼ teaspoon peppercorns	*2 tablespoons port*

Preheat the oven to 400°F.

Cut the thighs and legs off the pigeons and remove the breast meat; cover and refrigerate. Spread the boned carcasses on a roasting pan and roast at 400°F. until completely browned, about 35 to 45 minutes. Pour off the fat and reserve the pan to be deglazed later. Chop up the browned bones or, better yet, pound them in a big mortar or smash them up at low speed in the bowl of a standing electric mixer fitted with a paddle.

Heat a bit of olive oil in a heavy-bottomed stockpot and cook the carrot, onion, and celery until browned and softened. Add the red wine, peppercorns, clove, allspice, and thyme. Bring to a boil and reduce by half. Meanwhile, deglaze the roasting pan with a little chicken stock, scraping up all the brown bits, and add to the reducing wine along with the bones and the rest of the stock. Simmer, skimming off any scum that rises to the top. Cook for 2½ to 3 hours. Strain, pressing down on the bones to extract as much liquid and flavor as possible. This can all be done a day ahead.

Season the squab parts generously with salt and pepper and toss them in a bowl with the sweet and white wines. Marinate for at least 2 hours.

Simmer the huckleberries and port together until the berries are soft and juicy, about 10 to 15 minutes. Pass through a food mill.

Skim off any fat from the squab stock. Bring the stock to a boil and reduce to 1 cup. Season with salt and add the huckleberry purée to taste.

Prepare a wood or charcoal fire. Grill the squab over medium-hot coals. Start with the legs, skin side up; this helps seal the skin around the legs. Cook for 6 minutes, turn them over, and cook for 6 more minutes. Place the breasts on the grill, skin side down, and grill about 5 minutes, until golden; turn them over and grill just a minute or two more. Squab breasts taste the very best grilled medium-rare. Let them sit for 5 minutes before slicing. Serve the legs and sliced breasts on a warm platter with the sauce ladled over.

Serves 6.

HUCKLEBERRY ICE CREAM

Be sure to wear an apron: huckleberry stains are difficult to remove.

6 egg yolks
1 cup half-and-half
1¼ cups sugar
2 cups heavy cream, chilled

2 cups huckleberries
4 teaspoons lemon juice
Optional: 2 teaspoons kirsch

In a mixing bowl, whisk the egg yolks just enough to break them up. Gently heat the half-and-half and ¾ cup sugar in a nonreactive saucepan, stirring slowly over low heat until the half-and-half is steaming and the sugar is dissolved. Drizzle the warm mixture into the egg yolks, whisking constantly as you pour.

Measure the heavy cream into the mixing bowl. Return the half-and-half and egg yolk mixture to the saucepan and place over low heat. Stirring slowly and scraping the bottom of the pan with a wooden spoon or heat-resistant rubber spatula, cook the mixture until it thickens enough to coat the spoon. Immediately remove the mixture from the heat and strain through a fine-mesh sieve into the mixing bowl, whisking it into the cold heavy cream. Cover and chill thoroughly.

Stir together the berries and ½ cup sugar in a saucepan. Cook over medium heat until the sugar is dissolved and the berries have released their juices. Pass the berries through a food mill. Stir the berry purée into the chilled ice cream base. Stir in the lemon juice and kirsch, if using, and freeze according to the instructions for your ice cream maker.

Makes about 1 quart.

KIWIFRUIT 🦐

Season: Late fall through spring

The beautiful emerald-green, aromatic flesh of the kiwifruit has a flavor that has been compared to that of bananas, pineapples, strawberries, and melons. But, of course, their flavor is distinctively their own: refreshingly bright, slightly tart. We use the organically grown California kiwifruit available to us in winter and spring primarily for sherbet and in compotes with citrus or other tropical fruits. Kiwifruit are also good sliced into fruit salads and on the tops of tarts or simply cut in half and spooned out of the skin for a quick snack.

Kiwifruit are a bit odd-looking, with their thin, greenish-brown skin covered with fuzzy brown hair. The oblong fruit, two to three inches long and an inch or two across, has succulent pale to dark green flesh surrounding a soft, whitish, central core ringed with small, edible, purple-black seeds. Kiwifruit are harvested in late fall at a firm stage when they are not completely ripe but have enough sugar to ripen fully later on. After harvest they can be stored for months and brought to market as needed in winter and spring. Starch in the fruit is converted to sugar both during storage and when the fruit is later allowed to ripen at room temperature.

Wild kiwifruit vines climb over trees, bushes, and rocky hillsides throughout most of the forests of Asia, principally in India and China, but also as far north as eastern Siberia and as far south as Java. The fruit is eaten in China but seldom cultivated; about 1,000 tons are harvested each year from the wild. The kiwifruit was first introduced to the rest of the world in the mid-nineteenth century, becoming known as the Chinese gooseberry because its flesh resembles that of cultivated gooseberries in color and texture.

Outside Asia, Chinese gooseberries were first planted as ornamentals. Commercial production began in the 1930s in New Zealand, but it wasn't until 1960 that a southern California produce dealer started importing the fruit to the United States. Marketers renamed them kiwis, appropriately calling to mind both the small fuzzy bird and the use of its name as a nickname for a New Zealander. The first commercial harvests in California began in 1970. In 1974 marketers decreed a new "official" one-word name: kiwifruit.

Serious regard for kiwifruit has suffered from relentless marketing, beginning with the efforts of New Zealand growers in the 1960s and '70s. To spark exports, they promoted kiwifruit as an all-purpose garnish for savory dishes, as well as a dessert fruit, and chefs jumped on board. Kiwifruit became such a tiresome motif of French nouvelle cuisine that we still think twice before putting them on the menu.

Kiwifruit found in the market are varieties of *Actinidia deliciosa* that have been selected for large size and good flavor and storage characteristics; almost all are the Hayward variety or close relatives. This is the kind we get from the Four Sisters Farm, near the central coast of California. Their sweet, organic kiwifruit are left on the vine to ripen just a little longer than other commercial ones.

The Hayward variety grows best in subtropical areas that have a long growing season but a sufficient amount of winter cold to induce dormancy. Kiwifruit vines are either male or female, so growers must plant a few males to pollinate the female vines that bear fruit.

Kiwifruit vines are attractive and can be a part of an edible landscape for those who have room for robust climbers. Besides the tender *A. deliciosa*, there are several species of hardy kiwifruit, notably *A. arguta*, that can tolerate the cold of a midwestern winter. Hardy kiwifruit vines bear small, greenish-yellow, smooth-skinned fruits that are very sweet and juicy if picked when they are soft-ripe. Unlike fuzzy kiwifruit, they do not store well, but they can be eaten skin and all. Remember that if you want fruit, you must have both male and female vines.

When shopping for kiwifruit, buy plump ones that have unbroken skin and no dark areas that may indicate bruising. Fruit for immediate consumption should just give to gentle pressure, but firm fruit can easily be ripened at home, usually within a week, at room temperature.

Peeling the tender skin of kiwifruit is easy with a small paring knife. For serving, the fruit is usually sliced in rounds or quartered and cut into small chunks. It should be seasoned with a light sprinkling of sugar or a little orange juice and left to macerate for a half hour before serving.

122

Spring Fruit Compote with
Kiwifruit Sherbet and Coconut Meringue

¾ cup water
¼ cup sugar
3 blood oranges
¼ cup Champagne
1½ cups strawberries

3 kiwifruit
3½ cups kiwifruit sherbet
   (page 124)
12 shards of coconut meringue
   (recipe follows)

To make the compote, measure the water and sugar into a saucepan and grate the zest from one of the blood oranges into it. Heat the mixture just until the sugar dissolves. Remove from the heat and strain the syrup into a bowl to remove the zest. Add the Champagne. With a small, sharp knife, cut away all the orange rind, both the zest and the white pith below. Carefully cut out skinless orange segments, letting them drop into the syrup. Wash, hull, and slice the strawberries; peel, quarter, and slice the kiwifruit. Add to the orange segments in the syrup and serve in cold bowls with kiwifruit sherbet sandwiched between shards of coconut meringue.

Serves 6.

COCONUT MERINGUE
4 egg whites (about ½ cup),
   room temperature
¼ teaspoon cream of tartar
⅛ teaspoon salt

¾ cup sugar
½ cup unsweetened shredded
   coconut
¼ teaspoon vanilla extract
⅛ teaspoon almond extract

Preheat the oven to 275°F. Line a baking sheet with parchment paper.

In a clean, dry mixing bowl, beat the egg whites with the cream of tartar until frothy and beginning to hold soft peaks. Whisk in the salt and sugar and beat until glossy and firm but not dry. Fold in the coconut and vanilla and almond extracts. Spread the meringue about ¼ inch thick on the paper-lined baking sheet. Bake for 30 minutes, until the meringue is dry and beginning to turn golden. Let cool for a few minutes and peel off the parchment paper. Break into roughly 3-inch-square shards. Keep in an airtight container until ready to serve.

Makes about twelve 3-inch-square shards.

KIWIFRUIT SHERBET

1½ pounds kiwifruit (about 10)
½ cup sugar
Optional: A few drops kirsch

Peel the kiwifruit with a sharp knife and purée thoroughly in a food processor or blender. You should have about 2 cups of purée. In a small saucepan, heat the sugar with about ½ cup of the kiwifruit purée just long enough for the sugar to dissolve. Stir it into the rest of the purée and taste, adjusting the flavor with kirsch, if necessary. Cover and refrigerate.

When the sherbet base is cold, freeze according to the instructions for your ice cream maker.

Makes 3½ cups.

KUMQUATS ❧

Season: Winter

Kumquats start ripening around Christmastime, when the pretty little orange fruits are much in demand for interior decoration, especially the kumquats harvested on their stems with a few leaves attached. I sometimes wonder how many get tossed on the New Year's compost pile by people who don't really know what else to do with them.

But kumquats are the easiest citrus fruit to eat—after a quick rinse, just pop them in your mouth, skin, seeds, and all. These tiny round or oblong orange fruits, each about an inch across, are different from other citrus fruits in that the skin is sweet and the flesh is very tart.

Because kumquats are highly flavored, you probably would not want to eat a whole handful, but their sweet-tart flavor provides a nice accent in savory or sweet dishes. In the Café we use thinly sliced kumquats in salads with Belgian endive or onions and fennel. We also serve kumquats as a relish for grilled fish. Sliced kumquats are quick and easy to candy, and we like to sprinkle a few candied slices over lime sherbet and drizzle a little kumquat syrup on top, or fold chopped candied kumquats into ice cream. Kumquats make very good marmalade and preserves, either alone or in combination with other citrus fruits.

Kumquats originated in China and reached the United States by the mid-nineteenth century. Today they are grown commercially in Florida, California, and Texas. Besides having sweet skins, kumquats differ from other citrus fruits in having flowers that are distinctive in ways that perhaps only a botanist would appreciate; consequently, early in the twentieth century they were segregated from the other citrus in a new genus of their own, *Fortunella*.

Different kinds of kumquat were given their own species names, at least two of which can be found in our markets. Nagami (*F. margarita*) is the most widely grown variety, both here and in Asia. It has bright orange, oblong fruits with two to five seeds. The skin is highly flavored and the flesh quite tart. Meiwa (*F. crassifolia*) is harder to find but is much better for eating fresh. The round fruit is an inch or more across, and the pale orange skin is thick and sweet. The pulp is sweeter than that of Nagami and is sometimes seedless.

Kumquats are in season from November to March. They can be kept at room temperature for a week or for several weeks loosely covered in the refrigerator. At the market, choose fruits that are firm and shiny and have good color for their variety. Don't buy kumquats that have dull spots or any sign of mold. Wash them just before eating or cooking.

Slicing for salads or preserves is best done with a small, thin-bladed knife. Cut off the stem end and cut the fruit into ⅛-inch-thick slices. You can ignore the small white undeveloped seeds you find, but use the tip of the knife to pry out the larger hard seeds as you encounter them.

Kumquats may be preserved whole or sliced. Whole fruit should be blanched three times before preserving—covering with cold water, bringing to a boil, and draining each time. They should then be simmered in medium syrup (one part sugar to two parts water) until they become translucent. Sliced kumquats can be simmered in syrup until tender, without the preliminary blanching.

Kumquats grow on small compact trees; when grafted onto dwarf rootstock, they make very handsome container plants, especially when laden with fruit. Kumquats are the most cold-hardy of citrus and in warm climates can be grown outdoors all year. Where temperatures fall below 20°F., they should spend the winter indoors.

ENDIVE AND KUMQUAT SALAD

In California, hardier citrus varieties, such as tangerines, kumquats, and sour oranges, all thrive in the same climate as grapes, and many a vineyard owner has a few trees planted in the yard.

Belle Rhodes, who lives in the Napa Valley near Rutherford, gave us the idea for this salad. For each serving you will need 1 Belgian endive and 3 or 4 kumquats. Rinse the kumquats and slice them thin, picking out any seeds you encounter as you slice. Rinse the endive, cut away and discard about ¼ inch at the base, and separate the leaves. Rinse and drain the leaves, wrap loosely in a towel, and keep cool.

Just before serving, cut the endive leaves on the diagonal into inch-wide strips. Toss with the sliced kumquats, a sprinkling of salt, and a little good olive oil. Serve on chilled plates with a grind of black pepper and a little more olive oil drizzled over.

GILBERT'S SPRING ONION AND KUMQUAT RELISH

This simple relish, devised by Café chef Gilbert Pilgram, is fabulous with grilled tuna or baked halibut. It is also delicious as an element in an avocado salad, a combination that one of our waiters came up with during one of our daily tasting sessions.

20 kumquats
2 large red spring onions
1 pinch marash pepper or cayenne
Extra-virgin olive oil
Salt

Cut the kumquats crosswise into very thin round slices with a very sharp knife, prying out and discarding the seeds as you go. Cut the onions in half lengthwise, peel, and slice very thinly, cutting with the grain of the onion. Toss the kumquats and onions in a medium-size bowl, season with a pinch of marash pepper, and add enough olive oil to lightly coat the relish. Salt to taste and serve immediately.

Serves 6.

Candied Kumquat Ice Cream and Meyer Lemon Sherbet Tartlets

These tartlets are a cross between lemon meringue pie and baked Alaska. They're time-consuming to make but worth every bit of the effort. Prepare the tart dough and candied kumquats in advance to make the job easier.

5½ ounces pâte sucrée dough (page 296)
¾ cup half-and-half
1 cup sugar
4 egg yolks
1½ cups heavy cream
1 cup candied kumquat slices in their syrup (recipe follows)
1 teaspoon lemon juice
1 pint Meyer lemon sherbet (page 138)
6 egg whites

Roll out the dough to ¼-inch thickness on a lightly floured surface and cut into eight 4-inch circles. Carefully press each circle into a 3-inch tartlet pan. Press your thumb against the scalloped edge of each tartlet pan to pinch off the excess dough. Place the pans on a baking sheet and chill in the refrigerator for 30 minutes.

Preheat the oven to 325°F.

Bake the tartlet shells until golden, about 25 minutes. Let the shells cool, remove them from their pans, and place on a baking sheet. Cover the sheet of shells and place in the freezer for at least 30 minutes or overnight.

To make the candied kumquat ice cream, gently heat the half-and-half and ¼ cup sugar in a medium-size nonreactive saucepan, stirring occasionally, until the half-and-half is steaming and the sugar is dissolved. Whisk the yolks in a mixing bowl just enough to break them up. Whisk some of the hot liquid into the yolks and pour the yolk mixture into the saucepan. Stir with a wooden spoon over low heat until the mixture thickens and coats the spoon. Immediately remove from the heat and strain through a fine-mesh sieve. Whisk in the heavy cream to cool the mixture, cover, and chill thoroughly.

Drain the candied kumquat slices, reserving the syrup. Chop half the slices to stir into the ice cream and reserve the other half to garnish the tartlets. Stir the kumquat syrup and the lemon juice into the chilled ice cream base and freeze according to the instructions for your ice cream maker. Immediately after you take the ice cream out of the ice cream maker, stir in the chopped kumquats and spread about ¼ cup of ice cream into each frozen tartlet shell. Return the sheet of tartlets to the freezer for at least 30 minutes or overnight.

Put a 2-ounce scoop of Meyer lemon sherbet in the center of each frozen tartlet and freeze the tartlets again, this time for at least 2 hours.

Make a meringue by beating the egg whites until they begin to form soft peaks. Whisk in ¾ cup sugar and beat until the whites form stiff peaks that are glossy and firm but not dry. Spread a generous amount of meringue on top of each frozen tartlet, completely covering the ice cream and sherbet and touching the edges of the tartlet shells. Freeze the tartlets on their baking sheet for up to 2 hours, or bake immediately.

When ready to bake, preheat the oven to 500°F.

Put the baking sheet in the oven for 1½ to 2 minutes, just long enough for the meringue to firm up slightly and for its peaks to start to turn golden. Garnish the tartlets by sprinkling the reserved candied kumquat slices around the plate and serve them immediately.

Makes 8 tartlets.

CANDIED KUMQUATS

These little pinwheels are a bright addition to compotes made from dried fruits and tropical fruits. We serve them over ice cream as a garnish or chop and fold them into just-frozen vanilla ice cream to make kumquat ice cream.

Use a small, sharp paring knife to prepare the kumquats. Cut off and discard the little green stems. Slice the kumquats into ⅛-inch-thick rounds, removing and discarding the seeds as you slice. Put the slices in a small saucepan and cover with a mixture of two parts water and one part sugar. Simmer gently for 10 minutes, until tender. Let the kumquat slices cool in their syrup.

Kumquats and Prunes with Crème Fraîche

12 kumquats, sliced and seeded *1½ cups water*
1 pound dried prunes *⅔ cup sugar*
1 cup sweet white wine *½ cup crème fraîche*

Put all the ingredients except the crème fraîche in a medium-size saucepan. Simmer over low heat for 30 minutes, stirring occasionally, until the prunes are tender and plump. Remove from the heat and let the fruit cool in its juices. Serve with a dollop of crème fraîche.

Serves 6.

Kumquat Marmalade

This marmalade is easier to make than most because it requires no preliminary blanching of the fruit. We use it to fill cakes, tarts, and cookies.

1 pound kumquats
2½ cups sugar

Use a small, sharp paring knife to prepare the kumquats. First, cut off the little green stem and discard, then cut the fruit in half lengthwise and slice the halves crosswise into ⅛-inch-thick half rounds. Remove and discard the seeds as you slice. You should have about 3½ cups sliced kumquats. Put a plate in the freezer for testing the marmalade later.

Prepare three 8-ounce canning jars and their lids in boiling water, following the manufacturer's instructions.

Put the kumquats in a medium-size saucepan and cover with water. Measure in the sugar and boil over high heat for about 15 minutes, skimming off any white foam that rises to the top. As the marmalade starts to thicken and large bubbles form, start testing the consistency by putting a spoonful on the frozen plate to cool it quickly. When the marmalade has cooked to the thickness you want, turn off the heat and carefully ladle it into the prepared jars, allowing at least ¼ inch of headroom. Clean the lip of the jars with a damp clean towel, cover with the lids, and seal, following the manufacturer's instructions.

Makes 3 cups.

LEMONS 🦪

Season: Year-round, most abundant fall through spring

Cook without lemons? That would be like cooking without garlic or onions—unthinkable! Organically grown lemons are simply a given in our cooking. Lemons keep artichoke hearts from turning brown; they balance vinaigrettes, rich sauces, and mayonnaise; they add life to vegetables and fish. Lemons are important in desserts for accentuating the flavors of fruits such as peaches, nectarines, and strawberries; and the unmistakable perfume and flavor of Meyer lemons define several of our favorite desserts: lemon curd tart, lemon sherbet and ice cream, and lemon soufflé. After dessert, a thin strip of candied lemon peel is a most satisfying *mignardise*.

To those who have never tasted them, our recurring insistence on Meyer lemons may seem like an irritating California eccentricity, but I don't know many people who have tried one without getting hooked. Meyer lemons are widely planted as ornamentals in gardens throughout the state—backyard growers in the Bay Area always have big crops —but it wasn't until our longtime pastry chef Lindsey Shere started experimenting with them that our addiction and proselytization began. Now Meyer lemons have become so popular with restaurant chefs and home cooks alike that we suffer periodic shortages! Ripe Meyer lemons are sweeter than other lemons, and the skin has a distinctive floral fragrance, similar to a combination of lemon and orange. The fruits are rounder than common lemons and have golden yellow- to orange-tinged skin and tender, very juicy orange-yellow flesh. Meyer lemons can be used in many of the same ways as ordinary lemons, as long as you take into account their low acidity.

Imported from China in 1908 by the botanical adventurer whose name

they bear, Meyer lemons are most likely a hybrid of lemons and mandarins. One of the hardiest citrus varieties, they can be grown wherever temperatures rarely fall below 20°F. Meyer lemons should never be picked green or they will never develop their full, rich flavor. They are more fragile than other lemons and do not cure and color in storage as well; they are juicier and their skin is more tender. Meyer lemons are now available from a few growers in Texas and Florida, as well as California. The main season is from October through April, with fruit available sporadically through the summer months.

Over the centuries the lemon has traveled far from its home in Southeast Asia, arriving with Spanish colonization in Florida in the sixteenth century and in California in the mid-eighteenth. Lemons are one of the more frost-tender citrus. Major producers around the Mediterranean are in the warm coastal areas of Spain, Italy, Greece, and Turkey.

Lemons also grow well under conditions like those found along the central and southern California coast. These coastal areas have relatively even temperatures throughout the year, encouraging the year-round growth of flowers and fruit. California produces nearly a quarter of the world's lemons, from these coastal orchards as well as from orchards in inland valleys, where the harvest is more seasonal. Lemons are also grown in the Arizona desert, but in Florida a series of freezes and diseases has kept commercial production small.

Most of the lemons in California belong to one or the other of two common varieties of *Citrus limon*, Eureka and Lisbon. The fruits of these two are so similar to each other that only experts can tell them apart. Both have the typical oblong shape, bright yellow color, aromatic skin, and highly acid, juicy flesh that we expect from a lemon. Eureka was propagated from the seeds of an Italian variety planted in Los Angeles in the mid-nineteenth century. Eureka lemon trees tend to flower and set fruit throughout the year, but their yields are most plentiful from late winter to early summer. Lisbon, a variety from Portugal, produces its main crop in late winter and a second crop in early summer.

Midsummer to early fall, the low point of the harvest of both varieties, is the time when demand is highest, the season of lemonade and other summer drinks. Growers use cultural practices to encourage continuous production from the trees, but they also extend the season by harvesting lemons early, before they are completely ripe, and storing them until they are needed.

Once lemons reach a minimum size and juiciness, conventional growers harvest, sort, and treat them with fungicides. The yellow ones go to market immediately, and the others, sorted in grades from light to dark green, go into cool storage rooms where the fruit slowly matures. The darkest green lemons can be stored for as long as six months before they are sold, but ripening can be hastened by raising the temperature and introducing ethylene gas. Such techniques can ripen fruit in a matter of weeks.

Organic growers depend on beneficial insects to control pests, and they use cover crops and manure to improve the soil. Because they don't use fungicides for storage or shipping, or gas for ripening, organic farmers like Didar Singh at Guru Ram Das Orchards in the Sacramento Valley must wait until the fruit is ripe before picking. His Lisbon lemons have skin that is a deep, golden yellow and highly aromatic, and their juice is richer and less acidic than that of store-bought lemons. But we can get them for only a few months in the winter. The rest of the year we look to coastal growers for organic Eureka lemons, but even with year-round production, supplies run low in late summer.

At the market, choose lemons that are heavy for their size and have well-colored, smooth, thin rinds. Lightweight lemons with thick, rough rinds will not be as juicy. Avoid fruit that is obviously punctured or bruised or that has soft or watery-looking spots. Greenish lemons will be more acidic and less flavorful than solid yellow ones. Lemons will keep at room temperature for a week and in the refrigerator for a month.

MEYER LEMON LEMONADE

Lemon juice plus water plus sugar equals lemonade (although, according to the old children's rhyme, it should also be made in the shade, by an old maid, and stirred with a spade). Meyer lemon juice makes unusually fine lemonade. Start with equal parts lemon juice and water and sweeten to taste. Chill well and serve over ice, perhaps topped up with sparkling water. If you wish, crush a few sprigs of mint and steep them in the lemonade as it chills. Or for a further refinement well worth trying, sweeten the lemonade with sugar syrup in which you have steeped strips of lemon zest.

CRAB SALAD WITH MEYER LEMON, ENDIVE, AND WATERCRESS

Dungeness crab, Meyer lemons, and endive are all in season in the wintertime here in the Bay Area, so a simple, elegant salad like this one naturally suggests itself.

1 large Dungeness crab (about 1¾ pounds)	*Salt and freshly ground pepper*
2 large handfuls watercress (about 1 bunch)	*1½ teaspoons Champagne vinegar*
2 shallots	*6 tablespoons extra-virgin olive oil*
2 Meyer lemons	*4 Belgian endives*

Bring a large pot of salted water to a boil. Add the crab and cook for 13 minutes. Drain and let cool. Lift the carapace and clean the crab of all the "butter" and "lungs" inside. Break the crab in half. Separate the legs from the body and crack them open. Extract all the leg meat carefully; try to keep it intact. Next, split the body and pick out all its meat. Go through all the crabmeat after it is picked to remove any stray shell fragments. Set the crabmeat aside in the refrigerator.

Remove any tough stems from the watercress. Wash and dry it well. Peel and finely dice the shallots. Carefully peel the zest from the lemons with a sharp vegetable peeler, being sure to take only the yellow peel and none of bitter white pith. If you do end up with some pith, pare it away with a sharp paring knife. Cut the pieces of zest crosswise into a julienne and combine with the shallots in a small bowl. Season generously with salt and freshly ground pepper. Squeeze the lemons and add about 5 tablespoons of the juice to the bowl with the shallots and lemon zest. Add the Champagne vinegar, mix well, and let sit for at least ½ hour to macerate. Whisk in the olive oil; taste for salt, pepper, and acid and adjust as needed.

When you are ready to serve the salad, remove any blemished outer leaves from the endives. Cut them in half lengthwise and remove the cores, then cut lengthwise into strips. Put them in a serving bowl with the watercress, crab, and vinaigrette and toss well. Arrange on a platter or individual plates and serve immediately.

Serves 6.

MEYER LEMON RELISH

This relish is a welcome spot of brightness in the winter, delicious with fish and wonderful with a salad of cold roasted meats. The preserved lemon nicely complements the brininess of the olives.

1 preserved Meyer lemon (recipe follows)	2 teaspoons chopped parsley
	Extra-virgin olive oil
2 shallots	Freshly ground pepper
¼ cup picholine olives	Optional: Salt, if needed

Chop the preserved lemon, peel and dice the shallots, and pit and chop the olives. Stir together the lemon, shallots, and olives in a bowl. Add the parsley and thin out the mixture a little with 1 tablespoon or so of olive oil. Season with freshly ground black pepper. Taste for salt and add a bit, if needed.

Makes about ½ cup.

MOROCCAN PRESERVED LEMONS

Our favorite lemons to preserve are the thinner-skinned, sweeter Meyer lemons, but Eureka lemons work equally well. Preserved lemons make a wonderful condiment that adds a uniquely Moroccan flavor wherever lemon is called for. To make them, all that is required is lemons and salt. Additive-free kosher salt is especially recommended in this recipe because it seems to dissolve more quickly.

Wash the lemons well. While holding them over a plate to catch the juice, make four deep longitudinal cuts, evenly spaced around the lemon, effectively dividing it into four sections attached at the ends. Don't make the cuts so long (going into the ends) that the lemon separates into pieces; you want to keep the lemons whole. (Alternatively, cut the lemons into quarters, leaving them attached only at the stem end.) Pack the cuts generously with salt. Put a couple of tablespoons of salt in the bottom of a jar and pack the lemons in layers, sprinkling a thin layer of salt between each layer of lemons. Push the lemons down firmly to pack them tightly and to help express some of their juice. Finish with a final layer of salt. Pour in any juices that collected on the plate when the lemons were cut. Cover the jar tightly. Leave at room temperature for a few days, monitoring the level of liquid in the jar. The lemons should be submerged in juice after a few days. If they are not, add more lemon juice. The lemons will be ready to eat in a few weeks and will keep for up to a year. They do not absolutely require refrigeration, but we always keep them in the refrigerator at the restaurant.

Judy's Deep-Fried Lemons and Artichokes

Deep-fried Meyer lemon slices mingle the delightful flavor of a rich, crunchy, deep-fried exterior with the acid sweetness of the juice inside. We learned to fry lemons this way from Judy Rodgers, the gifted and enterprising chef of the Zuni Café in San Francisco. The most important thing in this simple recipe is the thickness of the lemon slices: they should be quite thin but not so thin that the flesh will separate from the sectioning membranes. When this happens, the slices will burn, but if they are too thick, they won't cook properly. The best thickness is about 1/16 inch. A sharp Japanese mandoline makes the job of slicing them to a uniform thickness much easier.

Dip the lemon slices in buttermilk and then into some flour. For lemon slices with a bit more texture, substitute 1 part semolina and 3 parts flour. Shake off the excess flour, but make sure that the slice is covered with an even, consistent coating. The slices can be dipped and floured a few minutes ahead of time, but not too far ahead or the coating will get soggy and stick to whatever it is resting on. Deep-fry the slices at 360°F. without crowding them, turning so they cook on both sides. They are done when they are crispy and golden. Drain on absorbent paper, sprinkle with salt, and serve immediately.

For deep-fried artichokes, choose baby ones. Trim away the darkest green, tough outer leaves and trim and peel the stem. Cut off the top of the artichoke leaves at the point where they turn darker green. If you are not cooking the artichokes right away, keep them in acidulated water or toss them in olive oil to retard oxidation and discoloration. When ready to fry, drain the artichokes well and cut into slices or quarters or sixths. Dip the artichoke pieces in the buttermilk and remove them with a slotted spoon, allowing the excess buttermilk to drain off. Toss them well in the flour, shake off the excess, and fry in the hot oil until golden and tender. Drain on absorbent paper, sprinkle with salt, and serve with the lemon slices.

Meyer Lemon Sherbet

1½ cups sugar
1½ cups water
1 cup Meyer lemon juice
1 tablespoon finely chopped
  Meyer lemon zest

¾ cup milk
1 teaspoon gelatin
2 tablespoons water

In a small saucepan, gently heat the sugar and water until the sugar is dissolved. Pour this syrup into a bowl with the lemon juice. Stir in the zest and milk. In the saucepan, combine the gelatin with the water and let it sit for 5 minutes. Once the gelatin has plumped up, heat it gently until there is no visible graininess. Add the melted gelatin to the lemon mixture and refrigerate.

When the sherbet base is cold, freeze it according to the instructions for your ice cream maker.

Makes 1 quart.

LIMES 🍋

Season: Year-round, best in summer and fall

Limes, like lemons, are too acidic to be enjoyed out of hand, but their juice can be used in small amounts to accentuate the flavor of other ingredients or diluted to tame its acidity while retaining its flavor in dishes. At the restaurant we add a squeeze of lemon to a dish almost automatically, to boost flavor or balance acidity. Limes must be used more carefully—although we have thought of writing a book called *Everything Tastes Better with Limes*. Their penetrating flavor and spicy fragrance can be too assertive and jarring if they are used indiscriminately.

Lime trees are more sensitive to cold weather than any other citrus and grow well only in the tropics. Not surprisingly, limes have become an essential element of tropical cooking worldwide, as ubiquitous as chilies.

At Chez Panisse we are most likely to use limes when we cook Latin American or East Indian food. Lime juice "cooks" and tenderizes raw fish in ceviche and tartare preparations. A squeeze of lime perks up low-acid tropical fruits such as avocados, mangos, and papayas. Lime meringue pie is sometimes more intriguing than lemon. Authentic margaritas, guacamole, and chutney are all impossible without Mexican limes. And what fruit drink is more refreshing in the heat of summer than limeade?

In the United States limes are grown commercially only where winters are warm and frost almost unknown, in southern California and southern Florida. There are two types of acid lime: the tiny round Mexican lime and the larger egg-shaped Tahiti lime.

Mexican limes, *Citrus aurantifolia*, also called West Indian limes, Key limes, or bartender's limes, are the more flavorful and interesting of the two. They are very tart and have a complex, spicy aroma. Never more than two inches in diameter and mostly round, they have a thin, smooth, leathery skin. The flesh is greenish yellow, juicy, seedy, and very acidic. This type of lime came to Europe from India; Spanish settlers brought it to the New World. It needs a uniformly warm, moist climate and is very sensitive to cold spells.

Although common throughout the tropics, Mexican limes can be grown in only the most sheltered parts of California and Florida. The scrubby trees have naturalized themselves in many areas where they have been cultivated, including the Florida Keys. Key limes are no longer a commercial crop, but they are still grown in many backyards. The world's biggest producer of limes is Mexico, which is also, per capita, the biggest consumer. Mexican limes grown in Dominica and Ghana end up in Rose's Lime Juice.

The peak of the Mexican lime season runs from early summer to late fall, although there is some production throughout the year. When they are to be sold as fresh fruit, they are harvested just before they are completely ripe, when the skin is light green. Workers must wear gloves to protect their hands from the exceedingly thorny trees. But when the fruit is fully ripe and yellow, the stage preferred for processing, it conveniently falls from the trees and is easily collected from the ground.

The Tahiti lime, *C. latifolia*, also called the Persian or Bearss lime, is probably a natural hybrid of Mexican lime and citron. The variety evidently came to California from Tahiti, although none of these limes are grown there now. A few are still grown in California, but most domestic production is in Florida. Tahiti limes are larger than Mexican limes and more oval in shape. They are the shiny dark green limes commonly seen in the supermarket produce section. Usually seedless, they have pale green juicy flesh but lack the intense fragrance of Mexican limes. Tahiti limes bear all year, with the peak of the harvest in summer.

Rangpur limes (*C. limonia*) are not really limes at all, but they are sometimes substituted for them. Probably a natural cross of lemon and mandarin orange, they were discovered growing in northwestern India and classified as a lime when their seeds were brought to Florida. Small and round, Rangpurs have very thin, rough, reddish-orange skin that peels easily from the fruit. The juicy, acidic flesh has some of the character of true lime, as well as sour orange.

Rangpurs are more cold-hardy than real limes. Gardeners in our neighborhood bring us fruit from backyard trees planted as ornamentals, but Rangpurs are also grown as a small-scale commercial crop in California. Look for them in the fall and winter. We use Rangpurs for sherbet as we would regular limes. The small fruits can be candied whole, and they are also very good for limeade and marmalade.

Buy organic limes that are firm, glossy, and heavy for their size. The color of Tahiti limes should be medium to dark green, and Mexican limes are usually pale green or yellow, but both kinds gradually turn yellow and lose acid during storage. Avoid limes that have dull, dry skin or soft spots or brown patches. Mexican limes should not be refrigerated but kept at room temperature, out of direct sunlight, and used within a week. Tahiti limes can be refrigerated for several weeks but will eventually change color.

To get the best yield of juice, make sure limes are at room temperature. Fruit taken from the fridge can be put in a bowl of hot tap water for ten minutes to warm up. Remember to grate or peel any zest you may want before juicing. Roll each lime firmly on the kitchen counter or table, bearing down with your palm, to soften it slightly; then cut in half and squeeze. Get yourself a Mexican lime squeezer. It may not be pretty, but it does the job better than any other tool, especially with tiny Mexican limes. A small handheld reamer works if you don't have a squeezer.

Samantha's Lime and Mint Cocktail

When the price of limes gets down to seven cents apiece, I harvest our backyard mint, break out the rum, and invite friends over. This recipe is a casual variation on the mojito, Cuba's quintessential cocktail. For an authentic mojito, use more mint and four times as much sugar (2 teaspoons per cocktail) and finish with soda water instead of tonic. Stir the sugar in a glass with a small handful of mint leaves and perhaps a splash of soda, lightly crushing the mint and dissolving the sugar. (This is called muddling, by the way, and is allegedly best done with a muddler, a small wooden baton made for this very purpose. Try using the handle of a wooden spoon and muddle until it smells powerfully of mint.)

Squeeze in the juice of a lime, leaving one of the juiced lime halves in the glass for more lime oil flavor. Add ¼ cup light rum, stir, fill with ice, top with soda water, garnish with more mint leaves, and serve.

1 handful fresh mint leaves
2 teaspoons sugar
5 limes (cut 1 into 4 wedges for
    serving)

1 cup light rum
1⅓ cups tonic water

Chill 4 highball glasses. When the glasses are cold, take them out of the refrigerator. In the bottom of each one, put 4 or 5 mint leaves, ½ teaspoon sugar, and the juice of 1 lime. Fill the glass with ice and pour in ¼ cup light rum and ⅓ cup tonic water. Stir each cocktail briskly with a long spoon so that the sugar dissolves and the mint releases its flavor. Garnish each drink with a lime wedge and serve immediately.

Makes 4 cocktails.

Silver Limeade

The so-called silver limes found in backyards in our part of California are a cold-hardy citrus, possibly a lemon-lime hybrid. Their small fruit is yellow-skinned, white-fleshed, and much spicier and juicier than Tahiti limes—and apparently unknown anywhere else. No matter; limeade made from any kind of lime will have complex, satisfying lime flavor if you briefly steep the lime rinds as described here.

10 silver limes
2½ cups water
1 cup sugar

1 small bunch mint
One 750-ml bottle sparkling
    water

Roll the limes on a cutting board, bearing down with the palm of your hand. This loosens the flesh a little and makes the limes easier to juice. Cut them in half and squeeze out the juice; there should be about 1 cup. Put the juiced lime halves in a nonreactive bowl, bring the water to a boil, and pour it over the lime rinds. Steep for 10 minutes but not much longer or the water will taste bitter. Strain this water into the lime juice and stir in the sugar.

Crush 5 or 6 mint leaves with your fingers and stir into the juice. Allow the mint to steep for at least 30 minutes. To serve, strain the limeade and dilute with half the sparkling water. Taste and adjust the sweetness and dilution to your liking. Serve poured over ice in tall glasses and garnished with sprigs of mint.

Makes about 2 quarts.

SCALLOP CEVICHE

If you can get live scallops still in their shells at the market, you will find that they make this dish even more delicious.

1¼ pounds very fresh scallops
Salt
1 cup lime juice (about 8 limes)
1 tomato
1 small red onion, finely
*   chopped*

2 jalapeño or serrano chilies,
*   thinly sliced*
6 to 8 sprigs cilantro, chopped,
*   plus more for garnish*
1 head romaine lettuce
1 avocado
Lime wedges

Slice the scallops horizontally into 2 or 3 disks about ¼ inch thick. Cut the disks into ¼-inch sticks and the sticks into ¼-inch dice. Put the diced scallops in a nonreactive dish and season well with salt. Cover with ¾ cup lime juice and refrigerate for 2 hours, until the lime juice has "cooked" the scallops. Meanwhile, peel and seed the tomato and cut into ¼-inch dice.

When the scallops are cooked, drain off and discard the lime juice. Add the diced tomato, chopped onion, sliced chilies, chopped cilantro, and remaining ¼ cup lime juice. Marinate, refrigerated, for a couple of hours. To serve, wash and dry the prettiest romaine leaves, make a nest with them, and arrange the ceviche over it. Garnish with slices of avocado, cilantro sprigs, and lime wedges. Serve with tortilla chips.

Serves 6.

Halibut Tartare with Lime, Coriander, and Shallots

¾ *pound halibut (Alaskan
    halibut is the best)*
2 limes
1 shallot, chopped fine
¼ *teaspoon coriander seeds,
    crushed*

Extra-virgin olive oil
Salt
2 tablespoons chopped cilantro
A few sprigs cilantro
*Toasted brioche or pain de mie
    triangles*

Slice the halibut very thinly across the grain, removing any fibrous connective tissue. Cut the slices into narrow strips and cut the strips crosswise into small dice. Grate the zest of 1 lime on the finest grater you have. Juice both limes into a bowl and add the zest, chopped shallot, and coriander seeds. Whisk in 2 tablespoons extra-virgin olive oil and season with salt.

When ready to serve, toss the diced halibut with a little salt. Add the sauce and toss again. Stir in the chopped cilantro and taste, adding more salt or lime juice, if necessary. Garnish with sprigs of cilantro and serve immediately with toasted triangles of brioche or pain de mie.

Serves 6.

Chinese Watermelon Radishes with Salt and Lime

This is a simple but stunning hors d'oeuvre. Chinese watermelon radishes are a dull white and green on the outside but an amazingly brilliant shade of pink on the inside. They are bulbous—usually around the size of a tennis ball—and are similar in flavor to the long white daikon radish. To prepare, peel the radishes, making sure you cut away all of the green outer layer, which has an overly strong, almost gassy flavor. Cut each radish in half and then into thin wedges or slices. Sprinkle with a bit of salt and squeeze some lime juice over, toss gently, and let sit a few minutes. A tiny pinch of cayenne adds zing, if wanted. Serve in a beautiful bowl. Another presentation is to serve the slices unadorned, with lime wedges and a ramekin of *fleur de sel* alongside.

KEY LIME MERINGUE PIE

¾ cup sugar
⅓ cup cornstarch
⅛ teaspoon salt
1½ cups water
1 tablespoon grated Key lime
    (Mexican lime) zest
⅔ cup Key lime juice
4 egg yolks
2 tablespoons unsalted butter
1 prebaked 9-inch pie shell
    (page 292)

MERINGUE
4 egg whites, room temperature
¼ teaspoon cream of tartar
½ cup sugar
1 pinch salt
½ teaspoon vanilla extract

Preheat the oven to 325°F.

In a nonreactive saucepan, whisk together the sugar, cornstarch, and salt. Whisk in the water, lime zest, and juice. Whisk in the yolks and add the butter. Cook the mixture over low heat, stirring constantly. Once it starts to thicken, simmer for 1 more minute and strain into the prebaked pie shell, spreading evenly in the shell.

To prepare the meringue, in a clean large bowl, beat the egg whites with the cream of tartar until they form soft peaks. Whisk in the sugar and beat until the whites are glossy and firm but not dry. Stir in the salt and vanilla. Gently spread the meringue over the custard, making sure that the meringue touches the edge of the pie crust all the way around, leaving no custard exposed. Bake the pie for 25 minutes, until the meringue is golden brown. Let cool for ½ hour before serving.

Serves 8.

LOQUATS 🍐

Season: Late winter through spring

Loquats, so very popular in Japan and China, ought to be more widely grown in North America. They ripen at a welcome time in late winter or early spring when apples and pears are winding down, before strawberries are really good, and while summer fruits are still green on the trees. Loquat fruits look a bit like small, lopsided pears, an inch or two long, with smooth to slightly downy skin. Depending on the variety, the skin color varies from yellow to reddish-orange, and the flesh may be white, yellow, or orange. Loquats have crisp, succulent flesh, well balanced between sweet and tart, and a mild tropical fragrance.

The loquat, *Eriobotrya japonica*, originated not in Japan but in China. There are some 800 known varieties, of which only a few are found in the United States. They grow best in subtropical climates, and the fruit is a springtime fixture not only in Asian but also in Mediterranean markets. Many of the small, handsome trees have been planted in California gardens as ornamentals since the late nineteenth century, and there are a few commercial orchards in Florida and California. The trees will survive outdoors as far north as the Carolinas, although they generally don't produce fruit north of Florida.

It is common to walk along the street near Chez Panisse and smell the dusky perfume of loquats blooming in winter and see the colorful fruits hanging in heavy clusters in spring. The Florida loquat season runs from February through May, while California fruit ripens from March through June. Loquats are best when allowed to ripen fully on the tree, when the color is fully developed and the fruit gives to gentle pressure.

Ripe loquats do not keep well and are easily bruised, so they don't ship well. In areas where they grow, the best places to look for loquats are farmers' markets and farm stands, and in other parts of the country you will find loquats in specialty produce stores and ethnic markets. Look for organically grown fruit that is well-colored and slightly soft. It should have a fragrance that hints of pineapple or banana. Avoid very hard fruit or those that are brown or bruised.

Loquats are fragile; don't count on keeping them for more than a couple days at room temperature or for longer than a week in the fridge. In either case, make sure they have good air circulation, which will inhibit mold and internal browning. Commercially marketed loquats may have been treated with fungicides, so always wash them carefully before using, and try to find untreated, organically grown ones.

Loquats are easy to eat out of hand; just cut them open and take out the seeds, which separate easily from the flesh. Peeling isn't really necessary. Quartered, peeled, and seeded, fresh loquats are an unusual addition to fruit salad, or they can be poached in sugar syrup and added to a macédoine of other fruits. Loquats are distant relatives of apples and have similar ratios of sugar, acid, and pectin. Slightly unripe loquats can be cooked in many of the same ways as apples to make pies, jam, jelly, sauce, and chutney. The sweet-tart character of loquats nicely complements grilled or roasted meat, especially duck, squab, and pork.

Sicilian Loquat Compote

1 pound ripe loquats	*¼ cup white wine*
1 cup water	*3 strips lemon zest*
⅓ cup sugar	

Peel and quarter the loquats and remove the seeds. Save a few seeds; they add a nice bitter almond flavor to the poaching liquid. If the skin on the inside of the fruit next to the seeds is tough, remove that as well. Measure the water, sugar, and white wine into a saucepan; add the lemon zest and reserved loquat seeds. Bring to a boil, reduce to a simmer, and cook for 4 minutes. Add the fruit and poach gently until tender, about 10 minutes. Remove from the heat and let the fruit cool in its liquid. Serve chilled.

Serves 6.

Note: This can be made with whole loquats, not just quartered ones. Wash the fruit well and poach for 20 minutes, until tender. You may need to make more poaching liquid to have enough to cover the fruit while it cooks.

Loquats and strawberries are in season at the same time and go together quite well. Hull and quarter a few strawberries and stir into the compote 15 minutes before serving.

CATHERINE'S LOQUAT SAUCE

Whenever I make this sauce, I think of Catherine Brandel, a beloved friend and longtime chef at Chez Panisse, who was so fond of loquats. She found many ways to use them when they were abundant, in late spring. The sauce is delicious served with any fatty meat, like pork or duck, and is especially good if you have pan juices from roasting the meat. Discard the fat from the roasting pan, add a little water, stock, or wine to help dissolve the brown bits, scrape the pan with a wooden spoon, and add the juices to the sauce.

Peeling loquats is not tedious if you have a willing helper—or if you are making this for people you really like. Don't peel the loquats more than a half hour before making the sauce or they will become unpleasantly oxidized.

3 tablespoons unsalted butter
⅓ cup finely chopped yellow onion
6 ounces fresh loquats, peeled, seeded, and quartered (about 1 cup)

⅛ teaspoon ground ginger, or 1 pinch grated nutmeg
¼ cup apple juice
¼ cup rich chicken stock or pan juices
Lemon juice
Salt and pepper

Melt 2 tablespoons of the butter in a saucepan over medium heat. When it is foaming but not yet brown, add the onion and reduce the heat to low. Cook, stirring occasionally, for about 5 minutes, until translucent. Add the loquats and ginger or nutmeg and continue cooking and stirring for another 5 minutes. Raise heat to high, add the apple juice and stock, and boil until slightly reduced. Off the heat, swirl in the remaining tablespoon of butter; season with lemon juice, salt, and pepper; and serve with roasted or grilled meat.

Serves 4.

MANDARINS AND TANGERINES ✦

Season: Early fall through late spring

In the Café we always have a bowl of fresh fruit available as a dessert alternative for those who want something simple and refreshing after dinner. In the summertime we have a superabundance of cherries, plums, apricots, peaches, and nectarines; the hard part is deciding which we will serve. In the fall, as choices dwindle, we start relying on citrus fruits, especially mandarins, to fill the fruit bowl.

No other fruit seems to provoke botanical discussion among restaurant staff the way that mandarins do. Waiters are forever asking cooks why some of these fruits are called mandarins and some tangerines and others clementines and still others satsumas and so on. The answer that never seems to stick is that all of these fruits are mandarins or have a mandarin somewhere in their family tree. They all have thin, loose peel and fruit segments that separate easily from each other. The ones with highly colored red-orange skin are often called tangerines. Clementine and satsuma are the names of two distinct families of mandarin varieties.

Of course, it doesn't help in sorting things out that this large group of citrus includes many man-made and natural hybrids, blurring lines that might have been distinct in the misty past. Nothing in nature is neat and tidy, but most mandarins belong to one of three groups: satsumas, "common" mandarins, and hybrids such as tangelos and tangors.

Mandarin season lasts more than half the year; the first varieties ripen in early fall, the last in late spring. Satsumas ripen first. They originated in Japan hundreds of years ago as seedlings of trees brought from China, and they now account for eighty percent of Japanese citrus production. The trees tolerate cold weather and produce good crops in the relatively chilly climates of northern Florida, the Gulf Coast, Texas, and the California Sierra foothills.

There are at least seventy varieties of satsuma, *Citrus unshiu*, but specific names are usually not noted in the market. They are mostly seedless and have loose and sometimes puffy orange skin that is very easy to peel. The early varieties that ripen in late September are never as good as the midseason Owari types, which start in November and continue through the winter. Every year our first really good satsumas, the kind with rich, tart-sweet flavor, come from the Johansen's organic farm in northern California.

Grouped with the common mandarins, *C. reticulata*, are the uncommonly good clementines. They may be a natural hybrid, discovered by Father Clement Rodier in Algeria at the turn of the last century, or they may have been brought to Algeria from China; in any event, they are often called Algerian tangerines. Before modern fruit breeders started working on them, clementines were always small, about two inches in diameter, and somewhat seedy; the newest members of the family are larger and often seedless. Clementines have smooth, bright red-orange skin and juicy, richly flavored flesh.

The sugar level of clementines depends on the climate and their maturity at harvest. The ones that we get from Full Belly Farm and Guru Ram Das Orchards, both to the north of us, are often rather tart, while those from Fairview Gardens, near Santa Barbara, are sweeter. Clementine harvest extends from late fall through early spring, depending on the growing area.

Dancy, the traditional Christmas tangerine, is another of the "common" mandarins. It was once widely grown in Florida, where it originated, but lately has been displaced by plantings of Sunburst, which ripens earlier, in November. Page is a very flavorful and juicy clementine-tangelo hybrid; because of its small size and sometimes tight skin, we use it more for juicing than for eating out of hand. Pixie is a late variety that comes to market in spring and usually finishes out mandarin season for us. Pixies have small- to medium-sized orange-colored fruit with a noticeably bumpy rind. They are perfect for eating out of hand because the skin peels easily and they are not excessively juicy.

Kishu is a tiny Japanese mandarin that we learned about from Jim Churchill, who farms in southern California, near Ojai. No more than an inch across, Kishus are very sweet and easy to peel. They were the most popular citrus in Japan until satsumas came along. Last New Year's Eve, Jim sent us many boxes of Kishus picked in clusters with their tiny dark green leaves, the first harvest from his newly planted trees. They were spectacularly beautiful set out on all the tables in the restaurant as one of the thirteen traditional Christmas desserts of Provence.

Some hybrid mandarins have been given names that hint at their parentage. Tangelos are man-made or accidental crosses of mandarins and grapefruit (think tangerine and pummelo). Tangelos are the size of an orange or larger and have thin, easily peeled skin that often tapers to a distinct neck at the stem end. In our experience the Minneola variety is best, although it may have a few seeds. Minneolas have brilliant red-orange skin and very juicy, tender flesh that is bracingly, deliciously sweet-tart. But beware: unripe Minneolas can be sour. They are best from late winter to early spring.

Tangors are mandarin and sweet orange hybrids. The well-known Honey tangerines of Florida (called Murcott elsewhere in the world) are thin-skinned tangors with a smooth, shiny peel that tends to cling to the flesh. The fruit segments of Honey tangerines are a little chewier than those of clementines or satsumas, but they are very high in sugar and have distinctively tasty juice. Buy them in late winter and early spring.

Another tangor is the Royal mandarin or Temple orange, which was discovered growing wild in Jamaica in 1896. Temple oranges have thick, pebbly, deep red-orange skin and orange flesh. The flesh of the medium-sized fruits is spicy, sweet, and tart. Temples are best in late winter.

When choosing mandarins at the market, it helps to be aware of varietal characteristics. Choose fruit that is heavy for its size and typically colored for the variety. Some, such as satsumas, have naturally loose skin, but don't buy mandarins that are very puffy; they may be overripe. Avoid fruits that have soft spots or watery areas.

Because of their thin skin and tender flesh, most mandarins don't keep well, but they can be stored at room temperature for up to a week. Ask for organically grown mandarins. Conventionally grown fruit is often packed in boxes with liners impregnated with fungicide. Even careful washing will not remove chemicals absorbed by the fruit during shipment and storage.

Mandarins seem designed for eating out of hand, but they have many other uses. Freshly squeezed mandarin juice is a quick refresher by itself or mixed with other citrus juice. The segments are easily added to fruit salads and compotes. Tart, highly flavored varieties such as Dancy tangerines, clementines, and Minneolas are excellent for sherbet and ice cream. Mandarins make brilliantly colored, delicious marmalades and candied peel, and small clementines are lovely candied whole.

Crêpes Suzette with Pixie Tangerine Sherbet

This classic dish is traditionally flambéed at tableside, the crêpes swirled in a rich sauce of orange juice, butter, and Grand Marnier. We often serve crêpes Suzette with tart, refreshing tangerine sherbet to balance the hot, buttery sauce. All the components are made in advance and then assembled in the kitchen when we are ready to serve.

Make the crêpe batter at least a day in advance to allow the batter to relax after mixing, and make the sherbet at least six hours in advance so it will be frozen solid. The crêpes can be fried, stacked, wrapped, and left at room temperature until you're ready to fill them. The sauce too can be made ahead and reheated to serve. Simply heat the crêpes in the oven, transfer them to individual plates, cover them with the sauce, and top with a scoop of sherbet, if you like.

LINDSEY SHERE'S
CRÊPE BATTER
(makes about 1 quart batter,
  enough for about 30 crêpes)
2 cups milk
¼ teaspoon salt
½ teaspoon sugar
4 tablespoons (½ stick)
  unsalted butter
1¼ cups unbleached
  all-purpose flour
1 tablespoon vegetable oil
3 eggs
½ cup beer

PIXIE TANGERINE SHERBET
Zest and juice of 4½ pounds
  Pixie tangerines
  (about 3½ cups juice)
1½ cups sugar

ORANGE BUTTER
CRÊPE FILLING
Zest of 2 Valencia or navel
  oranges (reserve juice for
  the orange sauce)
8 tablespoons (1 stick) unsalted
  butter, room temperature
2 tablespoons sugar
1 tablespoon Grand Marnier

ORANGE SAUCE
1½ cups Valencia or navel
  orange juice (about 3 oranges)
6 tablespoons sugar
2 teaspoons cornstarch
2 teaspoons water
2 tablespoons unsalted butter
2 tablespoons Grand Marnier
  plus more for the finished
  plates

Start the crêpe batter the day before. In a medium-size saucepan, heat the milk, salt, sugar, and butter until the butter has melted. Let cool to room temperature. Measure the flour into a mixing bowl, make a well in it, and add the oil and the eggs. Beat for a few minutes, until the batter is too stiff to beat and is smooth, with no lumps. Add the milk mixture little by little, beating until smooth. Strain the batter through a fine-mesh sieve and then whisk in the beer. Chill overnight.

To fry the crêpes, let the batter warm up a little. If the butter has congealed in a layer at the top, skim it off and melt it in a small saucepan over medium heat, stirring constantly. When it has melted, strain it back into the batter.

Heat a crêpe pan over medium-high heat until a drop of water sizzles in the pan. (The first crêpe may stick a little if your pan isn't quite the right temperature.) Rub the pan with a little butter, wiping out the excess with a paper towel. Ladle a thin layer of batter (about 2 tablespoons) into the center of the pan, tilting and rotating the pan to cover the bottom as thinly and evenly as possible. Lightly brown the first side for a minute or two. Gently flip the crêpe over and brown the other side for about a minute. Turn out onto plastic wrap.

Fry 12 large crêpes (or 18 small ones) to serve 6 people. Save the rest of the batter for a few days to make more crêpes, or fry all the crêpes now and reserve them for another use. Cover the crêpes and keep them at room temperature for a few hours, or wrap in plastic and refrigerate for up to 2 days. Tightly wrapped, crêpes can also be frozen for up to a week.

To make the sherbet, put the tangerine zest and the sugar in a food processor and pulse until the zest is finely chopped; or finely chop the zest by hand and pound it in a mortar with the sugar. This will release the tangerine oil and make the flavor of the sherbet more complex.

Transfer the sugar and zest to a medium-size saucepan, add about half the tangerine juice, and place over medium heat just long enough for the sugar to dissolve. Remove from the heat and stir in the remaining juice. Strain the mixture to remove the larger pieces of zest. Taste the mixture for sweetness and add more sugar or a squeeze of lemon juice to balance the flavors. Refrigerate until chilled, then freeze according to the instructions for your ice cream maker.

To make the orange-butter filling, chop the orange zest very fine and put it in a mixing bowl. Cut the butter into small pieces and mix with the orange zest until smooth. Add the sugar and Grand Marnier and stir until incorporated. The butter is now ready for spreading, but if it sits for more than half an hour, you'll need to stir the alcohol back into suspension. The filling can be made well ahead of time, chilled or even frozen, and then resoftened for spreading.

Unwrap the stack of crêpes and thinly spread about 1 teaspoon orange butter over each one. Fold into triangles and place in an ovenproof dish large enough to hold all the folded crêpes, slightly overlapping. Cover the dish with foil and chill until you are ready to serve. (There will be leftover butter for extra crêpes.)

The orange sauce takes only a few minutes, but if you make it in advance, the dessert can be assembled without too much bother after a meal. In a small saucepan, heat the orange juice and sugar until the mixture comes to a boil. In a small bowl, mix the cornstarch with the water to dissolve and add to the hot orange juice. Whisk the sauce over the heat until it boils again (to cook out the starchy flavor), then add the butter to melt. Take the sauce off the heat, pour through a fine-mesh sieve to remove any lumps of cornstarch, and add the Grand Marnier. Taste for sweetness and add more sugar or Grand Marnier to taste. Set aside to reheat later or proceed to assemble the crêpes.

Preheat the oven to 400°F.

Remove the prepared crêpes from the refrigerator and place the foil-covered dish in the oven to heat them through, 10 to 15 minutes. It's a good idea to warm your serving plates in the oven for about 5 minutes. Meanwhile, reheat the orange sauce just until it is hot, making sure it does not boil.

When the crêpes are hot, transfer them to warm plates and pour about ¼ cup sauce over each serving. Splash a little more Grand Marnier on each plate and top with a generous scoop of sherbet. Serve immediately.

Serves 6.

Tangerine and Chocolate Semifreddo

Despite the name, this is not the classic frozen parfait served all over Italy. It is more closely related to the equally ubiquitous tiramisù.

Italian pastry chefs are known for their use of the dense sponge cake they call *pane di Spagna*, or Spanish bread, which is probably a corruption of *pane di sponza*, Sicilian for sponge bread—a shift in nomenclature perhaps influenced by the fact that Sicily was under Spanish rule for centuries. The density of this cake lends itself to soaking without completely losing its identity in the moist interior of the semifreddo. Pane di Spagna need not be chocolate-flavored; for a golden sponge cake, simply omit the cocoa powder.

It is best to make this recipe a day in advance; it benefits from chilling overnight.

TANGERINE CURD
6 tangerines
3 tablespoons water
½ cup sugar
¼ pound (1 stick) unsalted
    butter, cut into small pieces
¼ teaspoon salt
3 whole eggs
3 egg yolks
1 cup heavy cream

PANE DI SPAGNA
4 eggs
4 egg yolks

1¼ cups sugar
1¼ cups plus 1 tablespoon
    unbleached all-purpose flour
¼ cup potato starch
¼ cup unsweetened cocoa plus
    more for dusting

SOAKING LIQUID
1 cup water
1 cup sugar
¼ cup orange liqueur or
    dark rum

To make the tangerine curd, first grate the zest from the tangerines and reserve to add later. Squeeze enough tangerines to yield ½ cup juice. Strain the juice into a heavy-bottomed nonreactive saucepan and add the water, sugar, butter, and salt. Heat slowly over low heat, stirring until the sugar dissolves and the butter melts. Briefly whisk the eggs and egg yolks together in a bowl. Drizzle the hot tangerine mixture into the eggs, whisking all the time, then scrape the contents of the bowl back into the saucepan. Cook over low heat, constantly stirring and scraping the bottom of the pan, until the mixture thickens, about 4 minutes. Strain the curd through a fine-mesh sieve, stir in the reserved zest, and chill in a small container with plastic wrap pressed onto the surface so that no skin forms as it cools.

Preheat the oven to 350°F.

To make the pane di Spagna, butter and flour the bottom and sides of a 9-inch round, 3-inch-deep cake pan. Line the bottom with parchment paper. Beat the eggs and egg yolks with the sugar until the mixture is pale lemon-colored and forms a ribbon when dropped from the beaters onto the surface, about 10 minutes. Combine the flour, potato starch, and cocoa powder in a large bowl. Sift the dry ingredients into the egg mixture a third at a time, folding in gently with a spatula after each addition. Continue folding just until all the flour mixture has been incorporated.

Pour the cake batter into the prepared pan, smooth the top evenly, and bake for 45 to 50 minutes, until the cake is springy and the edges have begun to pull away from the sides of the pan. Let cool on a rack, turn the cake out of the pan, and peel away the parchment paper.

Prepare the soaking liquid by stirring the water and sugar in a saucepan over low heat until the sugar dissolves. Let cool and stir in the orange liqueur.

To assemble the semifreddo, whip the heavy cream until it forms soft peaks and fold into the tangerine curd. Spoon a fourth of the lightened tangerine curd into the bottom of a 2-quart, 8-inch-square ceramic serving dish, spreading evenly. Slice the pane di Spagna horizontally into 6 or more layers about ¼ inch thick. Cutting pieces to fit snugly, make a single layer of cake in the serving dish. Use a pastry brush to moisten the cake with the soaking liquid.

Evenly spread a layer of lightened curd over the layer of cake, and continue alternating layers of cake with layers of curd until the dish is full, soaking each layer of cake as you go and ending with a smooth layer of tangerine curd. Cover with plastic wrap and chill thoroughly, preferably overnight, to allow the flavors to marry. To serve, dust lightly with cocoa, spoon the semifreddo onto chilled plates, and garnish with tangerine segments and chocolate shavings, if you wish.

Serves 6 to 8.

Clementine Sherbet in Its Shell à la Norvégienne

This fancy dessert offers dramatic contrasts of hot and cold, sweet and sour, soft and firm. It can also be made with Minneola tangelos, but you will need twice as much sherbet and meringue to fill the larger cups.

SHERBET
3 pounds clementines
½ teaspoon gelatin
2 tablespoons water
½ cup sugar

MERINGUE
2 egg whites (¼ cup), room
   temperature

¼ cup plus 2 tablespoons sugar
¼ teaspoon vanilla extract
1 pinch salt

GARNISH
Chopped pistachio nuts or
   chopped candied clementine
   peel (page 192)

To make the sherbet, grate the zest from 3 of the smaller clementines. Put the zest in a medium-size bowl and set aside. Carefully cut the clementines in half, keeping in mind that you will be saving the prettiest 12 to 18 halves of peel to use as cups for the sherbet. Sometimes if the fruits are very small, we cut off just the top third for a larger cup. Juice all the clementines, being careful not to tear the peel in the process. Choose the best-looking halves for cups. Depending on their size, decide if you want to serve 2 or 3 per person; discard the extras or save the extra peel to candy later. Using a soup spoon, scrape out the juiced flesh, core, and membranes and some of the white pith below. With a sharp paring knife, trim a tiny slice off the bottom of each cup so that it will rest steadily on the plate later. Arrange the cups snugly in a baking dish just big enough to hold them and put them in the freezer.

You should have about 2 cups of clementine juice. Pour the juice over the zest. Put the gelatin in a small saucepan with the water. Let sit for 5 minutes while the gelatin plumps, then warm it slightly over low heat until it is no longer grainy to the touch; do not boil. Measure in the sugar and add about ½ cup of the tangerine juice; continue to heat gently, stirring occasionally until the sugar dissolves. Pour the mixture into the bowl with the rest of the tangerine juice and strain through a fine sieve. Chill the sherbet base. Once it is cold, freeze it according to the instructions for your ice cream maker. When the sherbet is frozen, immediately fill the frozen cups, using a soup spoon to mold into dome shapes. Let the sherbet freeze in the cups until it is very firm, about 3 hours.

When the sherbet-filled cups are firm, prepare the meringue: In a clean, dry mixing bowl, whip the whites until they are frothy. Slowly beat in the sugar and beat until the whites are stiff and shiny but not dry. Mix in the vanilla and salt. Fit a pastry bag with a ½-inch star tip and fill it with the meringue. Remove the baking dish of sherbet cups from the freezer and, with a spiraling motion, pipe meringue onto the top of each cup, taking care to cover all the visible sherbet with meringue. Return the cups to the freezer. They may be held in the freezer in this oven-ready state for up to 2 hours.

Preheat the oven to 500°F.

Remove the baking dish of sherbet cups from the freezer and bake on the top rack of the oven for 3 to 4 minutes. (Baking them in the cold dish from the freezer helps insulate the sherbet from the heat while the meringue is browning. They are done when the meringue is golden. Transfer the cups to individual dessert plates, 2 or 3 per person, and garnish with chopped pistachios or candied peel.

Serves 6.

Tangerine Soufflés

⅓ cup finely chopped candied
   tangerine peel (page 192)
2 tablespoons orange-flavored
   liqueur (such as Grand
   Marnier or Cointreau)
1 tablespoon unsalted butter,
   melted and cooled slightly
½ cup granulated sugar plus
   more for coating the ramekins
   and sprinkling on top

1 cup pastry cream (page 302)
2 tangerines (clementine, Pixie,
   or mandarin)
1 cup egg whites (7 or 8 eggs,
   depending on their size),
   room temperature
1 tablespoon cornstarch
1 pinch salt
¼ teaspoon cream of tartar
Powdered sugar for dusting

Preheat the oven to 450°F.

Let the candied peel and orange liqueur steep together while you prepare eight 5-ounce ramekins. Brush the insides of the ramekins with the
butter, leaving a generous lip of butter around the inner rim. Pour in
some granulated sugar, coating the insides, and tap out any excess.
Touch up any uncovered spots with more melted butter and sugar. Set
the ramekins aside on a baking sheet.

In a large mixing bowl, stir together the pastry cream and candied
peel with a large rubber spatula. Finely grate the zest of the tangerines
into the pastry cream and stir it in. Cut the remaining peel from the tangerines with a small knife, then cut the individual segments free of their
membranes, dropping them into a small bowl. Sprinkle with a little
sugar and set aside for garnishing the finished soufflés.

In a clean, dry mixing bowl, whisk the egg whites until they are frothy.
Add the cornstarch, salt, and cream of tartar and beat until they are fluffy
and hold soft peaks. Gradually add ½ cup granulated sugar, whisking
until the peaks are firm and glossy but not dry. Gently fold the whites
into the pastry cream, deflating the whites as little as possible.

Spoon the soufflé mixture into the prepared ramekins, filling them
just to the lip of butter. Sprinkle the tops with a thin layer of sugar. Drag
your finger around the top and outer edge of the rim of each ramekin to
clean up any splattered excess soufflé mixture; this ensures that the
soufflés will rise straight up ½ inch or more without sticking to the sides.

Bake for 8 to 9 minutes, until the soufflés are tall, golden on top, and
still slightly soft to the touch in the center. Remove the baking sheet from
the oven and dust the tops of the soufflés with powdered sugar. Spoon a
few of the sweetened tangerine segments on top of each soufflé and serve

immediately on individual plates lined with napkins or doilies (to keep the ramekins from sliding around).

Serves 8.

SLICED MANDARINS WITH LAVENDER AND HONEY

A cook who was trying out for a position in the Café made this for us at his trial lunch. It was so good we had to put it on the menu—and we had to hire the cook. The sweet honey balances the tart flavor of the tangerines perfectly. A buttery cookie is a nice accompaniment.

*⅓ cup mild-flavored honey
(orange blossom and
star thistle are good choices)*

*1 teaspoon dried lavender
blossoms
1 pound satsumas or other
seedless mandarins*

Warm the honey in a small saucepan over low heat. Crush the lavender and add it to the honey. Let the mixture steep for 30 minutes off the heat, until it has a nice lavender flavor. Strain the honey before serving.

Peel the mandarins and cut horizontally into ¼-inch-thick slices. If you use a sharp, thin-bladed knife, the segments should not fall apart, but if they do, just reassemble them. Arrange the slices in a single layer on dessert plates.

Drizzle the honey over the mandarin slices and serve with cookies on the side.

Serves 4.

Note: If you are have a few stalks of fresh lavender, gently pull the tiny blossoms from the stalks and strew them over the mandarin slices just before serving.

MANGOS &

Season: Spring and summer

The soft, sweet, melting flesh and somehow pine-like aroma of a perfectly ripe mango make it totally understandable why it is called the king of fruits. There are people who say they don't like mangos, but I think they just haven't had a good one, full of flavor and with a perfect balance of sweetness and tartness. In Mexico and other areas where mangos grow, it's hard to find a bad one; whether purchased at a market or, peeled and ready to eat, from a sidewalk vendor, it will have been picked perfectly ripe. But even if you shop far from their tropical groves, you can still buy good, organically grown mangos.

We start looking for mangos in early spring. At this time of year, local fresh fruit is scarce and our desserts often have a tropical note. The early mangos, from Mexico and the Caribbean, go beautifully with papaya and pineapple in compotes or fruit soup, spiked with lemon or lime. Later in the season, we will serve mango more simply, peeled and sliced, with a few wedges of Mexican lime to squeeze over, or doused with Sauternes for an easy, slightly extravagant dessert. On the savory side, mangos go especially well with fish and shellfish and with highly flavored poultry, such as duck or squab. We also like to use green mangos, unripe fruits harvested still firm and spicy-tangy, in Indian- and Southeast Asian–inspired salads, pickles, and chutneys.

Although mangos start coming to market in March, the highest-quality fruits arrive in the greatest numbers in late spring and early summer, when there can be a bewildering number of different varieties available. Mangos come in various shapes (round, oblong, and kidney-shaped) and sizes (from a few ounces to several pounds each). All have smooth, waxy, beautifully colored skin, some completely yellow, some green or yellow splashed with orange, red, and purple. The flesh color ranges from pale yellow to dark orange. In India, where the mango (*Mangifera indica*) is native, there are more than 500 named varieties, and cultivated groves occupy nearly 2.5 million acres.

Of the fifty states, only Florida and Hawaii have weather warm enough to grow mangos for market. In Hawaii they are popular backyard trees, but fresh mangos cannot be shipped to the mainland because of problems with insect pests. During the peak of the season, we see some mangos from Florida, as well as imports from Central and South America, the Caribbean, and Mexico.

The two varieties most commonly grown in Florida these days are Tommy Atkins and Keitt. Tommy Atkins is popular for growers because of disease resistance, shipping qualities, and good looks; the flavor is only fair. The medium-size oval fruits have bright yellow flesh and thick yellow-orange skin strongly blushed with red. Organically grown Tommy Atkins mangos are shipped from Mexico in the spring and summer; the Florida harvest peaks in June and July.

Keitt, which comes a little later in the season, is a much better mango; richly flavored and sweet, it has yellow-orange, less fibrous flesh. Keitts are large oval fruits weighing a pound or more, with thickish yellow-green skin blushed with red. They are around until late summer.

Ataulfo, another delicious mango, originated as a seedling in Hawaii. The organic ones we get in late spring and early summer come from Mexico, where they seem particularly at home in the area around Veracruz. Ataulfo mangos are small, usually a half pound or so, and kidney-shaped. They have yellow skin and very sweet, smooth, buttery flesh with lots of flavor.

Two varieties to look for late in summer are Kent and Haden. At one time Haden was the predominant mango in southern Florida, but many trees were pulled out because of disease problems and housing development. Haden, which is still grown in Hawaii and South America, has yellow skin overlaid with orange and red, and its rich, tasty flesh contains only a little fiber. Kent is a large mango with greenish-yellow skin and a dark red blush, a small seed, and excellent flavor; it is rich, sweet, and nearly fiberless.

Use your sense of smell and touch when shopping for ripe mangos. They should have a mild, fruity aroma, especially at the stem end, and they should yield to gentle pressure, like a ripe peach. Don't buy mangos that are very soft or bruised. Color is not a reliable guide. The skin of many varieties develops a yellow or golden background color as the fruit ripens, but the skin of others stays green even when the mango is fully ripe. If you have a choice of sizes, large fruit has a higher proportion of usable flesh than small fruit. Mangos to be used green and immature should be just that, firm and green. Don't buy any that are soft, bruised, or wrinkled.

Firm ripe mangos should be allowed up to a week to soften at room temperature before eating. Placing the fruit in a paper bag with an apple can accelerate the process. Fully ripe fruit will keep for up to a week in the refrigerator. Mangos belong to the plant family Anacardiaceae, which includes cashews and sumac, as well as poison oak and poison ivy, and oils in the skin of the fruit and the tree's sap can irritate the skin. Mangos are usually washed after harvest, but it is wise to wash them again before handling.

Mangos have a single large, flat seed in the center of the fruit clinging tightly to the flesh, which must be cut away from the seed with a knife. This can be done before or after peeling. Stand the fruit on its stem end, narrow side facing you. Allowing about three-quarters of an inch as the thickest part of the pit, cut off the "cheeks" of flesh on either side of the pit, which is about three-quarters of an inch thick. Cut as close to the pit as possible, but avoid the very fibrous flesh near its surface. You can then cut away the two thinner strips of flesh that remain on the pit. Peel and cut or purée the fruit as needed.

I always consider any juicy flesh clinging to the pit as the cook's reward and eat as much as I can while leaning over the sink, hoping no one is watching. Mexicans sometimes employ a special three-pronged mango fork at this critical moment. The longer, center tine is pushed into the pit, the two shorter ones grip the flesh, and the rest of the fruit can be eaten as if on a lollipop. If you don't have a mango fork, plan on a certain amount of washing-up time.

Mango Salsa

This is a simple and refreshing sauce for fish that's especially good with grilled tuna and fish tacos. Peel and dice a large ripe mango and a large sweet onion. Remove the seeds from a medium-size jalapeño or another flavorful chili and chop it very fine. Combine the mango, onion, and chili and add about ½ cup chopped fresh cilantro. Squeeze 1 or 2 limes over the salsa, to taste, add salt to taste, and serve right away.

MANGO SALAD WITH HOT PEPPER

2 large ripe mangos
½ red onion
1 fresh habanero chili, or
   ½ teaspoon ground cayenne
   pepper

¼ cup lime juice (2 or 3 limes)
Salt
¼ cup chopped cilantro (leaves
   and stems, about ½ bunch)
A few sprigs cilantro

Peel the mangos with a small sharp knife. Cut the flesh away from the mangos following the directions on page 165. Cut the mangos lengthwise into ¼-inch-thick slices. Thinly slice the onion. Cut the habanero chili in half and remove the stem and seeds. Chop the chili into fine dice. Wear rubber gloves if you wish to protect your hands from the pepper.

Gently toss the mango, onion, and chili or cayenne pepper with the lime juice, a bit of salt, and the chopped cilantro. Taste for salt and acid and adjust as needed. Chill for half an hour. Garnish with cilantro sprigs before serving.

Serves 6.

GREEN MANGO SALAD WITH SHRIMP AND AVOCADO

4 small heads romaine lettuce,
   or 2 hearts of romaine
1 dozen white shrimp, peeled
   and deveined
Salt and pepper
1 tablespoon olive oil
1 green (underripe) mango
1 firm, ripe avocado
Grated zest and juice of 1 lime

1 shallot, diced fine
2 tablespoons Champagne
   vinegar
½ teaspoon grated fresh ginger
1 jalapeño chili, seeded and
   diced fine
½ cup extra-virgin olive oil
1 tablespoon chopped cilantro

Slice the heads of romaine in half lengthwise, remove the root end, and separate the leaves. Wash and dry them carefully.

Cut the shrimp in half lengthwise and season with salt and pepper. In a small skillet, sauté the shrimp in the olive oil over medium-low heat. As soon as they turn opaque, remove them from the pan and set aside to add to the finished salad.

Peel the mango with a vegetable peeler and cut the broad sides into

⅛-inch-thick slices. (The narrow sides tend to be fibrous and difficult to slice.) Cut these slices into ¼-inch-wide strips and set aside.

Cut the avocado in half lengthwise and remove the pit. Cut into ¼-inch-thick slices, leaving the skin intact. Sprinkle lightly with lime juice.

Put the shallot in a large bowl with the vinegar, remaining lime juice, ginger, and jalapeño. Season with salt and macerate for 15 minutes. Whisk in the extra-virgin olive oil and lime zest. Add the shrimp and mango strips and scoop the avocado slices out of their skin into the bowl. Toss gently and serve sprinkled with chopped cilantro.

Serves 4 to 6.

MANGO SHERBET WITH TROPICAL FRUIT MACÉDOINE

You may use any combination of tropical fruits—including the many kinds we have left out of this book—but do try to include passion fruit with its seeds and a variety of other colors, tastes, and textures.

MANGO SHERBET
1 pound very ripe mangos
1 juice orange (about ½ pound)
¼ cup sugar
1 dash vodka
Optional: A few drops lemon
   juice, to taste

FRUIT MACÉDOINE
2 cups water
½ cup sugar
1 large orange
1 small lemon

One 1-inch piece fresh ginger
2 blood oranges
   (about 8 ounces)
2 navel oranges
   (about 10 ounces)
1 small pineapple
   (about 14 ounces)
½ medium papaya
   (about 8 ounces)
2 small bananas
4 kumquats
2 or 3 passion fruit
1 or 2 kiwifruit

To make the mango sherbet, peel the mangos and slice the flesh off the pit. Purée in a food processor or blender or pass through a food mill. You should have 1¼ cup purée. Juice the orange and pass the juice through a strainer, forcing some of the pulp through as well. You should have a little less than ½ cup. Add to the mango purée. Stir in the sugar and flavor to taste with vodka and a few drops of lemon juice, if necessary. Pour into a container, cover, and chill.

Freeze the sherbet according to the instructions for your ice cream maker, or pour the mixture into a freezer tray and, when it is nearly frozen, beat with a hand mixer until light and return it to the freezer.

To make the macédoine, measure the water and sugar into a nonreactive saucepan. Peel all the zest from the orange and the lemon in very thin strips, being careful not to cut into the white part of the rind, and add to the syrup in the saucepan. Slice the ginger and add it to the syrup. Bring to a boil, lower the heat, and simmer for 5 minutes. Chill the syrup in the refrigerator.

Peel and section the blood and navel oranges into a bowl and squeeze the juice from the membranes over the segments. Peel, core, and cut the pineapple into small wedges and add to the bowl. Peel and seed the papaya and peel the bananas; cut into ½-inch cubes. Slice the kumquats as thin as you can, removing the seeds as you go, and add to the bowl. Cut the passion fruit in half, scoop out the flesh and seeds, and add to the fruit mixture. Add the kiwifruit, peeled and cut into small dice. You should have 4 cups or so of prepared fruit. Pouring through a strainer, add enough of the chilled syrup to make the mixture soupy. You may not need all of it. Cover and chill thoroughly.

When you are ready to serve the dessert, put a scoop of the sherbet into 4 to 6 soup plates and arrange the fruit around it. Serve immediately.

Serves 4 to 6.

MANGO WITH SAUTERNES

When time is short and you need an elegant dessert, try this one, especially in summer, when mangos are plentiful, delicious, and cooling. The rich, fruit flavors of Sauternes and mango are perfect together, and the lime adds an acid accent. A 1-pound mango is enough for 2 people.

Peel the mangos and slice off the "cheeks" and the remaining side strips of flesh, but avoid the fibrous area near the seed. Cut the large mango pieces into ¼-inch-thick slices and fan them out in shallow soup bowls. Slice the side strips and divide them among the bowls. Sprinkle a little sugar on the fruit and a generous squeeze of lime. Open a bottle of good Sauternes and pour several tablespoons of the wine over the fruit in each bowl. Cover the bowls and refrigerate until serving. Chill the rest of the wine in the bottle. Serve the chilled mango with a glass of Sauternes and a nutty cookie.

MELONS ❧

Season: Summer

Cool melons are a welcome sight for thirsty eyes in midsummer. And they slake that thirst straight away because they don't need much preparation: just cut them open, scoop out the seeds, and serve. At Chez Panisse we serve them very simply indeed. We arrange melon slices on plates with thin slices of prosciutto and add melon to salads. We take softball-size Charentais melons from the Chino Ranch in San Diego, cut them in half equatorially, and serve them with a little of the sweet Muscat wine called Beaumes-de-Venise poured into the cleaned-out seed cavity. We use various melons in an easy-to-make gelato. And on occasion we "juice" watermelons and make a refreshing drink (what in Mexico is called an *agua fresca*) and turn the leftover rind into sweet pickles.

The ancient cradle of melon cultivation is the Middle East, where melons have been growing for thousands of years from Egypt to India, but they will grow well in any temperate area that has a growing season long and hot enough. Melons were imported to the Western Hemisphere by Columbus on his second voyage. Their cultivation spread quickly from the Caribbean as far north as New England. Today most of the melons consumed in the United States are produced in California, followed by Texas, Arizona, Georgia, and the other southern states. Indeed, over half of the fifty states produce crops of commercial value, and there are melon vines in backyards just about everywhere.

Many different types of melons have been bred during their long history of cultivation, but all melons belong to one of two species. *Cucumis melo* includes muskmelons, cantaloupes, and honeydews. Watermelons belong to *Citrullus lanatus*. Both species are closely related to cucumbers, as will become instantly apparent if you bite into an unripe melon.

Many of the melons with aromatic, sweet orange flesh sold as cantaloupes are actually muskmelons. Regional preferences for muskmelons cause growers to refer to certain varieties as "eastern" or "western." Eastern farmers typically plant muskmelons that produce large fruit, round or slightly oval, with moderately netted rind that is segmented longitudinally by demarcations called sutures. Eastern muskmelons have soft flesh and do not ship very well, so they are usually marketed close to home. Western muskmelons are smaller and have firmer flesh. They usually have heavy raised netting but do not have obvious sutures.

One of our favorite muskmelons is the aptly named Ambrosia, an eastern type whose delicate yellow-orange flesh has intense musky fragrance and lovely flavor. The Passport melon is a green-fleshed muskmelon hybrid with a rind that turns light green or pale yellow when ripe. The rind of a Passport may have corky marks, but is not distinctly netted. The very sweet flesh is a pale light green—almost white.

True cantaloupes, which are not as widely grown in North America as they are in Europe and the Middle East, take their name from Cantalupo, a town outside Rome. These melons are smaller and more spherical than muskmelons, and they have harder skin. The rind is clearly segmented and usually smooth, sometimes scaly but rarely netted. Two delicious true cantaloupes that are becoming more common here are the French Charentais and the Israeli Haogen or Ogen. There are many named varieties of Charentais melons, but the best of them all have very aromatic dark orange flesh within a smooth gray-green rind. Charentais are always small, weighing no more than two pounds. Haogen melons have rich, creamy green flesh that tastes spicy when fully ripe and a greenish-orange rind with darker green sutures.

Local organically grown muskmelons and cantaloupes start coming to market in June, but July and August are the best months to try them. Honeydew, Crenshaw, and Canary melons usually ripen a little later and are at their best from midsummer through early fall. Honeydews have green or orange flesh contained in a very smooth, creamy white rind, sometimes splashed with yellow. While they are not as aromatic as muskmelons, their firm flesh can be very sweet when fully ripe. They keep better than muskmelons.

Crenshaws are some of the finest eating melons. They are oval in shape, a little pointy at the stem end, with thin, slightly wrinkled skin variously spotted and streaked with green and gold; their delicate orange-pink flesh is thick and juicy, very aromatic, and very sweet. Canary melons (also called Juan Canary melons) are Crenshaw-shaped but have bright, canary yellow skin; their almost white flesh is tender, juicy, and very sweet.

Among watermelons, Charleston Gray, Crimson Sweet, and Jubilee are three of the best of the traditional large varieties and are widely planted. Often weighing twenty-five to thirty-five pounds, they can easily take over a refrigerator. Many new varieties come in smaller sizes and still have the same sweet juiciness. Sugar Baby and Mickylee are delicious small red-fleshed watermelons, both local favorites; some of the newer yellow-fleshed watermelons, like Yellow Doll, are equally good.

If a watermelon is ripe, the patch on the bottom where it rested on the ground will be yellow, not white or pale green. Look also for skin that has a waxy bloom, dull rather than shiny. Watermelons that are large for their type and have a nice symmetrical shape are generally the best. Many farmers offer tastes at the farm stand or market to help you pick out a good one.

The best muskmelons and cantaloupes in the market are the ones that smell good. Look for organically grown ones with creamy gold or orange skin under the netted rind, and sniff out the most aromatic. Don't waste your time on melons with green skin. Ripe melons will often have a flattened side that is paler than the rest of the fruit. The stem end should be moist but not moldy. Honeydews and other late melons should give to gentle pressure on the blossom end. Ripe melons can be stored for several days at room temperature. Do not refrigerate them until several hours before using.

Pickled Watermelon Rind

We like the idea of using all the parts of the fruit. Watermelon pickles always used to turn up on Thanksgiving tables in the Midwest.

1 large watermelon (about 7 pounds)	*Two 3-inch pieces cinnamon stick*
½ cup kosher salt	*16 cloves*
5½ quarts water	*6 allspice berries*
2 cups Champagne vinegar	*1 Meyer lemon, sliced thin*
4 cups sugar	

Remove all the pink flesh and pare away the outer hard green layer of the rind. A sturdy vegetable peeler works well. Cut the rind into 1-inch cubes or batons, or cut it into rounds with a biscuit cutter. Dissolve the salt in 2 quarts water and add the melon rind. Place a plate over the rind to weigh it down and keep it completely submerged in the brine. Refrigerate overnight.

The next day, prepare six 8-ounce canning jars and lids in boiling water, following the manufacturer's instructions.

Take the rind out of the refrigerator, drain it, and rinse well. Put the rind in a pot with 3 quarts water, bring to a boil, and cook at a high simmer until half tender, about 10 minutes. Drain again.

Meanwhile, mix together 2 cups water, the vinegar, and the sugar in a heavy-bottomed pot. Tie the spices up in cheesecloth and add to the mixture. Bring to a boil and cook about 10 minutes. The syrup should be quite thick. Add the lemon slices and cook for 2 more minutes. Finally, add the rind, bring back to a boil, reduce the heat, and simmer until the rind is translucent, 5 to 10 minutes, depending on the size of the pieces. Ladle the rind into the prepared canning jars, cover with syrup, allowing ¼ inch of headroom, and seal, following the manufacturer's instructions.

Makes about 1½ quarts.

MELON GELATO

Make this with any fragrant, perfectly ripe muskmelon or cantaloupe—but not with watermelon.

1 small melon
  (about 2½ pounds)
6 egg yolks
⅓ cup plus 1 tablespoon sugar

5 ounces (½ cup plus
  1 tablespoon) light corn syrup
⅓ cup heavy cream
4 egg whites, room temperature
1 tablespoon lemon juice

Cut the melon in half, scoop out the seeds, peel off the rind, and cut the flesh into small pieces. Purée until smooth in a blender or food processor.

Beat together the egg yolks and ⅓ cup sugar until thick. Warm the corn syrup over low heat. Whisk the egg yolks and sugar into the corn syrup and cook over low heat, whisking just until warmed through. Remove from the heat and strain through a sieve. Whip the cream until it begins to mound up and peak softly, and fold it into the yolk mixture.

Beat the egg whites and 1 tablespoon sugar until they form soft peaks; fold into the yolk and cream mixture. Stir in the melon purée and lemon juice and freeze according to the instructions for your ice cream maker.

Makes about 1 quart.

WATERMELON AGUA FRESCA

Mexican *aguas frescas* (literally, "fresh waters") are fresh fruit drinks, and one of the most refreshing is watermelon. In fact, I have to say that I never liked watermelon until my friend Niloufer Ichaporia made this drink for me. To make about 2 quarts, cut a 7-pound watermelon into big chunks, carve away all the rind, and cut the flesh into smaller chunks. Working in batches, liquefy the melon in a food processor or blender, pulsing for about 1 minute in brief spurts so as not to grind up the seeds. Strain, pushing as much of the pulp through the strainer as you can. You should have about 5½ cups juice. Thin out with about 2 cups water and sweeten with about ¼ cup sugar, or to taste. Lime juice is vital: 1½ tablespoons, the amount in a small lime, is about right for 2 quarts. Chill over ice or in the refrigerator, and serve over ice, garnished with a slice of watermelon or lime.

Melon as a First Course

Serve melons in season as a first course, cut in half or peeled and sliced into wedges and sprinkled with Muscat de Beaumes-de-Venise (or another sweet wine) and freshly cracked black pepper. Or try strewing them with a chiffonade of mint leaves and a little extra-virgin olive oil. (Melon with mint is good for dessert too, drizzled with crème fraîche instead of oil.) And of course, melon slices can be draped with paper-thin slices of a cured ham such as prosciutto or Serrano.

MULBERRIES 🐝

Season: Midsummer

Mulberries are hard to find, but the unique flavor of these purple, juicy, musky berries makes the search worthwhile. About ten years ago we learned about a tree in the town of Sonoma, and now every summer we look forward to its sublime fruit. For years this big, handsome tree was tended by Charlie Grech, who built scaffolding so he could get up into its branches and pick the berries. After Charlie's passing, the picking was taken over by Charlie's widow, Salvina, and their daughters. Ripe mulberries are very soft and juicy and must be pulled or cut carefully from the branch; no matter how careful the pickers, their hands and clothes inevitably end up covered with purple juice. It is not a job for the faint of heart. Every year the Grech mulberry tree produces many, many mulberries, more than we can use fresh, but they freeze well, so we can enjoy them over a long season.

The black or Persian mulberry, *Morus nigra*, is native to western Asia. It has been grown in Europe for many centuries, and for centuries before that in the Middle East. There are two other main species of edible cultivated mulberry, one a native red American mulberry, but the black mulberry is the tree most commonly grown for its fruit, which looks very much like large blackberries that ripen from dark red to nearly black. Black mulberries are not very cold-hardy, so they are mostly found in orchards and gardens along the Pacific coast and in the South. Recently planted mulberries are starting to bear fruit in California, and organic growers have been taking pains to harvest them ripe and get them to farmers' markets, where they have attracted a loyal following.

You will almost never find mulberries in the supermarket because the fragile berries are highly perishable and must be harvested and handled carefully. Mulberries grow on handsome deciduous trees that tolerate drought and dust. A mulberry tree would be a welcome addition to any garden where winter temperatures don't fall below zero. They grow well in containers, but don't plant them near pavement, where the stains from falling fruit can be a problem.

Mulberries produce over a long season; a single tree will ripen fruit over a month or two, but they are at their peak in midsummer. There is little discernible difference in quality between black mulberry varieties. Black Persian and Noir of Spain are the most commonly grown. Illinois Everbearing is a cold-hardy variety that was found growing wild in Illinois in the 1950s, most likely a natural cross between red and white mulberries. Its berries are said to taste almost as good as black mulberries.

Mulberries are wonderful, if a bit messy, eaten out of hand. To capture their essence in a more civilized way, we often use their juice in a dessert soup (follow the boysenberry soup recipe on page 48, substituting mulberries), with sliced fresh summer fruit. The sweet tartness of mulberries is good with peaches and nectarines, and we put them together in tarts and cobblers. They also complement the flavors of late-summer apples and pears. The strong flavor of mulberries is beautifully tempered when they are served simply with sabayon or cream, and they make our best ice cream.

Try to use mulberries as soon as you get them home. Otherwise, they invariably start leaking juice and getting moldy. Unwashed mulberries will keep for a day or two in the refrigerator, laid out on a paper-lined baking sheet. Rinse the dust off them just before using. Mulberries can be frozen for longer storage or dried to use as a snack.

MULBERRY SHERBET

4 cups mulberries	*2 tablespoons lemon juice*
¾ cup sugar	*1 tablespoon kirsch*

Stir together the berries and sugar in a nonreactive saucepan and cook over medium heat just until the sugar dissolves and the berries begin to release their juice. Purée the berries in a food processor and pass through a medium sieve. Stir in the lemon juice and kirsch and freeze according to the instructions for your ice cream maker.

Makes 1 quart.

Mulberry Ice Cream

On the twenty-ninth birthday of Chez Panisse, we served mulberry ice cream cones on the sidewalk in front of the restaurant. One man who came by said it was the best thing he had ever tasted that cost only two dollars.

9 egg yolks
1½ cups half-and-half
1¾ cups sugar
3 cups heavy cream

3 cups mulberries
2 tablespoons lemon juice
1 tablespoon kirsch

Whisk the egg yolks in a mixing bowl just enough to break them up. Gently heat the half-and-half and 1 cup sugar in a medium-size nonreactive saucepan, stirring slowly over low heat until the half-and-half is steaming and the sugar is dissolved. Drizzle the warm sweetened half-and-half into the egg yolks, whisking constantly as you pour.

Return the mixture to the saucepan. Cook over low heat, stirring and scraping the bottom of the pan with a wooden spoon or heat-resistant rubber spatula, until the mixture is thick enough to coat the spoon. Immediately remove from the heat and strain through a fine-mesh sieve into a bowl with the heavy cream. Chill thoroughly.

Stir together the berries and ¾ cup sugar in a nonreactive saucepan over medium heat until the sugar dissolves and the berries begin to release their juice. Purée the berries in a food processor and pass through a sieve. (If you want texture in your sherbet, use a sieve with larger holes.) Stir the berry mixture into the chilled ice cream base. Stir in the lemon juice and kirsch. Freeze according to the instructions for your ice cream maker.

Makes 1½ quarts.

NECTARINES &

Season: Summer

Nectarines were named after the nectar consumed by the Olympian gods, and their flavor is widely acknowledged to be, in a word, divine. Although closely related to peaches, nectarines have smoother skins, firmer and finer-textured flesh, and a subtly different flavor. The genetic profile of peaches and nectarines differs by only a single gene, the one that makes peaches fuzzy, and nectarines are properly classified as a subspecies of peach, *Prunus persica* var. *nucipersica*. Nectarine and peach trees are indistinguishable both in flower and in leaf.

A beautiful ripe nectarine makes such pleasurable eating that we serve the very best nectarines of midsummer all by themselves or with a few raspberries. The rest we make into salads with other fruits; stuff with the same filling we use for peaches; bake into cobblers, crisps, tarts, and pies; and purée and freeze into sublime sherbet and ice cream.

If properly handled, ripe nectarines travel more successfully than peaches, and good ripe nectarines can be found in most parts of the country. In California we have an abundant supply of local nectarines; in fact, the state is responsible for nearly all the commercial production in the country. However, nectarines should thrive wherever peaches do well.

Depending on the variety, nectarines have either white or yellow flesh and are either cling or freestone. There has been a lot of interest recently in new varieties of sweet, low-acid, white-fleshed nectarines, which can be picked and shipped while quite hard, but many seem simply sweet, without any interesting contrast of sweet and tart. Ask if the white nectarine you are considering at the market is a low-acid variety.

Prime season for nectarines extends from June through September.

Do not miss one of the best white varieties, Arctic Glo, which ripens early in June. The sweet-tart flesh is richly flavored and often beautifully tinted with red near the pit. We particularly like Arctic Glo for sherbet, which turns out a lovely pale pink color. Before you buy other white varieties with Arctic as part of their name, taste carefully. Many, like the popular Arctic Rose, are low-acid, okay for eating but not for cooking.

Of the yellow-fleshed varieties, try Zee Grand and May Grand early in the season. Both ripen in June and have large, beautifully colored fruit with excellent flavor. Honey Kist is another favorite that comes in late June. In July we look for Ruby Grand, Flavortop, and Fantasia, and in August, August Red; these all come to us from Frog Hollow Farm in Brentwood. The season usually ends for us in September with Autumn Grand.

At the market, choose organically grown fruit that is plump and firm but not hard. Hard nectarines, which you will no doubt find, never ripen properly but shrivel and turn moldy after a few days. The background color of the skin of a ripe nectarine will be yellow or orange in the case of yellow-fleshed varieties, and white on white-fleshed ones. It should never be green. Most nectarines have a certain amount of red color in the skin, but that is only a varietal characteristic, not an indicator of ripeness.

Very ripe nectarines will give to gentle pressure along the suture, the seam that runs from top to bottom on the fruit, and should be used or refrigerated right away. Otherwise, plan to buy nectarines several days before you want to use them so that firm ones will have time to finish ripening. Don't put them in a plastic bag and don't leave them in the sun; they won't ripen properly. Nectarines that are ripe but still firm should be kept at room temperature in a paper bag. Over time the amount of acid in the fruit decreases, and the impression of sweetness increases. Check them every day.

Nectarines almost never need to be peeled; their skin is thin and tender. Just give them a quick rinse under cold water before using. To slice nectarines, cut along the suture from top to bottom, then along the opposite side back to the top. Gently try to twist the two halves apart. Freestone varieties will separate easily, and the pit can be removed cleanly. They can be left intact for stuffing or cut up as needed. The two halves of clingstone nectarines will not come apart, and the flesh must be cut away from the pit either in chunks or wedges, as you wish.

PISTACHIO-STUFFED NECTARINES

This versatile stuffing can also be used for peaches, apricots, pluots, apples, and pears.

6 tablespoons (¾ stick) unsalted
  butter, room temperature
4 tablespoons sugar
1 egg yolk
⅛ teaspoon salt
½ teaspoon orange liqueur

¾ cup chopped pistachio nuts
½ cup sponge cake crumbs
  (page 300)
6 medium nectarines
¼ cup dessert wine (Muscat or
  Sauternes)

Preheat the oven to 375°F.

To make the filling, cream the butter with 2 tablespoons sugar. Add the egg yolk and the salt and beat until fluffy. Beat in the orange liqueur, the chopped nuts, and the sponge cake crumbs.

Butter a 2-quart baking dish. Cut the nectarines in half and remove the pits. Arrange the nectarines in the dish, cut side up. Fill the cavity of each nectarine with stuffing. Drizzle the wine over and around the nectarines. Sprinkle the nectarines with the remaining 2 tablespoons sugar. Bake until the fruit is tender, about 30 minutes. Serve warm with vanilla ice cream (page 301) or crème anglaise.

Serves 6.

PRESERVED NECTARINES

We serve these over ice cream, in compotes, and with crêpes. The same method works well for peaches and apricots. Wash and halve nectarines, peeling them if you like. Prepare a light sugar syrup, enough to cover the fruit, of two parts water and one part sugar; heat until the sugar is dissolved. The syrup can be flavored with spices, citrus peel, or liqueur. Gently simmer the nectarine halves in the syrup until they are tender. Remove them from the syrup and pack into self-sealing canning jars prepared according to the manufacturer's instructions. Boil the syrup again, skim off the foam, and pour it over the fruit in the jars. Clean the lips of the jars and cover with the lids. Following the manufacturer's instructions, process pint jars for 15 minutes and quart jars for 25 minutes. These are best eaten within a few months.

Nectarine and Blackberry Crisp

Use white or yellow nectarines or a mixture for an exquisite late-summer dessert.

5 ripe nectarines, peeled, pitted, and cut into 1-inch cubes
1 cup blackberries
¼ cup sugar
3 tablespoons unbleached all-purpose flour
Zest of 1 lemon, chopped fine
1 tablespoon vin santo
3 cups crisp topping (page 289)

Preheat the oven to 375°F.

In a medium-size mixing bowl, toss together the nectarines, blackberries, sugar, and flour. Add the lemon zest and vin santo and mix briefly. Transfer to an ovenproof earthenware dish just big enough to hold the fruit slightly mounded at the center. Cover the fruit evenly with the crisp topping, pressing down lightly to form a crust and leaving no fruit exposed. Put the dish on a baking sheet to catch any overflowing juices, or wrap the bottom of the baking dish with aluminum foil, folding the sides up and around the rim to catch the drips.

Place on the center rack in the oven and bake for 50 to 60 minutes, rotating the dish once after 30 minutes for even coloring. When the crust is a deep golden brown and the juices have begun to bubble up the sides, remove the crisp from the oven and allow to cool slightly. Serve warm with bitter almond– or noyau-flavored ice cream.

Serves 6 to 8.

WHITE OR YELLOW NECTARINE SHERBET

We like to serve yellow and white nectarine sherbets together. They are made exactly the same way, but white nectarines tend to be sweeter and require a little less sugar than yellow ones. We use the same formula for making other stone fruit sherbets, such as plum and apricot.

1 pound ripe nectarines (about 4)
¾ cup water
⅓ to ½ cup sugar
Optional: A few drops lemon juice or kirsch

Cut the nectarines in half and remove the pits. Cut the fruit into 1-inch wedges and put them in a medium-size saucepan with ¼ cup water. Cook over medium heat for about 10 minutes, stirring occasionally, until the fruit softens and is just tender.

Working carefully with the hot mixture, purée the fruit in a blender or pass through a food mill. Strain the purée through a sieve. There should be about 1½ cups. Stir ½ cup water and ⅓ to ½ cup sugar into the mixture (less sugar for white nectarines). If the mixture is still warm, the sugar will dissolve easily; if not, you may have to heat it gently, stirring until the sugar dissolves.

Taste the purée and, if needed, add a few drops of lemon juice or kirsch—or both. Refrigerate the nectarine purée and freeze according to the instructions for your ice cream machine.

Makes 3 cups.

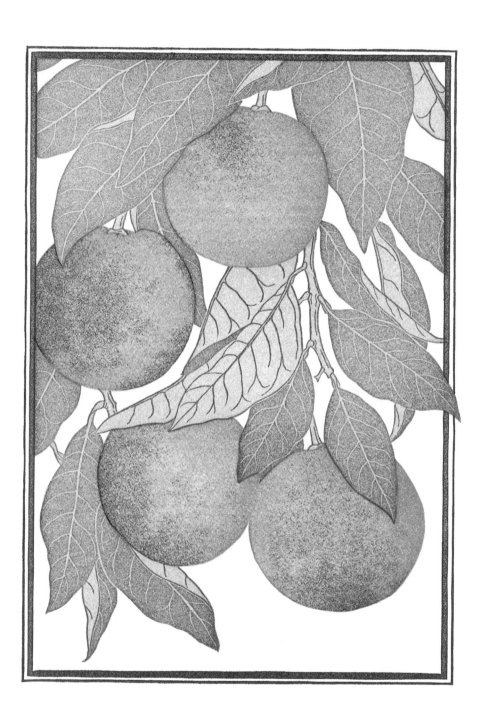

ORANGES &

Season: Year-round

Sometimes in the early winter, too much color has drained out of the kitchen, leaving behind a blanched spectrum made up of the browns, greens, and whites of mushrooms, root vegetables, cabbages, and winter fruits. But those dark days are soon brightened by the jewel-like colors of blood oranges. Their flashy flesh, streaked with purple, crimson, orange, and yellow, is as striking as any work of art, and when they reappear on our menus, the food begins to sparkle again. I remember the arrival thirty years ago, when Chez Panisse was in its infancy, of expensive little wooden boxes from Sicily, each holding a dozen or two precious blood oranges. Now blood oranges are grown in California, Texas, and Florida, and they're no more costly than most other oranges.

The orange, *Citrus sinensis*, has been a vital element in the cooking of the Mediterranean since at least the fifteenth century. Introduced to Europe from China, oranges continued westward to the New World as part of the great post-Columbian exchange of food plants between the hemispheres. Spanish padres planted oranges in the missions of California before 1800, and by 1900 land developers were luring settlers to southern California with the prospect of picking fresh oranges from backyard trees. Today suburbs have displaced the orange groves that once covered the southern California coastal valleys, and production has moved north and east, to California's central and northern valleys and deserts.

Oranges grow in several states other than California, and fresh oranges of some variety are always available. At the restaurant we use them year-round in upside-down cakes, fruit compotes, ice creams, and sherbets. The flavor of strawberries is deliciously complemented by that of oranges: try squeezing a little fresh orange juice over sliced berries or making strawberry-orange sherbet, one of our early-summer favorites. We sometimes make Italian orange granita as a summertime cooler, and we nearly always employ the Mediterranean trick of putting a little dried orange peel in such fish soups as bouillabaisse and in our beef stews too. Orange salads often appear on our menus, combining the fruit with olives, onions, or dates, Moroccan-style. On our drinks menu, freshly squeezed orange juice is a constant: Valencias in summer, blood oranges in winter. Winter is also the season to put up vin d'orange, the homemade apéritif flavored with sour oranges.

Florida produces the most oranges of any state, and California the next most. Large quantities come from Arizona and Texas, and a few smaller harvests are produced elsewhere along the Gulf Coast. Brazil has recently become the world's largest producer of oranges, most of them processed into frozen concentrate.

Oranges can be sorted into four main categories: blood oranges and navel oranges, both good for eating fresh; juice oranges, also called common oranges; and sour oranges.

Blood oranges have the most interesting and complex flavor of any orange, tart and rich, with hints of raspberry. The degree of red color in the flesh and peel varies according to variety, growing area, and degree of maturity. Blood oranges from California seem to have the most consistently bloody coloring, especially those from the inland valleys and the desert. Fruit from Texas and Florida is less colorful but has the same berry-like flavor.

Moro and Tarocco are the two varieties of blood orange most often found in the market. Moros are popular because they have the most reliably red flesh. They have medium-size fruit with orange skin, often blushing red. They are available from December to March or April, but their flavor changes noticeably during the season. Early Moros are almost unpleasantly tart; flavor and balance are much better in January and February. Late in the season you need to taste Moros carefully before buying. Left on the trees, they develop very dark purple flesh that can have an unpleasant musky flavor. Taroccos arrive a little later than Moros, from January to April. They are usually larger and have a pale red blush to their skin or none at all. The interior color of a Tarocco is not as bright or predictable as a Moro's, but the flavor is outstanding. Tarocco is the most popular orange in Italy.

The navel of a navel orange is actually a small secondary fruit that grows in the blossom end of the primary fruit. Navel oranges were known in Portugal and Spain in the seventeenth century, where they were called pregnant oranges. The variety known as the Washington navel orange arrived in California in 1873 via Brazil, and it has been the standard for eating oranges ever since. Navels grow especially well in California, where cool nights and warm days produce brilliant skin-color and the right balance of sugar and acid.

Washington navels have a thick, deep-colored rind that is easy to peel, and crisp, juicy segments that separate easily. They are almost always seedless, richly flavored, and just tart enough. The peak of the season runs from late fall through early spring. Navels make delicious juice, but be sure to drink it right away because a chemical compound in the fruit (limonene) will turn it bitter in short order. Cara Cara is a new navel variety with bright pink flesh and a sweet, spicy flavor.

Valencias are the most important of the common juice oranges. Their origin can be traced with certainty only as far as the Azores, where they were found in the early 1860s. They were propagated and planted widely, and now Valencia is the most commonly grown variety in the world. It does well in all citrus climates, from the tropics to the Mediterranean, South America, Australia, and South Africa. It is an important orange in Florida and the number-one orange in Texas and California. Valencias bear large, very juicy fruit with excellent flavor and few seeds. They ripen late in the citrus season but are slow to fall from the tree and can be harvested over a long period. Supplies are abundant from February through September. All oranges need cool temperatures to keep their orange color; ripe Valencias harvested in the summertime may have a certain amount of green in the skin, but the quality of the flesh is not affected.

Among the many other varieties of juice oranges, two in particular are produced in large numbers in Florida, the early Hamlin and the midseason Pineapple. Hamlin doesn't have particularly interesting flavor, but the juice is sweet, if a little pale; the harvest runs from October to December, when other juice oranges are scarce. Pineapple is very flavorful, and some tasters detect the scent of pineapple in the fruit. This orange is highly colored, and the juice is rich and flavorful, with a nice hit of tartness. Pineapple oranges are at their best in January and February, when their only drawback is their seediness: there are usually twenty or more seeds in each fruit.

Sour oranges belong to a distinct species, *C. aurantium*, native to Southeast Asia. Also called Seville oranges or bitter oranges, they arrived in Europe long before sweet oranges and were used for flavoring other foods; they are too sour and bitter to be eaten fresh. The blossoms, whose fragrance fills the springtime air of southern France, Spain, and North Africa, are harvested for perfume-making and orange flower water, which is made by boiling the flowers in water and distilling the steam. Sour oranges are essential for authentic orange marmalade, and boatloads of fruit are sent from Spain to England and Scotland for this purpose. Sour oranges are preferable to sweet ones for vin d'orange and such savory dishes as duck à l'orange. It is the oil from the peel of sour oranges that flavors such liqueurs as Cointreau and Curaçao.

Sour oranges can be found growing in California, Arizona, and Florida, where they are planted as street trees or backyard ornamentals; the attractive red-orange fruit is often left on the trees. A few are marketed commercially; the diligent shopper will find them in the winter in specialty produce stores.

Bergamots, sometimes called bergamot oranges, are related to sour oranges, possibly a hybrid of sour orange and lime. The yellow fruits, which look like small grapefruit, have intoxicatingly aromatic skin and very sour juice. The oil from the rind is used for cologne and other perfume-making and gives the characteristic flavor to Earl Grey tea. The peel is delicious candied, which is what we do whenever we can get our hands on a few bergamots. A small crop is grown in California; the only large-scale production is in Calabria, in southern Italy. Bergamots ripen in the winter.

Although most oranges are remarkably sturdy and can be harvested ripe and shipped to distant markets without damage, you must still be careful when shopping. Choose organically grown oranges that are firm but not hard and have relatively smooth skin for the variety. Avoid oranges that are soft or have dark, watery areas on the skin. Fruit that is heavy for its size will be the juiciest, but size itself is not an indication of quality, as larger fruit is often thick-skinned.

Nor is skin color a reliable sign of quality. Because oranges develop their deepest color only when grown in areas with warm days and cool nights, ripe oranges from Florida are often paler than oranges of the same variety grown in California or Arizona; they may even be greenish. The skin of Florida oranges also has more superficial blemishing, called russeting, which has no effect on flavor and may, in fact, indicate a thinner skin and superior juiciness. Fortunately, using vegetable dyes to color oranges is now prohibited in the United States.

Oranges stored at cool room temperature will keep at least a week. They will keep much longer in the refrigerator, but make sure they have good air circulation, and check them often, as one moldy orange will quickly spoil the lot.

For recipes that call for zest, remove only the thin, oily, pigmented outer layer of the skin; use a zester, a swivel-bladed vegetable peeler, a rasp, or a grater, and avoid the bitter white layer below (properly called the albedo and popularly called the pith). Smooth thin-skinned oranges are best for zest.

Navel oranges are easy to peel and segment without tools, unless you want skinless segments. In that case, peel and segment them as you would other varieties, using a small thin-bladed knife to slice off the stem and blossom ends of the fruit, exposing the flesh. Stand the orange on end and cut thin strips of peel from top to bottom, following the curve of the fruit and carefully removing as much white albedo as possible along with the skin. Continue around the fruit until most of the flesh is exposed. Pick up the orange and trim away any remaining bits of white.

Peeled oranges can be sliced more or less thin into little wheely disks, or they can be cut into skinless segments. To make segments, hold the peeled orange over a bowl and carefully cut toward the center, parallel to and just inside the membranes that separate each segment from its neighbor. Do this on each side of each segment, letting them drop into the bowl as they are cut. Make a fist and squeeze into the bowl all the juice that remains in the "carcass" of membranes.

DRIED ORANGE PEEL

Dried orange peel perfumes many a Provençal dish. Along with wild fennel, it is an obligatory part of the bouquet garni of an authentic bouillabaisse, and it adds character to beef daube, Provence's version of beef stew. *Boeuf à la Niçoise, estouffade, gardiane, soupe des pêcheurs*—all these classic dishes would be unthinkable without it. Orange peel when dried takes on a deep, earthy orange flavor different from the bright, lively flavor of fresh zest.

Orange peel is quite easy to dry: With a sharp swivel-bladed vegetable peeler, cut away long strips of zest from a deep-colored, thin-skinned orange. Run a needle and thread through one end of each piece and hang this garland up to dry out of direct sunlight. Once dried, store in a jar on your spice shelf for up to a year.

GRILLED DUCK BREAST WITH SEVILLE ORANGE SAUCE

2 large whole boneless duck   *2 Seville oranges*
    breasts, skin on   *1 cube Demerara sugar*
Salt and pepper   *2 tablespoons sherry vinegar*
1 quart duck stock

First, prepare the duck breasts for the grill. With the breasts skin side down, trim off the tenderloins (these can be added to the stock). Cut each whole breast in half down the center. Trim off any excess skin protruding from the edges, turn the breasts over, and score the skin with a sharp knife, making ⅛-inch-deep cuts on the diagonal, 3 or 4 times in one direction and then 3 or 4 times at a 45-degree angle, to create a crosshatch. This helps the fat to render quickly and the skin to brown. Season well with salt and pepper and refrigerate until about half an hour before you are ready to grill.

The sauce may be made ahead of time. Reduce the duck stock over medium heat to about 1 cup. Meanwhile, prepare the "gastric," the reduction of vinegar and orange juice that flavors the sauce. With a vegetable peeler, cut the zest away from the oranges in thin strips without taking any of the bitter white pith. Blanch the zest in boiling water for 4 minutes, drain, and slice lengthwise into fine julienne strips. Juice the oranges and strain out the seeds. Put the sugar and vinegar in a small heavy-bottomed saucepan and cook over medium-high heat until thick and caramelized. Add the orange juice and half the julienne and reduce to a thick syrup. Pour the gastric into the reduced stock, adjust the seasoning, and strain. Reheat before serving with the rest of the zest.

Prepare a wood or charcoal fire and let the coals burn down to medium heat; they should not quite be glowing incandescent red. (If they are too hot, the breasts burn; if not hot enough, the breasts will not render their fat and color nicely.) Grill the duck breasts, skin side down, for about 10 minutes, taking care that dripping duck fat does not flare up and burn the duck skin. To alleviate the problem of flaming fat, tilt the grill slightly so fat runs down and drips away from the actual cooking area. Move the breasts to a cooler part of the grill when nearly done. When the skin is golden brown and the fat has rendered away, turn the breasts over and grill 3 or 4 minutes more. The meat should be medium-rare. Let the breasts rest in a warm place for 10 minutes to stabilize their juices, slice, and serve immediately with the sauce ladled over.

Serves 4 to 6.

BLOOD ORANGE AND BEET SALAD

This salad is particularly beautiful when two or more colors of red, pink, or orange beets are paired with dark berry red and gold Moro blood oranges. An advantage of golden beets is that they don't bleed and run as their red counterparts do, making it easier to arrange the salad. Look for beets like these at your local farmers' market.

12 small or 6 medium beets (a mixture of Chioggia, golden, and red)
Extra-virgin olive oil
Salt and pepper

Red wine vinegar
5 Moro blood oranges
¼ teaspoon finely chopped rosemary
Optional: Niçoise olives

Preheat the oven to 375°F.

Trim off the beet tops, leaving 1 inch of stem and the root end intact. Wash them and put them in a roasting pan with a splash of water (enough to cover the bottom to a depth of ⅛ inch), a splash of olive oil, and a little salt. Cover and roast in the oven until tender, 45 minutes to 1 hour. If using a mixture of beets, roast the red ones separately to prevent staining. Let the beets cool until you can handle them, then peel them. Cut some of the beets into wedges and some into slices, always keeping the red ones separate from the others. Sprinkle with salt and 1 table-spoon vinegar and let stand for 10 minutes to absorb the flavor. Taste, add more salt and vinegar if needed, and add a little olive to coat them lightly.

Cut the tops and bottoms off 4 of the blood oranges with a sharp knife. Cut away strips of peel from end to end, removing the peel all the way down to the flesh. Set the oranges aside.

Make a vinaigrette by grating half the zest from the remaining orange into a small bowl. Squeeze 3 tablespoons juice from the orange and add to the bowl along with the chopped rosemary and 1 teaspoon vinegar. Season with salt and generous amount of pepper and mix together. Let this macerate for ½ hour, then whisk in ¼ cup olive oil. Taste and adjust the salt and acid as needed.

When ready to serve, carefully slice the peeled oranges into ¼-inch-thick rounds. Arrange them on a platter with the golden and pink beets; carefully place the red beets around the platter. Spoon the vinaigrette over the salad and serve, garnished with a few Niçoise olives, if you wish.

Serves 6.

Candied Orange Peel Dipped in Chocolate

When my friends in Provence took me shopping in Nice, I was delighted to find this irresistible candy sold everywhere. Lemon, lime, mandarin, or tangerine peel can be candied in exactly the same way.

5 oranges
4 cups sugar plus more for tossing
2 cups water
¼ pound bittersweet chocolate, chopped

Wash the oranges. Cut them in half and juice them. Drink the juice or save it to make sherbet. Put the halves of peel in a medium-size saucepan and cover with cold water. Bring to a boil over low heat and simmer for 10 minutes. Drain the peel, return it to the saucepan, and cover with cold water; bring to a boil and simmer 10 more minutes. Repeat this blanching process a third time, simmering until the peel can easily be pierced with the point of a knife. After this third blanching, let the soggy peel cool. Scrape out most of the white part of the peel with a spoon and slice the peel into long ¼-inch-thick strips.

Put the strips of orange peel in the saucepan and add the sugar and 2 cups water. Stir the mixture over low heat until the sugar is dissolved. Allow the peel to continue to cook slowly in the sugar syrup until it becomes translucent and the syrup is boiling in fast small bubbles; the temperature of the syrup should reach 230°F.

Turn off the heat and let the fruit sit in the syrup for ½ hour. Drain the peel and arrange the strips, not touching one another, on a rack or on a baking sheet lined with parchment paper. The next day, toss them with about ½ cup of sugar and store them in an airtight container, refrigerated, for up to 6 months.

Four ounces of chocolate will cover about 60 pieces of orange peel. There are two ways in which we treat chocolate for dipping peel. If we are going to serve the peel immediately, we gently melt the chocolate in a double boiler, remove it from the heat, and carefully dip the long strips into it, leaving the end of each strip uncoated. Let the excess chocolate drain back into the bowl and lay the strips on a parchment-lined baking sheet. Refrigerate until firm and serve cold.

If the strips of peel need to stay at room temperature for a long time—or if we want them to be very shiny—we temper the chocolate before dipping. Start by chopping all the chocolate. Gently melt about three-quarters of the chocolate and pour it into a room-temperature bowl. Add the unmelted chocolate, stirring until it is a little cooler than body temperature. Dip the strips of peel into the chocolate as described above. This chocolate will solidify at room temperature.

Makes 4 cups.

BLOOD ORANGE SPONGE CAKE TART

This vibrant tart is so visually appealing you will hate to cut into it, but after your first bite you won't care. The cake tucked under the oranges is a surprise. The tart dough, the shell, and the cake can all be prepared in advance, leaving the simple assembly for the last minute.

10 or 11 blood oranges	*1 sponge cake (page 300)*
¼ cup sugar	*1 prebaked 11-inch pâte sucrée*
¼ cup Cointreau	*tart shell (page 296)*
½ cup water	

Combine the grated zest of 1 blood orange, the juice of 2 blood oranges, and the sugar, Cointreau, and water; stir to dissolve the sugar.

If the sponge cake is a 9-inch round, cut it horizontally into two 1-inch-thick layers. Center 1 layer in the baked tart shell and cut arcs from the other layer to fill the shell snugly right up to its edge. If the cake is a 12- by 18-inch rectangle, simply cut out a 10½-inch round and place it in the shell. (In either case, save the leftover sponge cake for another use.)

Strain the zest out of the soaking liquid and spoon about ¾ cup of the liquid over the cake. Lift the cake and make sure it is thoroughly and evenly soaked.

Cut the top and bottom off the remaining blood oranges. Carefully cut away all the peel, and slice the oranges into ¼-inch-thick pinwheel rounds. Arrange them on top of the soaked cake in slightly overlapping concentric circles.

Pour the remaining soaking liquid into a small nonreactive saucepan and simmer for about 10 minutes to reduce and thicken it a little. Taste and, if necessary, adjust the sweetness with some lemon juice or blood orange juice. Let cool slightly. Brush the glaze over the blood oranges. Cut the tart into wedges and serve.

Makes one 11-inch tart; serves 8 to 10.

Candied Orange and Almond Tart

The candied orange slices can also be chopped up and folded into just-frozen vanilla ice cream.

CANDIED ORANGE SLICES
1 Valencia, blood, or navel
   orange
2 cups water
1 cup sugar

1 tablespoon kirsch or orange
   liqueur
1 pinch salt
2 tablespoons unbleached
   all-purpose flour

ALMOND FILLING
6 ounces almond paste
4 teaspoons sugar
4 tablespoons (½ stick) unsalted
   butter
2 eggs

Two 10-ounce pieces galette
   dough (page 290)
2 tablespoons unsalted butter,
   melted
2 tablespoons sugar

To make the candied orange slices, cut the orange horizontally into ⅛-inch-thick pinwheel slices, removing the seeds as you go. Put the orange slices in a medium-size saucepan with the water and sugar. Cook for 15 minutes, simmering gently so as not to break up the slices, until tender and translucent. Let them cool in their syrup.

To make the almond filling, mix together the almond paste and sugar. Thoroughly beat in the butter. Add the eggs, kirsch or orange liqueur, and salt and beat until fluffy and smooth. Stir in the flour.

Roll out the galette dough into two 14-inch circles about ⅛ inch thick and refrigerate them for about 10 minutes.

Preheat the oven to 400°F.

Put one circle of galette dough on a parchment paper–lined baking sheet. Spread the almond filling evenly over the dough, leaving a 1½-inch border at the edge uncovered. Drain the candied orange slices.

Arrange the slices in an even layer on top of the almond filling. Brush the exposed border with melted butter and lay the second piece of dough on top. Use a small paring knife to trim away any excess overhanging dough. Gently press around the circumference so that the top and bottom pieces seal together, then work your way around the tart, folding over the layers of dough on themselves and crimping to make a sealed rim that resembles a length of rope. Brush the top with melted butter and sprinkle with 2 tablespoons sugar.

Bake in the lower third of the oven, rotating occasionally for even col-oration, for 45 minutes. Immediately slide the tart off its paper-lined baking sheet onto a cooling rack. Cool 15 minutes before serving with lightly whipped cream.

Makes one 12-inch tart; serves 8.

Orange Ice Cream

6 egg yolks
3 medium oranges
1 cup half-and-half
⅔ cup sugar

2 cups heavy cream
Optional: ¼ teaspoon orange
 liqueur

Whisk the egg yolks lightly in a mixing bowl, just enough to break them up. Remove the zest of 2 oranges with a zester (the kind with tiny holes) or peel off strips of zest with a swivel-bladed vegetable peeler and cut into a fine julienne. Put the half-and-half and sugar into a medium-size saucepan, add the zest, and heat gently, stirring slowly, until the half-and-half is steaming and the sugar is dissolved. Drizzle the warm mix-ture into the egg yolks, whisking constantly as you pour.

Pour the mixture back into the saucepan. Measure the heavy cream into the mixing bowl. Cook the egg yolk mixture over low heat, stirring slowly and scraping the bottom of the pan with a wooden spoon or heat-resistant rubber spatula, until the mixture thickens enough to coat the spoon. (This happens at a temperature of about 170°F.) Immediately remove from the heat and strain through a fine-mesh sieve into the bowl with the heavy cream. Whisk together to cool the mixture, cover, and chill thoroughly.

Juice the 3 oranges, strain out the seeds, and chill the juice. (You should have about ⅔ cup.) Just before freezing the ice cream, stir the juice and the orange liqueur, if using, into the chilled ice cream base. Freeze according to the instructions for your ice cream maker.

Makes 1 quart.

Blood Orange Tartlets with Caramel

4 blood oranges	*1½ cup orange-flavored pastry*
¾ cup plus 1 tablespoon sugar	*cream (page 302)*
¼ cup water	*6 prebaked 4-inch pâte sucrée*
2 teaspoons orange liqueur,	*tartlet shells (page 296)*
such as Grand Marnier	

Cut off the tops and bottoms of 3 of the oranges with a sharp paring knife. Cut away thick strips of peel from end to end, removing the peel all the way down to the flesh. Cut the oranges into ¼-inch-thick pinwheel slices, removing the seeds as you go. Spread out the orange slices on a plate and sprinkle with 1 tablespoon sugar.

For the caramel-making, you will need a bowl large enough to hold your small saucepan. Fill it with ice water and set it right next to the stove. Put ¾ cup sugar in the small saucepan with ¼ cup water. Cook the sugar over high heat, swirling the pan occasionally, until it starts turning a light gold color and smoking a bit. When the caramel is amber-colored, remove the saucepan from the heat and plunge the bottom of the pan into the ice water bath. This will stop the cooking immediately. As it cools, the caramel will harden in the pan.

Stir the orange liqueur into the pastry cream.

To assemble the tartlets, first remove the prebaked shells from their pans and place them on a cooling rack. Gently rewarm the caramel over low heat, letting it liquefy enough so that it forms threads when pulled with a fork, but not letting it get so hot that it starts to burn again. Working close to the stove, use the fork to drizzle thin threads of caramel into the bottom of each tartlet. If the caramel gets too thick to drizzle, return it to the heat; if it gets too hot, return it to the ice bath. Thick droplets of caramel will harden and be difficult to eat. If there are big droplets or too much caramel in a tartlet shell, let the caramel cool; the entire web will release easily and you can try again.

Once the tartlets are lined with a crisp, delicate web of caramel, fill each one with ¼ cup pastry cream, and arrange 4 or 5 orange slices on top. Thin out the leftover caramel with the juice left on the plate that held the sugared orange slices and the juice of the remaining orange. Heat gently, stirring to blend the sauce and juice. Transfer the tartlets to individual dessert plates and drizzle some of the orange caramel over them and on the plates as a sauce.

Makes six 4-inch tartlets.

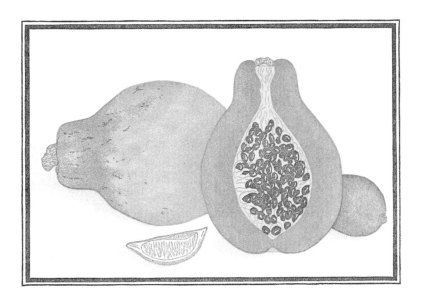

PAPAYAS 🎨

Season: Year-round, best in summer and fall

Papayas are a bit like melons—they have thick, sweet, juicy flesh that is low in acidity. The very ripest papayas have a slightly odd, strong musky scent, but the flavor remains muted, and much of the pleasure of eating a papaya is tactile as the luscious melting flesh slides easily down your throat. This may be why papaya with lime is such a refreshing breakfast, especially on a sultry summer morning.

Ripe papayas have tender flesh that needs no cooking. Slices of raw papaya can be served at the beginning of a meal, seasoned with lemon or lime and salt and pepper, perhaps draped with thin slices of pro-sciutto, and sliced papaya with lime can be served after a rich dinner, when it is as refreshing and satisfying as it is at breakfast. When papaya is combined with higher-acid tropical fruits, such as passion fruit, cit-rus, and pineapple, perhaps in a macédoine, its flavor is enhanced and its soft texture makes a pleasing contrast. Puréed, it imparts velvety soft-ness and body to tropical fruit sherbets.

In southern Asia green papaya is popular used as a vegetable, shred-ded or sliced thin and seasoned with lime and hot pepper in salads. In the Thai dish *sohm taam*, a cooling snack offered by street vendors, green papaya is crushed in a mortar with garlic, chilies, palm sugar, green beans, and dried shrimp, and finished with lime juice and crushed peanuts. Green papayas are also cooked like summer squash.

Carica papaya, a native of Central America and southern Mexico, was cultivated across much of tropical America by the time of Columbus's first visit. Now papayas are grown in the tropical zone worldwide. A good number of the papayas we see in California come from Hawaii, and a few fruits are produced for sale in southern Florida, but Mexico is the source of most of the papayas marketed in the United States.

Papayas grow on rapidly maturing trees of confusing sexuality, with some varieties having male and female trees and others having only hermaphrodites and females. Growers sex the trees and aggressively thin them out, leaving only a few of the nonbearing males to pollinate the females, which start producing when they are only a few feet tall. The fruits hang in clusters just below a tuft of large fan-shaped leaves that tops the tree's single slim, straight trunk. The trees quickly grow too tall for easy picking and are usually replaced after three years. In the wild, papayas can grow as tall as twenty-five or thirty feet. Although papayas bear some fruit year-round, they are most prolific in summer and fall.

As a papaya ripens, the thin, waxy skin turns from dark green to yellow or orange and the flesh begins to soften. Its flavor is best if it is harvested when the skin is mostly yellow with a few streaks of green. In practice, most fruit harvested for shipping is picked well before this point, and the skin is mostly green with a few streaks of yellow. The fruits soften and turn color during storage but get no sweeter.

Cut into a ripe papaya and you will find yellow, orange, or salmon-pink flesh, depending on the variety. The center of the fruit is hollow, but clinging to the flesh and looking like so many large grains of caviar are dozens of black seeds, shiny in their gelatinous coating. The seeds are edible and very spicy, having the peppery taste of watercress.

There are two types of papaya, Mexican and Hawaiian. Hawaiian papayas are small, about the size of a grapefruit. They are descended from a fruit found in Barbados in 1911 and given the name Solo because it was a good size to be eaten by one person. Solo and its offspring quickly came to dominate the Hawaiian market. The fruits weigh a pound or two and have yellow or orange skin and very sweet flesh. They are either round or pear-shaped, depending on the sexual orientation of their parent tree. The Kapoho variety has yellow-orange flesh, while Sunrise is reddish-orange.

The introduction in the mid-1990s of two genetically modified papayas, Rainbow and SunUp, has caused concern among organic growers in Hawaii. The new varieties have a gene inserted for resistance to a serious viral disease, and many conventional papaya growers have rushed to plant them. Organic farmers fear that pollen drifting from nearby genetically altered plants will fertilize flowers on their organic plants, causing them to bear fruit with seeds having the engineered gene. Farmers who plant these seeds could be growing genetically modified fruit, which by definition is not organic. Be sure to ask your produce dealer if he or she sells genetically engineered papayas.

Papayas from Mexico are much larger than the Solo types and often grow to the size of small watermelons, weighing upwards of five pounds. The flesh of these large fruits is very tender, highly colored, and flavorful, but often not as sweet as Solo.

When shopping for papayas, choose well-colored, organically grown fruit that gives to gentle pressure. Don't buy any that have cuts, soft spots, or bruises or show any signs of mold. The texture and color of underripe fruit will improve if the papayas are kept at room temperature for several days, but they will not get sweeter. Papayas should never be refrigerated; don't try to store them past the point when they're ready to eat.

To prepare a papaya, cut it in half from stem to bottom and scrape out the seeds with a spoon. Taste a seed, and if you like it, save a few to sprinkle over the fruit when you serve it. A small papaya can be peeled at this point; larger fruit should be cut into manageable pieces before peeling. Slice the flesh or cut it in chunks or cubes, sprinkle with a little lime juice, and refrigerate for an hour or two before serving. Don't use raw papaya in gelatin desserts! Papaya contains an enzyme that prevents the gelatin from setting.

TROPICAL FRUIT SHERBET

We make this sherbet when tropical fruits are just coming into season. Select fruit that is perfectly ripe and delicious. Try experimenting with different types of mangos and bananas. Red bananas have a delicate tropical flavor and a texture that produces an especially velvety sherbet.

2 medium bananas
1 cup chopped mango
½ cup chopped papaya
2 cups chopped pineapple

1 kiwifruit
1 cup frozen passion fruit purée
2½ cups orange juice
Juice of 1 lime

Put all the ingredients in a food processor and blend until smooth. Freeze according to the instructions for your ice cream maker.

Makes 1 quart.

PASSION FRUIT 🦋

Season: Late summer through fall

European missionaries saw symbols of the passion of Christ (by which is meant his suffering and crucifixion) in the showy flowers of the passion fruit vines they encountered in Brazil and elsewhere in tropical South America—with flower parts standing for the five wounds, the three nails, the crown of thorns, and so forth—and thus the fruits became known as passion fruit. Today most people are ignorant of the passion fruit's symbolic past and associate the fruit with passion only in the sense of secular desire. Understandably so: the alluring passion fruit captivates almost everyone who tastes or smells its spicy, unmistakably tropical aroma.

Passion fruit has a concentrated and acidic flavor that blends well with those of other fruits. Its most celebrated use must certainly be in Pavlova, a dessert named for the ballerina Anna Pavlova during her visit to Australia in 1935, although it was a popular dessert in Australia and New Zealand before that. Pavlova has many variations, but they all include a tender meringue shell, crisp on the outside and soft in the middle, filled with whipped cream and fruit, most often strawberries and kiwifruit. The classic Pavlova is topped with passion fruit pulp, including seeds.

Pavlova at Chez Panisse changes a little every time we make it. The basic flavors stay the same, but we have fun putting them together differently. We might fill meringues with strawberry ice cream and fresh kiwifruit and pour passion fruit sauce on top, or we might use passion fruit ice cream garnished with fresh pineapple and oranges. Only rarely do we make a version of this dish without passion fruit in it somewhere.

Passion fruit is especially good with citrus, and our passion fruit sherbet always includes orange juice. It also makes a sprightly sauce for sliced oranges and other tropical fruits with a savarin or rum baba. Passion fruit makes an interesting soufflé, and our most elegant baked Alaska is filled with passion fruit sherbet and vanilla ice cream. But you don't need to make fancy desserts to enjoy passion fruit. Add some passion to fruit salad, try a little spooned over ice cream, or make a refreshing drink with sweetened passion fruit stirred into orange or pineapple juice.

There are two main commercial types of passion fruit, one yellow-skinned, the other purple. Both have round or oblong fruits, two or three inches in diameter; yellow-skinned ones tend to be larger. Inside the tough outer shell, the golden yellow, juicy pulp contains many small edible seeds, about the size of grape seeds. Purple passion fruit have black seeds; yellow passion fruit have brown seeds.

Purple passion fruit, *Passiflora edulis,* is sometimes called purple granadilla, Spanish for "little pomegranate." The vines thrive in subtropical climates and are particularly popular in Australia and New Zealand. They grow and flower well in our part of the Bay Area but don't produce much edible fruit here. They have long been cultivated in Hawaii, which has become a major producer and where they have escaped from cultivation to grow in the wild. Most of the organic passion fruit in our markets comes from a few farms in southern California, but passion fruit is also imported from South America and New Zealand.

Purple passion fruit are preferred for the fresh market because they are richer, sweeter, and juicier than the yellow types. Yellow passion fruit, *P. edulis* var. *flavicarpa,* are preferred for processing because the fruits are bigger and easier to handle; much frozen passion fruit pulp and juice comes from yellow passion fruit. Australia, Brazil, and Central America are important producers of yellow passion fruit, which require true tropical conditions.

Because of their widely dispersed growing areas, fresh passion fruit are available periodically throughout the year, but the best domestic ones come to market from late summer to late fall. Fruits with dimpled and wrinkled skin will be the ripest and sweetest. Choose ones that are organically grown and heavy for their size. Underripe fruits will be smooth-skinned; keep them at warm room temperature until they are wrinkled. Ripe fruit can be stored in the refrigerator for a week or so and can be frozen.

The easiest way to enjoy passion fruit is to cut the fruit in half and scoop out the pulp and seeds with a spoon. Since the seeds are small and edible, all you need to do is add a little cream and sugar. Some recipes require seedless pulp, obtained by forcing the pulp through a nonreactive fine-mesh strainer with a rubber spatula or wooden spoon. Heating the pulp gently with a little sugar before you strain it will cause it to release more juice, but too much heat will adversely affect the flavor. Figure on getting about a tablespoon of usable pulp from a medium-size, heavy passion fruit, less from a lighter one.

Passion Fruit Sherbet

Passion fruit have such intensity of flavor that only a few are needed to make a flavorful sherbet. Be careful not to overheat the passion fruit purée, or it will lose its remarkable bouquet.

3 pounds oranges, or	*¾ cup plus 2 tablespoons sugar*
enough to make 3 cups juice	*¼ teaspoon vanilla extract*
8 passion fruit	*Optional: 1 teaspoon Cointreau*

Juice the oranges, strain, and measure 3 cups. Cut passion fruit in half and scoop out the pulp and seeds into a small nonreactive saucepan. Add the sugar and 1 cup orange juice. Heat gently and stir until sugar is dissolved. Press and scrape through a nonreactive fine-mesh strainer with a wooden spoon or rubber spatula, and add the remaining orange juice, the vanilla, and the Cointreau, if using. Chill thoroughly.

Freeze according to the instructions for your ice cream maker. Serve with delicate butter cookies or coconut macaroons.

Makes about 1 quart.

Passion Fruit Soufflés

This recipe is derived from the raspberry soufflé recipe published by Michel Guérard in his 1978 cookbook, *Cuisine Gourmande*.

1 tablespoon unsalted butter, melted and cooled slightly
½ cup granulated sugar plus more for coating the ramekins and sprinkling on top
½ cup seedless passion fruit pulp (page 203)

½ teaspoon vanilla extract
2 egg yolks
4 egg whites, room temperature
1½ teaspoons cornstarch
1 pinch salt
¼ teaspoon cream of tartar
Powdered sugar for dusting

Preheat the oven to 450°F.

Brush the insides of six 5-ounce ramekins with the butter, leaving a generous lip of butter around the inner rim. Pour in some granulated sugar, coating the insides, and tap out any excess. Touch up any uncovered spots with more melted butter and sugar. Set the ramekins aside on a baking sheet.

Whisk together ¼ cup sugar and the passion fruit purée, vanilla, and egg yolks in a large mixing bowl.

In another clean, dry mixing bowl, whisk the egg whites until they are frothy. Add the cornstarch, salt, and cream of tartar and beat until the whites are fluffy and hold soft peaks. Add the remaining ¼ cup granulated sugar and keep whisking until the peaks are firm and glossy but not dry. Gently fold the whites into the passion fruit mixture, deflating the whites as little as possible.

Spoon the soufflé mixture into the prepared ramekins, filling them just to the lip of butter. Sprinkle the tops with a thin layer of sugar. Drag your finger around the top and outer edge of the rim of each ramekin to clean up any splattered excess soufflé mixture; this ensures that the soufflés will rise straight up ½ inch or more without sticking to the sides.

Bake for 8 to 9 minutes, until the soufflés are tall, golden on top, and still slightly soft to the touch in the center. Remove the baking sheet from the oven and dust the tops of the soufflés with powdered sugar. Serve immediately on individual plates lined with napkins or doilies (to keep the ramekins from sliding around).

Serves 6.

PEACHES ❧

Season: Summer

We've said it many times before: the perfect dessert after a rich and satisfying meal is a perfect piece of fruit, and the most perfect fruit has to be a perfect peach. Its texture is luscious, its aroma is intoxicating, its flavor is ravishing, and its juice runs everywhere. A perfectly ripe peach is a special, fleeting thing, and it has to have been grown and harvested nearby because ripe peaches are fragile and easily damaged if mishandled. We have a number of special growers we look to year after year for carefully tended and harvested organic fruit, farmers like Al Courchesne in the Sacramento delta and Ernie Bierwagen in the Sierra foothills. And for years we looked forward to our August visit from Kimi, a backyard grower in the Central Valley who always brought us a box or two of her exquisite Elbertas, each one hand-selected and always at the point of perfect ripeness.

Even amid the abundance of other summertime fruits, peaches are our favorite for desserts. Most of our peach desserts are simple preparations designed to enhance the natural characteristics of the fruit. We don't poach the fruit for our peach Melba but use sliced fresh peaches instead. Our peach galettes are paired with ice cream flavored with noyaux, the kernels extracted from peach or apricot pits. Peach leaf parfait is scented with just a handful of crushed peach leaves. And what could be simpler, or better, than a freshly baked peach pie?

Peaches and their leaves have a place in other parts of the menu too. We often make a Provençal-style vin de pêche, a stimulating apéritif flavored with the tender peach leaves of early summer, and we make pickled peaches to accent the flavor of game or pork.

Peaches appear in markets earlier every year, but the first good ones don't show up in California and the South until June and in the Midwest and East until late June or early July. The peak of the season comes in late July and August, when a different variety seems to ripen every day. Peach season winds down in September but can extend into early October in the most favored spots. Early peaches are almost always clings, that is, peaches with firm flesh that doesn't part easily from the pit. They are the best peaches for canning. The peaches of midsummer and fall are usually freestones, which have softer, more delicate flesh that separates easily from the pit.

Peaches were first cultivated in China, but they were introduced to southern Europe from Persia, whence they take their Latin name, *Prunus persica*. They have been grown in this country from the time of the first European settlers, and they were adopted and widely planted by Native Americans, as well as the colonists. However, many varieties that we think of as heirlooms were developed fairly recently. Elberta is only about 130 years old.

Commercial quantities of peaches are grown in thirty states, but more than two-thirds of the annual aggregate production comes from California. Other important growing areas are in Georgia, South Carolina, Texas, and New Jersey, and growers in each state have their favorite varieties.

Among the early peaches, Flordaking, Spring Lady, and Queencrest are all flavorful clings and widely available; after these come several delicious varieties that are considered semiclings: Gold Dust, Flavorcrest, and Coronet.

The peak of peach season in July and August brings both yellow- and white-fleshed varieties, most of them freestone. Belle of Georgia is a large, firm, very flavorful white peach popular in the Southeast. Carolina Belle is a newer variety, a little firmer and less likely to bruise. In California, we look for Babcock, a semifreestone white peach that is extraordinarily aromatic when picked ripe. Other midseason white peaches with exceptional aroma, taste, and texture are Silver Logan, Nectar, and White Lady.

Peach connoisseurs in Michigan wait for Red Haven, a variety developed there, which ripens in early August. It is considered to be the quality standard for yellow-fleshed peaches in the Midwest. Red Haven is freestone when fully ripe, but may cling to its stone if underripe. Elberta, the most widely planted peach in the United States, is considered to be the quality standard in California. Its large yellow, red-blushed

fruit is firm and juicy, has a hint of lemon, and is good whether used fresh, canned, or made into preserves.

Sun Crest is a peach we look for every year, one whose reputation was rescued by our friend Mas Masumoto. His book *Epitaph for a Peach* poetically describes life on his farm and his family's efforts to save Sun Crest. This delicious, very juicy variety was in danger of being lost because produce sellers passed it by, ignoring its excellent flavor and preferring instead less fragile, redder-skinned peaches—although I cannot imagine how anyone could fail to be charmed by Sun Crest's lovely golden skin overlaid by a brilliant red blush. Rio Oso Gem is another wonderful peach that has marketing problems. Although this exceptionally well-flavored, large yellow peach is of the highest quality for eating and cooking, it bruises easily and drops from the tree as soon as it gets ripe, making it feasible only for small growers who can keep an eye on every tree and sell to a local market.

August also brings O'Henry, a beautiful red-skinned peach with very good flavor, and Indian Blood, a peach variety that comes in both a cling and a freestone type. These have very dark red skin and tart, dark red flesh; they make beautiful pickled peaches and brilliant pink sherbet. Good late-season peaches include Summerset, Fair Time, Autumn Flame, and the appropriately named Last Chance.

Look for any of these peaches at farm stands and at farmers' markets. And try other local favorites too. The aroma of a peach is the best indicator of ripeness; one of the most pleasurable aspects of selecting peaches is smelling them. If you get a hit of deep peachy aroma, buy that peach. Avoid those with obvious bruises or cuts in the skin and any that are soft all over. A ripe peach will feel firm, just beginning to yield to gentle pressure on its shoulder. Check the color at the stem end of the fruit. The background color should be creamy white or yellow. Except for nectar white peaches, which can be a creamy pale green even when fully ripe, do not buy peaches that show any green color. Red skin color is only a varietal characteristic, not an indicator of quality.

At home, firm ripe peaches should be stored at room temperature until they begin to soften along the suture, the line running from the stem to the blossom end; then they are ready to eat. Any not used at this point can be refrigerated, but plan to use them within several days.

Peaches to be eaten fresh should be peeled with a small sharp knife. Cut into the fruit following the suture from stem to blossom end and continuing up the opposite side. Twist the two halves gently; if the peach is a freestone, they will separate easily; if it is a cling, they will not. Clings should be peeled whole and the slices cut away from the pit. Freestones should first be halved, then peeled and cut. Sliced fresh peaches should be eaten as soon as possible, or they will oxidize and turn brown. At the restaurant we retard this process by keeping the peaches in a bowl nestled in ice, arranging the sliced fruit in layers with sprinklings of sugar and thin shavings of ice. You can also submerge sliced peaches in chilled sugar syrup.

To peel peaches for cooking, gently lower them, a few at a time, into a pot of rapidly boiling water. Let them parboil for a minute or so, and as they are done, plunge them into a bowl of ice water. The peels should come off easily.

PICKLED PEACHES

3 peaches	*½ teaspoon peppercorns*
2 cups water	*4 cloves*
½ cup red wine vinegar	*2 allspice berries*
¼ cup red wine	*½ stick cinnamon*
2 tablespoons honey	*1 bay leaf*

Pickle the peaches at least a day before you plan to serve them. First peel them; if the skins don't come off easily, plunge the peaches into boiling water for less than a minute and immediately refresh them in cold water to loosen their skins. Cut the peaches in half and remove the pits.

Measure the water into a heavy-bottomed saucepan. Add the vinegar, red wine, honey, peppercorns, cloves, allspice, cinnamon, and bay leaf. Bring to a boil, then reduce the heat and simmer for 5 minutes. Add the peach halves and cook just until tender, 3 to 5 minutes: test with a toothpick or sharp knife. Carefully remove the peaches with a slotted spoon; they will be quite delicate. Let the pickling mixture cool slightly and then strain over the peaches. Cover and refrigerate overnight or for up to a week.

Makes 6 pickled peach halves.

Grilled Cured Duck Breast with Pickled Peaches

2 whole large duck breasts
5 quarts cold water
½ cup salt
¼ cup sugar
1 bay leaf

½ teaspoon peppercorns
1 clove
3 allspice berries
2 small dried chili peppers
6 pickled peach halves (page 209)

First, prepare the duck breasts for the brine. With the breasts skin side down, trim off the tenderloins and save them for another purpose. Cut each whole breast in half down the center. Trim off any excess skin protruding from the edges, turn the breasts over, and score the skin with a sharp knife, making ¼-inch-deep parallel cuts on the diagonal, 3 or 4 times in one direction and then 3 or 4 times at a 45-degree angle, to create a crosshatch. This helps the fat to render and the skin to brown.

To make the brine, put the cold water in a nonreactive container large enough to hold the duck breasts and brine. Stir in the salt and sugar until dissolved. Lightly crush the bay leaf, peppercorns, clove, allspice, and chili peppers and stir into the brine. Immerse the duck breasts, keeping them weighted down and submerged underneath a plate. Cover and refrigerate for 2 days. (Or 3 days at the most in the brine. Once removed, dried, and wrapped well, the duck breasts will keep for another day or two in the refrigerator.)

When you are ready to grill the duck breasts, take them out of the refrigerator and dry them well. Prepare wood or charcoal fire and let the coals burn down to medium heat; the coals should not quite be glowing incandescent red. (If the coals are too hot, the breasts will burn, but if they are not hot enough, the breasts will not render out their fat and turn golden brown.) Grill the breasts, skin side down, for 10 minutes, being careful that dripping fat does not flare up and burn the duck skin, ruining it. When they are nearly done, move the breasts to a cooler part of the grill. To alleviate the problem of flaming duck fat, tilt the grill at a slight angle so the fat runs down and drips away from the actual cooking area. After 10 minutes, when the fat is rendered and the skin has browned nicely, turn the breasts over and cook for 3 or 4 minutes more. The duck should be medium-rare. To allow the juices to stabilize, let the duck breasts rest in a warm place for 10 minutes before slicing. Before serving, gently warm the peach slices in their pickling juice and arrange them alongside the sliced duck breast.

Serves 6.

VIN DE PÊCHE

120 fresh peach leaves, picked
    in late spring or early
    summer, washed and dried
One 750-ml bottle red wine
    (preferably a light, fruity
    Zinfandel)

½ cup Cognac
2 cups sugar

Combine all the ingredients in a nonreactive container and cover tightly.
Store in a cool, dark cellar or in the refrigerator for 30 days. Strain out the
leaves and bottle in a clean wine bottle. Serve as an apéritif, well chilled
or over ice.

Makes about 6 cups.

PEACH MELBA

Named for the legendary Australian diva Nellie Melba, this classic dessert is a perfectly balanced trio of flavors and textures. We serve it with
a generous plate of delicate crispy almond cookies.

5 medium firm ripe peaches
¼ cup sugar
1 quart vanilla ice cream (page 301)
¾ cup raspberry coulis (page 271)

Chill serving bowls or glasses. Gently peel the peaches with a sharp paring knife. Slice them ⅓-inch thick into a medium-size bowl and toss
with the sugar. Cover the bowl and let stand at least 10 minutes, until the
sugar dissolves.

When you are ready to serve the dessert, remove the bowls from the
refrigerator. Put 3 small scoops of vanilla ice cream in each bowl, drizzle
with a few tablespoons of raspberry coulis, and top with sliced peaches.
Drizzle a few more spoonfuls of coulis over the peaches and serve immediately.

Serves 6.

Peach Pie

2½ pounds peaches, peeled
  and sliced (about 6 cups)
3 tablespoons quick-cooking
  tapioca
2 teaspoons lemon juice
1 pinch salt
¼ cup sugar plus more
  for sprinkling

1 tablespoon unsalted butter,
  cut in thin slices
Two 9-ounce pieces pie dough
  (page 292)
1 tablespoon heavy cream
  or milk

Toss the sliced peaches in a large bowl with the tapioca, lemon juice, salt, sugar, and butter. Cover the fruit mixture with a sheet of plastic wrap pressed against its surface (this prevents the fruit from oxidizing and discoloring). Let stand for 30 minutes so the peaches release their juice, plumping the tapioca and dissolving the sugar.

Preheat the oven to 400°F.

Roll out each piece of pie dough into a 13-inch circle, ⅛ inch thick. Line a pie plate with the first piece, letting the edges hang over. Pour the fruit mixture into the dough-lined plate. Cover with the second piece of dough. Using a small knife or scissors, trim the edges of the dough so that there is a ¾-inch overhang. To seal the pie, neatly fold up the overhanging dough so that it rests on the rim of the pie plate and pinch a wavy scalloped edge all around the pie by making indentations in the crust with your thumb and fingers. Roll out the scraps, cut out pretty decorations, and stick them to the top of the pie with a dab of water. Poke a few holes in the top of the pie to let the steam escape during baking. Lightly brush the pie with cream and sprinkle with sugar.

Bake in the lower third of the oven until the top of the pie is golden brown and thick juices bubble from the holes, about 1 hour. Let the pie cool on a rack for 1 hour. Serve with vanilla ice cream (page 301) or vanilla-flavored sweetened whipped cream.

Makes one 9-inch pie.

Variation: For ginger-peach pie, add either 1 tablespoon finely chopped fresh ginger or 2 tablespoons chopped candied ginger (page 303) to the peaches.

PEACH AND RASPBERRY GRATIN

The peaches should be the freestones, which are usually sweeter and more aromatic than the earlier clings. Raspberries lend a nice tartness to the gratin. You can substitute Beaumes-de-Venise, vin santo, or Sauternes for the rum in the sabayon. If you like, serve sprinkled with freshly toasted almonds.

¾ cup sugar	*1 basket (½ pint) raspberries*
Splash of kirsch	*1½ cups rum sabayon*
1 pound peaches	*(page 298)*
1 sponge cake (page 300)	*¾ cup pastry cream (page 302)*

Stir together ¼ cup sugar and ½ cup water in a small saucepan and heat just until the sugar dissolves. Let the syrup cool, then add a splash of kirsch.

Halve, pit, and peel the peaches and cut them into ½-inch-thick slices. Sprinkle the slices with ¼ cup sugar, more or less, depending on their sweetness, and let them macerate while you prepare the other components.

Cut the sponge cake into ¼-inch-thick slices. Line the bottom of 6 individual gratin dishes (or 1 large one) with slices of cake. (You will have plenty of sponge cake left over for another use.) Moisten the cake with the sugar syrup and evenly distribute the peach slices and raspberries on top.

Preheat the broiler.

Gently fold together 1½ cups sabayon and ¾ cup pastry cream in a mixing bowl. Pour the mixture into the gratin dishes and spread over the peaches and raspberries, allowing some fruit to show through. With the remaining ¼ cup or so of sugar, sprinkle the tops of the gratins in an even layer, then place directly under the broiler. Cook for about 2 minutes, checking often, until the tops are browned and bubbling. Serve warm.

Serves 8.

Peach Shortcake

1½ pounds peaches
  (about 6 medium)
¼ cup plus 1½ tablespoons
  granulated sugar
1 cup heavy cream

¼ teaspoon vanilla extract
6 baked 2-inch biscuits
  (page 291)
Powdered sugar for dusting

Peel and slice the peaches; toss with ¼ cup sugar. Whip the cream with 1½ tablespoons sugar and the vanilla until it holds soft peaks. Slice the biscuits in half.

To assemble each shortcake, place the bottom of a biscuit on a plate, cover with a scoop of peaches and a dollop of cream, top with the other half of the biscuit, and dust with powdered sugar. Serve immediately.

Serves 6.

Almond Tartlets with Peaches

These tartlets are also notably tasty served with sugared strawberries or nectarines.

11 ounces pâte sucrée dough
  (page 296)
2 eggs
¾ cup sugar
¾ cup almonds

Grated zest and juice of 1 lemon
¼ teaspoon almond extract
⅛ teaspoon salt
5 medium peaches

Line eight 4-inch tartlet pans with pâte sucrée and let them chill in the freezer for at least 10 minutes.

Preheat the oven to 350°F.

Bake the shells for 15 minutes, just until they start to color. To make the almond filling, beat the eggs with ¼ cup sugar until they are pale yellow and form a thick ribbon when dropped from the beaters. Pulverize ½ cup of the almonds with ¼ cup sugar. Beat the almonds into the eggs mixture for 1 minute. Stir in the lemon zest and juice, almond extract, and salt. Chop the remaining ¼ cup almonds and fold them in.

Carefully fill the tartlet shells without letting any filling spill between the shells and the tartlet pans. Bake for 20 minutes, until golden. Let cool for 10 minutes and remove the tartlets from their pans.

While the tartlets are baking and cooling, peel and slice the peaches. Toss them with ¼ cup sugar. Serve the tartlets warm with the sugared peaches and lightly sweetened, softly whipped cream.

Makes eight 4-inch tartlets.

PEACH LEAF PARFAIT

There is something crisply refreshing about the bitter-almond flavor of this frozen dessert. It is delightful with peaches, but when they are not ready yet and we are eager for summer fruit, we serve it with berries.

4 cups whole milk
¾ cup plus 2 tablespoons sugar
2 cups tender young peach leaves, loosely packed
3 egg whites, room temperature

Heat the milk and ¾ cup sugar to just under a boil. Crush peach leaves with your hands, stir into the hot milk, and steep for about 5 minutes. Start tasting the mixture; you are striving for a slightly floral almond flavor. Take heed! If the leaves infuse too long, the mixture can become offputtingly bitter and astringent. Strain out the peach leaves and refrigerate the mixture until chilled.

Whip the egg whites with 2 tablespoons sugar until they are shiny and form firm peaks. Fold into the chilled milk mixture. Freeze according to the instructions for your ice cream maker. This sherbet is best the day it is frozen.

Makes 1½ quarts; serves 6 to 8.

Variation: Other flavors may be substituted for the peach leaves. Lemon verbena is wonderful, and so is 1 cup toasted coconut or 1 scraped vanilla bean. Or for a bitter-almond flavor, try steeping 2 tablespoons coarsely chopped noyau kernels (page 19).

PEARS, EUROPEAN AND ASIAN ❧

Season: Late summer through winter

Getting a perfect pear from farm to table is a risky and complicated business. Each step along the way requires the attention of someone with knowledge and skill. First the pear must be picked from the tree when it is mature but not fully ripe. It must experience a period of cool storage, the optimal length of which varies according to the variety. Then it must be brought out to room temperature to finish ripening. At every step of the way, from tree to market to kitchen, it must be handled gently to avoid bruising. Determining the point of perfect ripeness isn't easy at a glance; most pears do not indicate by their color when they are ready. The signal is a slight yielding to gentle pressure at the neck. And then, what wonderful eating from a carefully tended pear!

Given so many things that must be done right, a perfect pear should be treasured. At Filoli, the historic estate south of San Francisco with an orchard full of heirloom pear trees, the gardeners say that a fine pear is a work of art and deserves to be eaten with proper respect. In good years they bring us a few of their finest.

There are two main classes of pears, one European, one Asian. The best European pears have buttery smooth, fine-grained, juicy flesh with a minimum of gritty cells in the fruit. The flavor is usually sweet, sometimes musky, and nicely balanced with acid. European pears need time to cure and ripen after harvest. Most fruits of European pears are, to some extent, well, pear-shaped—or pyriform, botanically speaking.

Asian pears are very crisp, juicy, and sweet, but they do not have the acid balance of European pears and the flavors seem milder. They are appreciated for their sweet juiciness and crunchy texture, often accented by gritty "stone" cells; another name for Asian pears is sand pear.

They ripen completely on the tree, and although they don't need curing, they do keep well in cool storage. They are also called apple pears, both because of their crunchiness and because most Asian pear varieties are pomiform—apple-shaped.

Both kinds of pears are wonderful in salads, where their sweetness makes them good partners with bitter greens, such as the endives. Slices of ripe pear with prosciutto are an appetizing first course; pears marry well with walnuts and hazelnuts, and they are ideal with blue-veined cheeses, like Roquefort and Gorgonzola, and soft-ripened Camembert-style cheeses. Pears enhance the flavor of sweet winter vegetables; try adding some diced pear to a purée of sweet potatoes or winter squash. The mild tanginess of European pears goes especially well with grilled or roasted fatty meats, such as pork, duck, or squab.

In the pale days of winter, pears poached in wine make brilliant desserts: poached in red wine and served with their reduced ruby-colored syrup and a dollop of cream, or poached in white wine and served with vanilla ice cream—either with chocolate sauce for pears Belle Hélène, or with the last of the raspberries in late fall for pears Melba. We also bake pears drizzled with Marsala or dusted with spices, and serve them warm with fresh mascarpone. Pears and almonds are good together, and we like to bake pear-almond tarts and spicy crisps and pear halves stuffed with almond filling. Upside-down cakes and tartes Tatin sparkle with the beautiful maroon of Zinfandel-poached pears.

The European pear, *Pyrus communis*, was cultivated before written history, but most of its modern varieties were developed in Europe in the eighteenth and nineteenth centuries. The French especially devoted much horticultural energy to breeding new varieties. Most of our familiar pears have descended from French cultivars, losing at least part of their poetic French names in the process.

The Bartlett, for example, got its sturdy American name early in the nineteenth century, a few years after it arrived in New England from Europe, where it is better known as Williams' Bon Chrétien or just plain Williams. It is the most widely planted pear in North America and one of the most popular pears in the world. With their juicy, sweet, buttery flesh and familiar musky aroma, Bartletts are the classic summer pear. They are medium to large in size and have a thick neck but are clearly pear-shaped. When ripe, their skin is golden yellow, sometimes blushed with red. Red Bartlett has similar eating qualities but completely red skin. Bartletts need only a few weeks off the tree to ripen. Their season goes from late July through September.

The harvest for most pears peaks in late summer and early fall in a flurry of picking. Much of the fruit won't be seen in the market until after months of storage, but the pears must be picked and packed before they become too mature.

Comice (short for Doyenne du Comice) is the most perfect pear for eating. Its very juicy flesh is fine-textured and rich-tasting and has a lovely winey aroma. Individual fruits can be quite large and portly, rounder than Bartletts and slightly lopsided; their tender skin is a pale greenish-yellow when ripe, blushed with red. The best Comice pears come from Oregon and coastal northern California.

D'Anjou (Beurré d'Anjou) is widely grown in the United States, not so much for its flavor, which I find lacking, but because it keeps very well. You may see d'Anjou in the market in late spring, fruit that was picked the previous fall. D'Anjou pears are short-necked and almost cone-shaped and have fine-textured, tender flesh and pale green skin when ripe. There is also a red variety.

Bosc (Beurré Bosc), perhaps the most useful and commonly available variety for cooking, is a graceful fruit with a long, tapering neck that is often charmingly inclined. There are several strains of Bosc that differ in the degree of russeting, the bronze coloration on the skin. A ripe Bosc has dense, tender flesh that is sweet, rich, and aromatic. The skin of fruit with light russeting will turn yellow when ripe, but heavily russeted Boscs will not show a change in color and must be tested by pressing gently on the neck area. Because they are firm-fleshed, a ripe Bosc will give only slightly.

French Butter pears, another Beurré-type variety, come to our markets every fall from the Pettigrew Fruit Company, a family farm on the Sacramento River delta; they have been a favorite at Chez Panisse for years. This variety, usually planted as a pollinizer for Bartlett, bears delicious pears of its own. Known in France as Beurré Hardy, the medium to large, greenish-yellow fruits with bronze russeting have high-quality, juicy, aromatic flesh with a flavor that hints of rose water.

Several notable pears actually originated in the United States. Seckel is a small, roundish pear from Pennsylvania, with olive green and maroon skin and a fine spicy flavor; its small size makes it ideal for poaching or pickling whole. Warren pears originated in Mississippi: pale green when ripe, with a red blush, they have tender, juicy flesh, very good for eating out of hand. Warrens are good keepers that store well until ripened. Kieffer is another Pennsylvania variety, a hybrid of European and Asian pears, one of a number of such blends called "southern-cross" pears, which grow particularly well in the southeastern United States. Kieffers have firm flesh that is crisp and juicy but coarser in texture than that of European pears. They will soften some if allowed to ripen completely. They make an interesting sherbet when cooked and are very good for canning and preserves.

There are as many as 3,000 known varieties of Asian pears, all of them offspring of two Asian wild pears, *P. pyrifolia* and *P. ussuriensis*. Harvested at the same time as most European pears, Asian pears come to market earlier because they are ready to eat right away. We use them at Chez Panisse mostly as a table fruit or in salads. Their mild flavor and crisp texture suffer when they are cooked. Their season peaks in the summer but lingers into winter with fruit that has been stored.

Chinese immigrants planted Asian pears in California as early as the Gold Rush, but the number of varieties grown here has remained small. Farmers' markets in western and southeastern states and Asian produce markets in big cities will have the widest range of choices. Most popular here and in Japan is Nijisseiki (Twentieth Century), notable for its sweet, slightly tart flavor and juicy, crisp flesh. The round fruits have thin, easily bruised yellow skin and must be handled carefully. Shinseiki, which has Nijisseiki as one of its parents, is a little firmer and grittier. Chojuro has yellow-brown russeted skin and a distinctive flavor that doesn't appeal to everyone. Hosui is a large, round, very juicy, sweet pear with bronze russeted skin. Shinko grows well in hot climates, producing flavorful fruits that have beautiful bronze russeted golden skin. Ya Li, a popular Chinese variety with very tender green skin, is distinctly pear-shaped. Its crisp, juicy flesh has fewer stone cells than other varieties.

Nearly all the European pears sold in this country come from Washington, Oregon, and northern California, but they are grown for market in many other parts of the country, notably New York, Michigan, Pennsylvania, and Connecticut. Disease problems make the going tough for farmers in the humid East, but in some places Asian pears succeed where European pears have not, especially in the Southeast. Some organic farmers maintain that pears are easier to grow than other fruit trees, that they are adapted to a wider range of climates and soils, and that they have fewer pest and disease problems.

Because they keep so well, European pears have a very long season, extending from midsummer through the following spring. Early pears such as Bartlett don't keep as well as others and make a briefer appearance at the market than pears that store well, such as d'Anjou and Bosc, which are available for months.

There are differences among varieties, but a few general rules apply to choosing pears at the market. Remember that pears are fragile and that even unripe pears suffer from bruising, so handle them carefully. It is best to buy green pears and ripen them at home; this ensures that they were not picked overripe and decreases the chances of bruising. Choose organically grown fruit that is firm, intact, and unbruised; a few brown marks on the skin are almost inevitable.

At home pears should be ripened at room temperature in a loosely closed paper bag. Very firm green pears may take a week to ten days to ripen, while riper ones may need only a couple of days, so check daily for that slight give at the neck when you press gently. Ripening time depends on maturity at harvest, length and temperature of storage, and other circumstances beyond your control, and you do not want to miss that moment of perfect ripeness. If you must, you can store ripe pears in the refrigerator for several days, but they will gradually lose quality.

Asian pears are ready to eat when they are harvested, but they can be stored without harm. Ask for a taste at the market if you have a choice of several varieties; pick fruit that is firm but not hard and is free from bruises and holes in the skin. Asian pears keep well at cool room temperature for a week or two.

Asian pears can be peeled first, then quartered and cored as you would an apple, but ripe European pears are too fragile for such treatment. Cut them in halves or quarters first; the skin makes the fruit easier to handle. Remove the core and the fibrous strings that run from the stem end to the core. (A melon baller is a useful coring tool for halved pears.) Peel with a very sharp paring knife or vegetable peeler.

Pears will start turning brown as soon as they are cut and peeled and should be used right away. Those for a salad can be tossed with a little lemon juice or some of the vinegar that will be used for the dressing if they must wait a bit. If you are preparing more than a few pears for cooking, toss with lemon juice and a little sugar as you go. If they are to be poached, have the poaching liquid ready before you start to peel, and drop in the pears one by one as they are peeled.

For poaching, choose naturally firm pears—Bosc, Seckel, and winter Nellis are good; slightly underripe Bartletts will work too. Firm-ripe Bartletts, d'Anjous, and Comices are best for baking. For salads, use Asian pears and firm-ripe European pears.

BUTTERNUT SQUASH AND PEAR PURÉE

Cut a medium-size butternut squash in half lengthwise and scoop out and discard the seeds. Place the halves on an oiled baking sheet, cut side down, and bake at 375°F. until tender and easily pierced with a sharp knife at the stem end, about 1 hour. When the squash is cool enough to handle, scoop out the flesh and pass through a food mill. Into the purée stir 2 perfectly ripe pears, peeled, cored, and diced fine. Reheat and serve, seasoned with salt and enriched with a little butter or olive oil, if desired. A purée of sweet potatoes can be livened up the same way.

ASIAN PEAR AND NEW-CROP WALNUT SALAD

*⅓ pound new-crop walnuts
  in the shell
1 tablespoon Banyuls vinegar
  or Champagne vinegar
Salt and pepper*

*¼ cup extra-virgin olive oil
3 Asian pears
4 Belgian endives*

Preheat the oven to 350°F.

Shell the walnuts, carefully extracting them as whole as possible. Spread out on a baking sheet and toast in the oven just until turning golden, a little over 5 minutes; do not overtoast. Put them in a clean kitchen towel and rub gently to remove the skins. They will come off relatively easily.

Make a vinaigrette by mixing the vinegar with salt and pepper and whisking in the olive oil. Taste and adjust the acid and seasoning as needed. Peel and core the pears. Remove any blemished leaves from the endives. Cut in half lengthwise and remove the core with a V-shaped cut.

When ready to toss and serve the salad, slice the pears and cut the endive lengthwise into julienne. Toss the pears and endive with the vinaigrette and then gently crumble in the walnuts. Arrange prettily on a plate and serve immediately.

Serves 6.

Upside-Down Pear and Red Wine Tart

Few desserts ever pleased our mentor, the writer Richard Olney, but this is one of them. I have to agree that the balance of tart and sweet is especially pleasing when there is still red wine in your glass.

One 750-ml bottle red wine
1 cup sugar
Two 2-inch pieces cinnamon
    stick
7 peppercorns
4 cloves

1 orange
6 large pears (Bosc, Bartlett,
    or d'Anjou)
One 10-ounce piece galette
    dough (page 290) or
    puff pastry (page 294)

In a medium-size saucepan over low heat, combine the wine, sugar, cinnamon sticks, peppercorns, and cloves. Shave long strips of zest from the orange with a swivel-bladed peeler and add them to the wine mixture. Slice the orange in half and squeeze in the juice. Quarter, core, and peel the pears. Add the pears to the wine mixture and simmer over low heat for 20 to 30 minutes, until tender. Remove from the heat and let the pears cool in their poaching liquid. They can be stored in the refrigerator for up to 2 days at this point.

Preheat the oven to 400°F.

Remove the pears from the liquid and set them aside. Strain the poaching liquid, return it to the saucepan, and reduce to about 1 cup. Roll out the dough about ⅛ inch thick into an 11- to 12-inch circle. In a 10-inch ovenproof sauté pan or cast-iron frying pan, arrange the pear pieces in concentric circles, core side facing up. Pour ½ cup of the reduced poaching liquid over the pears. Cover the pears with the circle of dough, tucking the overhang between the sides of the pan and the pears.

Bake for about 40 minutes, until the dough is golden-brown. Let cool for 10 minutes. Remove the tart from the pan by placing a rack over the pan and inverting it. Some of the hot juice may come off the tart, so it is best to invert it over a baking sheet to avoid making a sticky mess. Push the pears back into place if necessary, and let the tart cool for another 15 minutes on the rack. Serve with crème fraîche or vanilla ice cream and pass the leftover wine reduction as a sauce.

Makes one 10-inch tart; serves 6 to 8.

Wine-Poached Pears with Warm Chocolate Fondant

2 tablespoons unsalted butter,
   melted, for the molds
5 teaspoons granulated sugar
   plus extra for the molds
6 tablespoons (¾ stick) unsalted
   butter
2 ounces bittersweet chocolate
3 ounces semisweet chocolate

1 pinch salt
¼ cup cocoa powder
3 egg whites
¼ teaspoon cream of tartar
Powdered sugar for dusting
6 white wine-poached pears
   and their sauce (page 225)
Whipped cream

Generously brush 6 individual brioche molds with the melted butter, and coat with sugar, knocking out the excess.

Melt the butter and the bittersweet and semisweet chocolate together in the upper part of a double boiler, stirring frequently. Do not allow the water to boil, or the chocolate will burn. When it has melted, remove from the heat, add the salt, and sift in the cocoa. Stir together carefully and keep in a warm place while you prepare the egg whites.

If the egg whites are cold, place them in a mixing bowl and set over the double boiler briefly to take the chill off, stirring continuously; remove once they have reached room temperature. Begin whisking the egg whites, and as they start to foam, add the cream of tartar. Slowly add the sugar and continue whisking until they hold soft peaks. Gently fold the egg whites into the chocolate, one-third at a time, and immediately fill the brioche molds. Once they're filled, they can sit for a couple of hours until you're ready.

Preheat the oven to 400°F.

Set the brioche molds on a baking sheet and bake on the center rack of the oven for about 12 minutes, until the top is crusty and set but not burning. Remove the fondants from the oven and let them sit for a minute. With your hands protected by oven mitts, flip the molds over onto a cutting board. If they stick, use a paring knife to loosen the edges and try again. Dust with powdered sugar.

While the fondants are baking, slice the poached pears in half and remove the seeds with a pear corer or melon baller. Cut the pear halves into ½-inch thick slices, leaving them joined at the stem end. Fan them out, drizzle with the reduced pear syrup, and top with a small dollop of whipped cream, if you wish. Serve with a fondant alongside.

Serves 6.

Pear-Shaped Pear Tartlets

We sometimes make individual pear tartlets for dessert in the restaurant using a pear-shaped cutter to cut out individual tartlet shells from rolled-out puff pastry. We fill them with wine-poached pears, sliced thin, fanned out over a base of frangipane (page 299), and sprinkled with sugar, and bake them just long enough for the puff pastry to turn golden-brown.

Pears Poached in White Wine

Pears are best poached whole, completely submerged in wine and syrup or in wine alone.

3 cups (1 bottle) fruity white wine (such as a Marsanne)
1½ cups water
1½ cups sugar
One 2-inch piece vanilla bean, split in half lengthwise

½ cinnamon stick, broken into pieces
Grated zest and juice of 1 lemon
6 firm, not-quite-ripe Bosc pears, peeled, stems intact

Pour the wine, water, and sugar into a nonreactive pot or saucepan that will hold the pears snugly. Stir over medium heat until the sugar is dissolved. Scrape the vanilla bean seeds into the syrup. Add the bean pods, cinnamon stick, and lemon zest and juice. Arrange the pears in the liquid and cover with a piece of parchment paper and a plate to keep the fruit submerged. Bring to a boil, reduce the heat, and maintain the liquid at a slow simmer, cooking the pears until tender, about 45 minutes, depending on ripeness. A paring knife should slice into the center of a pear without resistance.

Serve the pears warm, or let cool to room temperature, still weighted and submerged in the liquid, and refrigerate to serve later, chilled. Or serve alongside chocolate fondant (see page 224).

To make a sauce, measure out 3 cups of the poaching liquid, return to the saucepan, and reduce to a thick syrup over medium heat. A last-minute splash of fresh wine or pear eau-de-vie will brighten the flavor.

Serves 10.

Spiced Pears

Here is another poached-pear recipe, this one reproduced from memory after one of our chefs visited a three-star restaurant in France. Unfortunately, no one seems to remember which chef or which restaurant.

3 cups (1 bottle) dry white wine	1 cup heavy cream
1½ cups sugar	Two 3-inch pieces
1 cup water	cinnamon stick
Zest and juice of 1 lemon	10 cloves
½ vanilla bean,	1 star anise
split in half lengthwise	1 teaspoon peppercorns
6 firm, not-quite-ripe Bosc,	¼ cup honey
Bartlett, or d'Anjou pears,	4 tablespoons (½ stick)
quartered, cored, and peeled	unsalted butter

Pour the wine, sugar, and water into a medium-size saucepan and stir over low heat until the sugar is dissolved. Remove the lemon zest with a zester (the kind with tiny holes) or peel off strips of zest with a swivel-bladed vegetable peeler and cut into a fine julienne. Add the zest and lemon juice to the syrup, scrape the vanilla bean seeds into it, and add the bean pieces. Add the pears and simmer gently until they are tender and cooked through, about 30 minutes. Remove the pears and set aside. Over high heat, reduce the poaching liquid to about 1 cup of thick syrup. Add the cream, lower the heat, and simmer for 5 minutes. Strain the sauce and keep it warm.

Crush the cinnamon sticks, cloves, star anise, and peppercorns together with a mortar and pestle. The spices should be coarsely ground until the pieces are small enough to be edible. Melt the honey and butter together in a large sauté pan. Add the pear pieces, sprinkle with the spice mixture, and sauté over high heat until the pears are browned and the spices are stuck to them. Arrange 3 or 4 pieces of pear on each plate and drizzle with the pear sauce. Serve warm, with a scoop of vanilla ice cream alongside.

Serves 6.

Marsala-Baked Pears

6 medium Bosc pears
1½ cups Marsala wine
½ cup sugar

Preheat the oven to 425°F.

Slice ⅛ inch off the bottom of each pear so it will sit flat. Arrange the pears in a ceramic baking dish just large enough to hold them snugly. Pour the Marsala over the pears and sprinkle with sugar. Bake the pears for about 1 hour, basting them every 15 minutes with their cooking juices. They are done when they can easily be pierced with a knife and look caramelized and golden. Serve the pears on individual dessert plates, drizzled with the juices from the baking dish and with a dollop of crème fraîche or mascarpone alongside.

Serves 6.

PERSIMMONS ❧

Season: Fall

Persimmons ripen late in the fall, and the brilliant orange fruits hang on the trees even after the leaves have fallen. A persimmon tree full of fruit can be a spectacular sight sparkling against a deep blue autumn sky. The fruits sparkle in the kitchen, too, as they are peeled and sliced for salad or arranged on trays to soften and ripen before going into puddings and cookies.

The persimmons that grow in California and are found in markets across the country are varieties of *Diospyros kaki,* a species that originated in China and made its way to Japan well over a thousand years ago. Today the trees are cultivated in every part of that country where the climate supports them.

Dried persimmons are an integral part of traditional Japanese New Year's celebrations. We learned about this from the Chino family, whose meticulously grown vegetables have shaped the kind of food we serve at Chez Panisse. It has become a tradition for me to travel to the Chinos' beautiful farm north of San Diego a few days before our own New Year's celebration and join a large group of friends and family in a bustle of cooking and ritual preparation for the new year. The foods all have symbolic significance for the new year's outcome. The main event is the making of mochi, bun-shaped rice cakes made from steamed glutinous rice that is pounded in a huge stone mortar with a heavy wooden mallet. The pounding, which starts at the crack of dawn, is customarily done by men, but they let me take a whack at it too. Dried persimmons are an auspicious part of the ritual decorations for the mochi, and everyone takes some home.

There are only a handful of California growers who dry persimmons the traditional way. The peeled fruit of the Hachiya variety is laid out in the sun for a month or more. While drying, each fruit is massaged to even out the texture, tenderize the fibers, and bring some of the sugar to the surface of the fruit, where it dries into a silvery sheen.

Oriental persimmons are subtropical plants, and at least 500 of the several thousand known varieties were brought to California during an exuberant planting spree between 1870 and 1920. Although only a few varieties are now grown in commercial quantities, many others survive in backyards and in the corners of orchards. Persimmon fanciers have devised several complicated systems for classifying varieties, but the most important thing to remember is that there are persimmons that are unpleasantly astringent until they are completely soft and ripe, and there are persimmons that are never astringent, even when firm and crisp. The names that have become generic for these two types are Hachiya for the astringent kind and Fuyu for the nonastringent.

During the persimmon's heyday in California, Hachiya was the most popular kind, but after reaching a peak in the 1940s, Hachiya production has declined. Hachiyas are harvested in the fall while still firm, but they must be allowed to ripen and soften completely before they are eaten or they will be inedibly astringent. The bright orange acorn-shaped fruit are about the size of an apple. They have thin, satiny, translucent orange-red skin that may be streaked with black. The sweet, mildly aromatic deep orange flesh of a ripe Hachiya has a jelly-like consistency and seems to be bursting from its skin.

While Hachiya production has been declining, production of Fuyu persimmons has been increasing, mostly as a result of demand from Southeast Asian immigrants. The name Fuyu is rather loosely applied to any of several similar varieties, the most common being the one known in Japan as Jiro. These persimmons are roughly four-sided and have the roundish, squat shape of certain tomatoes; some have a shallow crease in the side. They are picked from late October into December, after they have developed their reddish-orange color. They are not astringent and can be eaten as soon as they are picked, when the light orange flesh is crisp as an apple's, or they can be left to soften slightly before eating. They are best for eating fresh and in salads.

Although most persimmons are grown in California, they are sold in many parts of the country, particularly in Asian markets and specialty produce stores in the big cities. It can be difficult to find organically grown ones. In California and the Southeast, farmers' markets are more likely to have organically grown fruit from local farms. Look for some of the less common varieties, like Maru or Hayakame, which has rich, cinnamon-colored flesh.

Persimmons are also native to a large area of the United States, from Connecticut south to the Gulf Coast and west to Kansas and Texas. The small, orange-colored fruit of the American persimmon, *D. virginiana*, was an important food for Native Americans, who dried it and baked it into a kind of bread. (Our word for persimmon comes from the Algon-quin.) Indians taught European settlers that the fruit is best eaten only after the leaves have fallen and the fruit has become very ripe and soft. The flesh of persimmons has such high levels of astringent tannins that your mouth will be given an extraordinarily puckery feeling if they have not been allowed to moderate through ripening.

Wild American persimmons can be found along the edges of open fields and abandoned pastures, but there is a score of cultivated varieties that have larger fruit and fewer and smaller seeds than the wild species.

Peak of the season for all persimmons is from mid-October through December. Mature Hachiyas will be deeply colored, showing no patches of yellow skin. Some farmers will ripen Hachiyas before bringing them to market, but ripe fruit is very fragile and most produce stores sell firm ones that must be ripened at home. Persimmons should not have cracks or bruises. If you choose fruit that is starting to soften a little, it will take about a week or so to ripen at room temperature. Firmer fruit will take longer. This process is not for the impatient; you must wait until the fruit is completely jelly-like to enjoy its honey sweetness. Ripe Hachiyas can be stored in the refrigerator for several days.

Ripe Hachiyas are so soft, the smartest way to eat them is to cut them in half and spoon the flesh out of the skin. You may find an occasional seed, which should be discarded. To prepare Hachiya pulp for cooking, scrape it from the skin into a bowl and pass the flesh through a strainer or potato ricer, or whirl it for a moment in the food processor. The pu-rée can be frozen if your persimmons ripen before you are ready to use them.

Buy Fuyus that are very firm and have well-colored, glossy skin. The calyx should be pale green, not brown. Avoid fruits with any touches of green or yellow; they will be immature. Very firm ripe Fuyus can be left for a few days to soften slightly before eating. Some people don't bother with peeling Fuyus, but at the restaurant we always do. Use a sharp par-ing knife to remove a cone-shaped piece around the calyx at the stem end of the fruit. Peel away the skin and cut the fruit into thin slices or wedges, discarding any seeds you may encounter. Do not peel and slice Fuyus more than a half hour before using them, or they will oxidize and gradually start to turn brown.

FUYU PERSIMMON SALAD WITH POMEGRANATES, BELGIAN ENDIVE, AND WALNUTS

6 Belgian endives	1½ tablespoons Banyuls or
4 ripe Fuyu persimmons	sherry vinegar
1 pomegranate	Salt and pepper
⅓ cup walnuts	6 tablespoons extra-virgin
	olive oil

Preheat the oven to 375°F.

Trim the bottom end of the endives, discard any blemished outer leaves, and separate into leaves. Cut the persimmons in quarters and peel. Remove any seeds and cut the quarters into thin wedges. Roll the pomegranate firmly on the countertop to loosen its seeds. Cut it in half crosswise and, one at a time, invert the halves cut side down onto the palm of your hand. Hold over a bowl and pound on the back with a large spoon to dislodge the seeds, which will fall through your fingers. Pick out and discard any white pith that may have fallen out with the seeds. Toast the walnuts in the oven for 8 minutes. While they are still warm, rub the walnuts in a clean dishtowel to remove some of the skins, then coarsely crumble them.

Make a vinaigrette by whisking the vinegar with ½ teaspoon salt and a few grinds of pepper. Whisk in the olive oil, taste for acid and salt, and adjust as needed. Put the endives, persimmons, walnuts, and pomegranate seeds in a large salad bowl, toss with the vinaigrette, and serve.

Serves 6.

Salad of Persimmons, Pears, and Pomegranates with Wine Grape Vinaigrette

2 heads very young curly endive
(frisée) no more than
8 inches in diameter, with
tender white centers
1 head radicchio
2 ripe Fuyu persimmons
1 pomegranate
(about ½ cup seeds)

¼ pound red wine grapes,
stemmed
1 tablespoon red wine vinegar
Salt and pepper
¼ cup extra-virgin olive oil
2 ripe pears (Bartlett, d'Anjou,
or Comice)

Tear off and discard the tough green outer leaves of the curly endives. Cut out the tough core, separate the leaves, and wash and dry them well. Cut the root end off the radicchio, remove any blemished outer leaves, and separate, wash, and dry the inner leaves. Cut the persimmons in quarters and peel. Remove any seeds and cut the quarters into thin wedges.

Roll the pomegranate firmly on the countertop to loosen its seeds. Cut it in half crosswise and, one at a time, invert the halves cut side down on the palm of your hand. Hold over a bowl and pound on the back with a large spoon to dislodge the seeds, which will fall through your fingers. Pick out and discard any white pith that may have fallen out with the seeds.

Reserve 12 of the wine grapes and crush the rest in a bowl with a whisk or a potato masher. Add the vinegar and a pinch of salt. Let sit for at least ½ hour. Strain, pressing on the grapes to extract all the juice. Add a few grinds of pepper and whisk in the olive oil. Cut the reserved grapes in quarters and remove and discard the seeds. Add the grape quarters to the vinaigrette.

When ready to serve, put the lettuces and persimmons in a large mixing bowl. Peel and core the pears, cut them into thin wedges, and add to the bowl. Dress carefully with the vinaigrette, adding a pinch of salt if needed. Arrange on a plate and garnish with the pomegranate seeds.

Serves 6.

Persimmon Cookies

We serve these delicate nutty cookies alongside winter fruit compote or Cognac-flavored crème brûlée.

1½ cups dried persimmons
* (page 236)*
¼ pound plus 6 tablespoons
* (1¾ sticks) unsalted butter,*
* room temperature*
1 cup light brown sugar, firmly
* packed*
1 egg

½ teaspoon vanilla extract
1 tablespoon dark rum
½ teaspoon salt
2 cups unbleached
* all-purpose flour*
¼ teaspoon ground cinnamon
1 cup pecans, roughly chopped

To prepare the persimmons, carefully trim off any skin with a lightly oiled knife or scissors. Cut into ¼-inch pieces.

In a large mixing bowl, cream together the butter and brown sugar. Beat in the egg, vanilla, rum, and salt. Sift together the flour and cinnamon and beat into the batter. Add the pecans and persimmons and stir just until combined. Divide the dough into 2 pieces and roll each piece into a 9-inch log about 1½ inches in diameter. Wrap the logs in plastic and freeze. The logs will keep up to 2 weeks in the freezer.

To bake, preheat the oven to 350°F. Line a baking sheet with parchment paper.

Remove the logs from the freezer, unwrap them, and slice the dough into thin cookies (a little less than ¼ inch thick). Arrange the cookies ½ inch apart on the baking sheet and bake for about 12 minutes, until they are just starting to turn golden around the edges. Serve the same day.

Makes 60 cookies.

PERSIMMON PUDDING

We use Hachiya persimmons at their peak of ripeness for this pudding; their flesh should be so soft it nearly falls off the skin. If you find persimmons in this fragile state, make this pudding! It is moist and flavorful, and wants only a spoonful of gently whipped cream.

1½ pounds persimmons
1½ cups milk
¼ cup heavy cream
3 eggs
1 tablespoon honey
1¼ cups unbleached
  all-purpose flour
¾ cup sugar
1 teaspoon ground cinnamon

¾ teaspoon baking soda
¾ teaspoon baking powder
⅛ teaspoon salt
6 tablespoons (¾ stick) unsalted
  butter, melted and slightly
  cooled
1 cup walnuts (about 6 ounces),
  toasted and chopped

Preheat the oven to 325°F. Butter a 9-inch round cake pan and line with parchment paper.

Cut out a cone from the stem end of each persimmon as you would from a tomato. Cut the persimmons in half and scoop out the pulpy flesh with a spoon. Put the flesh through a strainer or purée in a blender or food processor; you should have 1½ cups of purée.

Combine the persimmon purée, milk, cream, eggs, and honey and lightly whisk until smooth. In another bowl, sift together the flour, sugar, cinnamon, baking soda, baking powder, and salt.

A little at a time, add the persimmon mixture to the flour mixture, whisking until smooth after each addition. Let the batter stand about 15 minutes to thicken. Stir in the melted butter and the walnuts and pour the batter into the prepared pan. Bake in the center of the oven for 1 to 1½ hours, until completely set, the pudding pulling away from the sides of the pan. Serve the pudding warm, with lightly sweetened, Cognac-flavored whipped cream.

Serves 8.

Dried Persimmons

This is a wonderful way to use very ripe, translucent Hachiya or over-ripe Fuyu persimmons. In their freshly dried state, they are bright orange and chewy and have a date-like sweetness. They are delicious in cookies or diced in a salad. We get the best results by using a food dehydrator, although a very low oven works too.

Gently wash and dry ripe, gelatinous persimmons. With a very sharp paring knife, remove the leaf and stem by cutting around the top, sacrificing as little fruit as possible, then cut the fruit lengthwise into ½-inch-thick slices. (Leaving the skin on makes the slices easy to handle.)

Arrange the persimmon slices on the racks of your dehydrator. The slices should not touch once another. Dry at 135°F. for 8 hours, or until they are no longer mushy. If you use an oven, arrange the slices on a rack and bake at 150°F. (or at your oven's lowest setting) for about 3 hours. Turn off the oven and let it cool down without opening. Check the persimmons after another hour or so; if they are not dry enough, reheat the oven and bake for another hour. Remove the persimmons from the oven and air-dry for another few hours. (If your oven has a pilot light, the persimmons will keep drying slowly if left in the turned-off oven overnight.) Store the slices in airtight containers in the refrigerator. They are best used within a few weeks.

PINEAPPLES 🍂

Season: Year-round; best in spring and summer

As winter gives way to spring around the beginning of March, we start tiring of dried fruits and the last of the previous season's harvest of apples and pears. The first tender spinach and watercress are sprouting up in the markets, and the farmers are promising that asparagus is just around the corner, but fresh, lush, warm-weather fruit still seems far, far away. So we simply grant ourselves an exemption from our rule of relying only on local produce and look to the tropics, from whence ripe pineapples are being sent in our direction.

The pineapple, *Ananas comosus*, is native to Central and South America. Christopher Columbus's men found pineapples being cultivated on the island now called Guadeloupe in 1493; whole fruits or their leafy tops were displayed outside homes as symbols of hospitality. The Spanish called them simply *piñas*, or "pinecones"; our English word for them acknowledges the resemblance and adds the suffix "-apple," reminding us that they are, in fact, fruits. More poetically, the indigenous South

American name, *ananas* (adopted as the pineapple's official botanical generic name and as its common name in French and several other languages), means "fragrant excellent fruit."

Soon after their discovery in the New World, pineapples were growing in greenhouses across Europe and spreading through the tropics. Although Hawaii and pineapples are inextricably linked in the minds of mainland Americans, pineapples did not arrive there until after European contact, late in the eighteenth century. The Hawaiian word for pineapple, *halakahiki*, means "foreign fruit."

Because the majority of commercial pineapple growers rely on chemical fungicides, herbicides, and pesticides, it is especially important to find and encourage sources of organically grown fruit. Quantities of delicious organic pineapples are beginning to come to market from Hawaii (mainly Maui) and from Mexico and Central America. Pineapples are in markets all year long, but in our experience they are sweetest and most abundant in spring, from March through June.

To be good, pineapples must be picked ripe. Although the fruits typically spend a year or so developing, the final concentration of sugar happens in a matter of days, and the fruit must be harvested at the last moment. Only air freight can deliver the freshest, ripest Hawaiian pineapples. Mexican pineapples can be delicious, but they are less consistently good than Hawaiian pineapples.

Most pineapples in the market are a variation of one type, the Cayenne, which has large fruit with yellow flesh that is not too fibrous. Esmeralda is a Cayenne type we like that comes from Mexico. You may also find Sugarloaf, which has smaller fruit and white to pale yellow flesh.

Columbus's men were "astonished and delighted" by the flavor and aroma of the pineapples they discovered, and so should you be when you buy one. The best way to choose a good pineapple is to pick it up and smell it. There should be a definite aroma of pineapple, with no sour or fermented odors that would indicate spoilage. The fruit should give just a little when pressed gently, but there should be no soft spots. Reject fruit with watery or dark patches on the skin, and check the stem end for mold.

The color of the skin is not an indicator of ripeness. A green-skinned pineapple can be as ripe and sweet as a golden one. Deep green leaves are a good sign of freshness, but checking if they can be pulled out easily is not a true test of ripeness. Shun fruit that has dried or brown leaves. Choose a size that makes sense for you, but remember that larger pineapples yield a higher proportion of usable flesh for the same amount of prep work. Once you get them home, very firm pineapples will benefit from softening a day or two at room temperature, but they won't get sweeter.

Trimming and peeling a fresh pineapple is not difficult if you have a sharp knife. Cut the crown of leaves and a bit more off the top, then cut off the bottom. Stand the pineapple on end and cut off a thickish layer of the skin. I like to use a boning knife to do this because it follows the shape of the fruit better. There are several good ways to trim out the "eyes." Use the point of a stainless-steel potato peeler to dig them out, or remove them by using a small sharp knife to cut V-shaped grooves that follow the spiral patterning of the eyes. Cut the peeled fruit into wedges and trim out the fibrous core, then slice or cut into chunks, as the recipe directs.

The sweet-tart flavor of fresh pineapple is welcome after a rich meal, either by itself or with other tropical fruits in a macédoine. We often caramelize pineapple in a pan with butter and sugar to heighten its flavor before using it in more elaborate desserts. A sprinkling of kirsch is also a nice complementary flavor booster. Never use raw pineapple in dishes that contain gelatin: an enzyme in the fruit will disable its gelling properties. Cooking the pineapple deactivates the enzyme.

Ginger Pineapple Upside-Down Cake

TOPPING
4 tablespoons (½ stick)
  unsalted butter
¾ cup brown sugar, firmly
  packed
2¼ cups quarter slices fresh
  pineapple (peel, quarter, core,
  and slice ¼ inch thick)
2 tablespoons chopped candied
  ginger (page 303)

BATTER
1½ cups unbleached
  all-purpose flour

2 teaspoons baking powder
¼ teaspoon salt
¼ pound (1 stick) unsalted
  butter, room temperature
1 cup granulated sugar
1 teaspoon vanilla extract
2 tablespoons chopped
  candied ginger
2 eggs, separated, room
  temperature
½ cup whole milk
¼ teaspoon cream of tartar

Use a 9-inch round or an 8-inch square cake pan with 3-inch sides. To make the topping, put the butter and brown sugar in the cake pan, place the pan on a stovetop burner over low heat, and melt, stirring with a wooden spoon. When the mixture starts to caramelize, turning a slightly darker shade of brown, remove from the heat and let cool. Arrange the slices of pineapple evenly in the bottom of the pan and scatter the candied ginger over it. Set aside.

Preheat the oven to 350°F.

To make the cake batter, sift the flour, baking powder, and salt into a bowl. In a large mixing bowl, cream together the butter and granulated sugar with an electric mixer until pale and fluffy. Mix in the vanilla and ginger. Add the egg yolks one at a time, scraping down the sides of the bowl after each to make sure everything is thoroughly incorporated. Gradually add the dry ingredients and milk in stages: mix in about a third of the flour mixture, followed by about half the milk; mix in another third of the flour, then the rest of the milk; finally, add the last third of the dry ingredients.

In another large mixing bowl, whisk together the egg whites and cream of tartar. Beat the whites until they form firm peaks. Fold the whites into the batter in two batches to lighten it. Pour the batter over the topping in the prepared pan and bake until the top is slightly brown and the cake pulls away from the sides of the pan, about 50 to 60 minutes. Let the cake cool for 15 minutes. Run a knife around the edge of the pan and invert the cake onto a serving plate. Serve with lightly sweet-ened whipped cream flavored with a little vanilla.

Makes one 9-inch round cake or one 8-inch square cake; serves 8.

Pineapple Frangipane Tart

  3 tablespoons unsalted butter
  3½ cups quarter slices fresh
      pineapple (peel, quarter,
      core, and slice ¼ inch thick)
  ¼ cup sugar

  10 ounces galette dough
      (page 290), rolled into a
      14-inch circle
  ½ cup frangipane (page 299)

Preheat the oven to 400°F. Place a pizza stone, if you have one, on a lower rack in the oven. Line a baking sheet with parchment paper.

Melt 2 tablespoons butter in a large sauté pan over high heat. Add the pineapple slices and 2 tablespoons sugar and sauté until the pineapple is tender and translucent. With a slotted spoon, gently transfer the pineap-ple to a bowl to cool, leaving the juice behind. Cook the juice down into a thick syrup to glaze the tart with—there should be about 3 tablespoons.

Put the round of galette dough on the paper-lined baking sheet. Spread the frangipane evenly over the dough, leaving about a 1½-inch border uncovered at the edge. Arrange the cooked pineapple in one layer on top of the frangipane. While rotating the tart, fold the border of exposed dough up and over itself at regular intervals, crimping and pushing it up against the outer circle of fruit, creating a containing rim that resembles a length of rope. Pinch off any excess dough. Melt the re-maining 1 tablespoon butter and brush it on the edge of the tart. Sprin-kle the edge with the remaining 2 tablespoons sugar.

Bake the tart in the lower third of the oven, preferably on a pizza stone, for about 45 minutes, rotating about halfway through for even cooking. The crust should be brown and caramelized when done. Slide the tart off the pan and paper onto a cooling rack and let cool for 10 minutes. Serve warm, with lightly whipped cream or ice cream flavored with vanilla, rum, or kirsch.

Makes one 13-inch tart; serves 8.

PLUMS AND PLUOTS &

Season: Late spring through early fall

In late January and early February, many of the street trees in our Berkeley neighborhood are bare and dormant, except for the many flowering plums, whose brown branches have started showing hints of pink buds. Soon the branches are covered in clouds of blossoms. On sunny days the light takes on a distinctly pink quality and the air is delicately scented with the fragrance of plum blossoms. When the ornamental plums have finished, seedling and wild plums growing in deserted dooryards and vacant lots follow with their snow-white blooms. The flowers of all these plums make lovely, delicately flavored custards and ice creams, capturing the aroma of the blossoms and the flavor of bitter almonds, which come from the same stone fruit family as plums, peaches, and apricots. Later in the summer we collect some of the tiny yellow fruits of these wild plums to make jam, sherbet, and ice cream.

Plum trees thrive in our part of the Bay Area, and we depend on several Berkeley backyard growers, as well as on farmers at the market, for our summer supply of organic fruit. Our own lettuce growers pick Santa Rosa plums from a tree in the corner of their garden, and neighbors bring plums to the back door of the restaurant, several paper bags full at a time. Plum season starts in late spring, when the first of the Santa Rosa and other Japanese plums start ripening, and lasts until early fall. During the peak of the season, we use plums for galettes, crisps, clafoutis, and custardy tarts. Cultivated and wild plums also go into jam, ice cream, sherbet, and dessert soups and sauces.

Many varieties of plums were developed nearby in the Sonoma Valley by Luther Burbank, a brilliantly intuitive plant breeder who started importing Japanese plum trees in 1885. He eventually released 113 new varieties of plums and prunes, including many we use today, such as the giant Elephant Heart and the tiny sugar plum. His best-known plum is the Santa Rosa, which accounts for about a third of the plums grown in California. Burbank also crossed plums and apricots, calling the new fruits plumcots. This kind of breeding continues today, notably by Floyd Zaiger in the Central Valley, who has developed many new varieties of plums, pluots, and apriums.

Plums themselves are the most diverse group of the stone fruits. Their color ranges from green through yellow to red, purple, and blue; their flavor from sour to very sweet. Shape and size are variable too. Some are best eaten fresh, and some will dry naturally to become prunes. Even with such variability, cultivated plums can be classified into four main groups: European, Japanese, damson, and native American.

European plums, *Prunus domestica*, have small to medium oval fruits with sweet, dense flesh, usually greenish or golden yellow, and skin that is either yellow or blue, covered with a silvery bloom. They are often freestone—that is, the flesh separates easily from the pit. Prunes can be made from the many varieties of European plums that will not ferment if dried while still containing their pits. European plums are also very good for baking, poaching, and for eating fresh. Their season peaks in late summer.

Most of the European plums we find at the market are prune plums with purple skin and sweet yellow flesh. These include sugar plums and Italian and French prunes related to the French variety La Petite d'Agen. Tragedy and the beautiful President are also excellent varieties. The most widely grown plum in the East, Midwest, and South is Stanley, a freestone plum that ripens in early September. It has dark blue skin and yellow-green flesh that is sweet and flavorful.

Closely related to the common European plums is a group of yellow and green plums called Gages in England and Reine Claude in France. These are delicious eating, with their tender, sweet, rich-tasting flesh that may be green or gold. Most have a slightly flattened shape and are often freestone or nearly so. Green Gage is the best known, but also look for Golden Transparent Gage—a transcendentally beautiful plum with a stone that shows through the skin and flesh when it is held up to the light—as well as Imperial Gage and the purplish Count Althann's Gage.

Japanese plums, *P. salicina*, originated in China but have been cultivated and appreciated in Japan for hundreds of years. They come in many sizes, shapes, and colors, all with very juicy, fibrous flesh that is highly flavored but not as sweet as that of European plums and rather acid near the peel and the pit. The round or heart-shaped fruit comes to a point at the end and is always clingstone. Japanese plums are best used fresh; they do not dry successfully. They have a long season, from mid-spring to the first days of fall.

Santa Rosa, the best of the Japanese plums, has a rich and distinctive flavor that comes across well in desserts. The large, round purple-red fruit has amber flesh that shades to red near the skin. True Santa Rosas ripen in early summer, but there is a late type that comes at the end of July. When the Santa Rosas are finished, other good Japanese plums to look for are Laroda, with purple skin and light amber flesh; Satsuma, red with blood-red flesh; and Casselman, red with amber flesh.

Toward the end of the season, we look for Emerald Beaut, a full-flavored green plum with yellow or orange flesh; Howard Miracle, a yellow plum extravagantly blushed with red, which has flavorful yellow flesh; and Elephant Heart, with dark purple skin and rich, juicy, blood-red flesh.

Damsons and Mirabelles are both wild European plums that were cultivated before modern plums developed in Europe. A few damsons are grown here, but they are most popular in England, where they are widely appreciated for jams, jellies, and preserves. The small, intensely flavored oval fruits can be blue or green. Tiny yellow Mirabelles are very popular in France, where they are used in tarts and preserves and for making eau-de-vie.

A number of wild native American plum species have been collected, and about a hundred varieties have been selected for cultivation. These plums and some of their hybrids with Japanese varieties are very cold-hardy, surviving winter temperatures of -50°F. The fruit is small and used for preserves and sauces.

At Chez Panisse we have found pluots to be the most interesting of the interspecies hybrids. They have many of the color and flavor characteristics of plums combined with the sweetness and texture of apricots, reflecting a parentage that is three-quarters plum and one-quarter apricot. To our taste, Flavor King is the most successful of the pluots. The large dark red fruit has red flesh with rich, sweet, spicy flavor similar to that of a Santa Rosa plum but without the acid bite. Flavor King is featured every summer on our fruit plate in the Café upstairs, and it also is very good cooked, especially in tarts and clafoutis.

Flavor King ripens in late summer, but several interesting varieties appear earlier, including Flavor Queen, ripening in mid-July, which has light green or yellow skin and sweet amber flesh; and the whimsically named Dapple Dandy, ripening a little later, which has skin speckled and streaked with red, green, and yellow and sweet flesh that is red and white.

Thousands of acres of pluots have been planted in California recently; if you haven't seen them in the market yet, you will soon. California already produces 99 percent of the nation's prunes (and more than two-thirds of the rest of the world's) and dominates the plum market as well. This is a shame because good plums are grown in the Pacific Northwest, Michigan, and New York, and many varieties produce delicious fruit in other parts of the country. Encourage your local growers by shopping at farmers' markets and roadside stands and by asking for locally and organically grown fruit at your produce store.

Choose plums and pluots that look plump and well-colored for their variety. If they are aromatic and give to gentle pressure, they're ripe and ready to eat. Fruit that is firm but not hard will soften and ripen further at home, but it won't get any sweeter. Do not buy rock-hard fruit; it will never ripen properly. Also shun fruit that has wrinkled skin, soft spots, and cuts or breaks in the skin.

At home, store firm plums at room temperature, out of direct sunlight. Softening can be speeded up a bit by keeping the fruit in a loosely closed paper bag, but check daily and eat them as soon as they are ripe. Ripe plums and pluots will keep for a few days in the refrigerator.

Plums and pluots should be washed before eating or cooking. For the best texture and flavor, allow them to come to room temperature. To prepare them for cooking, find out first if the fruit is cling or freestone: Cut around the fruit from stem to bottom and back up the other side and twist the two halves gently. If freestone, the halves separate easily, and you can continue to halve the fruit, removing the pits and slicing the fruit as needed. To slice clingstone plums, use a small knife and cut toward the center of the fruit, freeing the flesh from the pit in wedges. If you want to peel plums, dunk them in boiling water for half a minute. Fish them out with a strainer or slotted spoon and submerge in ice water. The skins should slip right off.

Rabbit Stew with Prunes

1 whole rabbit (3½ pounds),
   cleaned
Salt and pepper
8 prunes, pitted
¼ cup hot water
⅓ cup white balsamic vinegar
2 thick slices bacon

3 carrots, peeled
2 medium onions, peeled
Olive oil
3 sprigs thyme
½ cup white wine
1½ cups chicken stock

Cut the rabbit into 8 pieces. Remove the forelegs and cut across the body to remove the hind legs in one piece; cut down the backbone to separate them. Cut the saddle, or loin end, crosswise into 2 pieces. Cut the rib section into 2 pieces; the long ribs can be trimmed down if you wish. Season generously with salt and pepper.

Plump the prunes in the hot water and vinegar. Slice the bacon crosswise into ½-inch lardons. Cut the carrots into large chunks and the onions into thick wedges.

Heat 2 tablespoons olive oil in a heavy-bottomed pot and cook the bacon until lightly browned but not crisp. Remove with a slotted spoon and set aside. Add the rabbit pieces and carefully brown them on all sides over medium heat. When all the rabbit is browned, set it aside, pour off most of the fat, and add the carrots, onions, and thyme. Cook for a few minutes to soften slightly. Add the wine and the prune soaking liquid and cook over high heat until reduced by half. Add the rabbit pieces, bacon, and prunes. Pour in the chicken stock and bring to a boil. Reduce the heat and simmer, covered, for 15 minutes. Remove the saddle pieces and cook the remainder for another 25 minutes. Remove the pan from the heat and skim any fat off the surface of the liquid. Taste for seasoning and add salt as needed. Return the saddle pieces to the pan, warm through, and serve.

Serves 4.

Note: This is wonderful served with sautéed spinach and steamed potatoes with butter and parsley. This recipe also works well with chicken, but remember to remove the breast pieces before the legs and thighs so as not to overcook them.

PORK LOIN STUFFED WITH WILD PLUMS AND ROSEMARY

Once again, we advise you to avoid eating pork unless you can find a local certified organic farmer who takes care of his hogs the right way.

*1½ pounds wild plums or
    Santa Rosa plums*
2 shallots
1 bunch rosemary
2 tablespoons olive oil
2 tablespoons brandy

*2 tablespoons sweet wine
    (Beaumes-de-Venise and
    port are good choices)*
½ cup water
Salt and pepper
2 lemons
*1 standing 6-rib pork loin,
    chine bone removed*

The plums can be prepared a day in advance. Split the plums in half and remove the pits. Cut the halves into small wedges. Peel and chop the shallots fine. Strip enough rosemary leaves off the stems to make a scant ½ teaspoon, chopped.

Heat the olive oil in a heavy-bottomed pot, add the shallots and the rosemary, and cook for 5 minutes over medium heat, until wilted. Add the brandy and flame. Add the sweet wine, bring to a boil, add the plums, and cook for 3 minutes. Add the water and mash the plums with a potato masher or whisk. Add ¼ teaspoon salt, a generous amount of freshly ground pepper, the grated zest of ¼ lemon, and a squeeze of lemon juice. Cook at a simmer until thickened, about 10 minutes, stirring often to keep the plum paste from sticking and burning. Taste and adjust the salt as needed. Let cool completely before stuffing the pork loin.

To stuff the loin, take a sharp knife and cut along the rib bones to separate them from meat. Cut almost all the way down, leaving only 1 inch of the loin attached to the bones. Make a lengthwise pocket for the stuffing, cutting halfway into the roast, where the meat has been exposed from the bones. Liberally season the roast all over with salt and pepper; this will give it a delicious crust. Season the inside of the pocket and stuff it with the plum paste. Press the pocket closed. Slice the second lemon as thin as you can. Arrange the lemon slices and rosemary sprigs between the bones and the meat. Gently push the roast back into its original shape. Using cotton twine, tie up the roast with one tie between each rib. Now the loin is stuffed with the plums in the middle and the lemon and rosemary between the ribs and the meat. It can be roasted now or covered and refrigerated for up to a day.

If the loin has been refrigerated, take it out of the refrigerator at least 1 hour before roasting. Preheat the oven to 375°F.

Put the loin in a roasting pan, bone side down, and roast for about 1½ hours, until an internal temperature of 130°F. is reached. Start checking the temperature with an instant-read thermometer after an hour, but be sure to insert the thermometer into the meat, avoiding the line of stuffing. When the roast is done, remove it from the oven and let it rest for at least 20 minutes in a warm place. Remove the twine, carve into individual chops, and serve.

Serves 6.

TEA-POACHED PRUNES

These prunes are served with fresh slices of blood orange and candied kumquat slices or in winter fruit compotes with poached quinces, pears, and apples. We like using the black teas that are flavored naturally with fruit, but you can certainly experiment with other teas.

4 cups water
4 tablespoons loose black tea
  (preferably peach, black
  currant, or Earl Grey)

1¼ pounds pitted prunes
¾ cup sugar
¼ cup Cognac

Bring the water to a boil in a nonreactive saucepan. Remove from the heat, add the tea, and steep for 3 minutes. Strain out the tea leaves and pour back into the saucepan over the prunes. Stir in the sugar and Cognac and heat gently for about 10 minutes, until the prunes are tender. Transfer to a glass or porcelain bowl and allow to cool in the refrigerator, uncovered. When cold, cover tightly and keep refrigerated until serving, up to 1 week.

Serves 6.

Prune-Armagnac Ice Cream

When you stir the Armagnac-soaked prunes into the ice cream, you can do so rapidly, creating a swirl of prune pieces, or more thoroughly for a more homogeneous appearance.

½ cup pitted dried prunes	*1¼ cups whole milk*
2 cups Armagnac	*¾ cup sugar*
6 egg yolks	*2¼ cups heavy cream, chilled*

Several days or weeks in advance, put the dried prunes in a container and cover with the Armagnac.

In a mixing bowl, whisk the egg yolks just enough to break them up. Gently heat the milk and sugar in a medium-size saucepan over low heat, stirring occasionally, until the milk is steaming and the sugar is dissolved. Pour the cold heavy cream into a separate container large enough to hold the finished custard. Drizzle the warm milk mixture into the egg yolks, whisking constantly as you pour.

Return the milk and egg yolk mixture to the saucepan. Cook over low heat, stirring constantly and scraping the bottom and sides of the pan with a wooden spoon or heat-resistant rubber spatula, until the mixture is thick enough to coat the spoon. Immediately remove from the heat and strain through a fine-mesh sieve into the heavy cream, whisking to cool the mixture. Cover and chill thoroughly.

While the ice cream base is chilling, strain the prunes, reserving the Armagnac, and chop roughly. Add 2 tablespoons of the reserved Armagnac to the chilled ice cream base and freeze according to the instructions for your ice cream maker. When the ice cream is frozen, stir in the prunes, more or less thoroughly, according to your preference, and adjust the flavor with more Armagnac, if desired.

Makes about 1 quart.

WILD PLUM JAM

Wild plum trees line the streets of Berkeley, and their pink and white buds often start blooming in early January. These plum trees have been planted by human hands, of course, primarily as ornamentals, but they are genetically closer to wild plums than to the common commercial varieties. The only way to tell if their fruit will be good for baking is to taste one cooked, with its skin on. Slice a plum and heat it gently in a sauté pan with a little water. When it is tender, let it cool and taste it; this will give you the best indication of how the flavor of the skin will affect what you are cooking. In general, bitterness cannot be corrected, but if the plums are too sweet or sour, you can adjust the sugar in the recipe. This recipe works well with Santa Rosa plums if you don't have wild ones.

2½ pounds plums (about 5 cups diced)
3 cups sugar

Wash and pit the plums. Cut them into ½-inch pieces. In a large heavy-bottomed pot, stir the fruit and sugar together and let stand for 15 minutes. Put a small plate in the freezer to use later to test the consistency of the jam.

Prepare four 8-ounce canning jars and lids in boiling water, following the manufacturer's instructions.

Bring the pot of fruit to a boil over high heat, stirring occasionally to make sure it isn't sticking to the bottom. As the mixture comes to a boil, it will rise up in the pot with big bubbles. During the first 5 minutes, skim off the foam that rises to the top. When the jam subsides but is still bubbling thickly, start to monitor it closely, testing frequently by putting small spoonfuls of jam on the cold plate. When it has cooked to the consistency you like, remove from the heat and carefully ladle the jam into the prepared jars, allowing at least ¼ inch of headroom, and seal with the lids, following the manufacturer's instructions. The jam will keep for about a year.

Makes 4 cups.

Variation: For wild plum and raspberry jam, substitute 2 or 3 cups of raspberries for the same quantity of plums.

Plum Paste

3 pounds plums
½ cup water
3 cups sugar plus more for tossing
Juice of 1 lemon

Line a baking pan with parchment paper and lightly oil the paper.

Wash and dry the plums. Cut them in half and remove the pits. Put the plum pieces in a large nonreactive pot with the water. Cover the pot and cook over medium heat until the fruit is soft and falling apart. Remove the pot from the heat and purée the fruit by passing it through a food mill or pressing it through a sieve.

Return the purée to the pot and add the sugar. Stirring constantly, cook over low heat for about 45 minutes, until the purée has turned into a thick paste. The paste should be boiling thickly, forming large bubbles, and it should hold a mounding shape. If it starts to burn before the texture is right, turn off the heat and let it rest a few minutes; then stir again, and the part sticking to the bottom should release. When the mixture reaches the desired texture, stir in the lemon juice.

Pour the paste onto the paper-lined pan. Spread the mixture into an 8- by 10-inch rectangle, about ¼ inch thick. Let it cool completely. Invert the sheet of paste onto another piece of parchment and carefully peel off the older parchment paper. Let the paste dry uncovered overnight. (If the paste is not firm enough to cut at this point, try drying it out for an hour in the oven at 150°F. or the lowest setting.) Once the paste is cool and firm, cut it into 1-inch squares and toss them in sugar. Store uncovered in a dry place. Keeps for 1 week.

Makes eighty 1-inch-square pieces.

Santa Rosa Plum Tart

10 ripe Santa Rosa plums
  (about 1½ pounds)
1 prebaked 11-inch pâte sucrée
  tart shell (page 296)
¼ pound (1 stick) unsalted
  butter
Juice of 1 lemon
2 eggs

¾ cup sugar
1½ teaspoons plum brandy,
  grappa, or kirsch
¼ teaspoon vanilla extract
⅛ teaspoon salt
3 tablespoons flour
2 tablespoons heavy cream

Preheat the oven to 375°F.

Cut the plums in half, remove the pits, and slice into ½-inch wedges. Arrange the wedges in concentric circles in the prebaked tart shell. Melt the butter in a small saucepan over low heat. Let it bubble gently and cook until the milk solids turn a toasty light brown. Remove the butter from the heat, add the lemon juice to stop the cooking, and set aside to cool.

Beat the eggs and sugar together with an electric mixer until the mixture is thick and forms a ribbon when dropped from the beaters, about 5 minutes. Add the butter, brandy, vanilla, salt, flour, and cream. Stir just until mixed. Pour the mixture over the plums, filling the tart shell. Bake in the top third of the oven until the top is golden brown, about 35 to 40 minutes. Let cool on a rack for 15 minutes. Serve warm or at room temperature, with lightly whipped cream.

Makes one 10-inch tart; serves 6 to 8.

Variations: Replace the plums with 3 cups of fresh raspberries, or substitute wine-poached pear slices and serve with a sauce made from the reduced poaching liquid.

POMEGRANATES 🍂

Season: Fall

Around the Mediterranean and in the Middle East, the plump wine-red seeds of pomegranates have been part of the human diet for millennia. Their sweet-tart juice flavors and tenderizes meats, especially lamb; and the seeds are sprinkled over salads, cooked greens, and desserts to add color, flavor, and a crunchy texture. Pomegranate molasses—syrupy thick, concentrated pomegranate juice—is produced commercially in the Middle East and used in marinades, splashed into drinks, and drizzled over cooked foods whenever fresh pomegranates are out of season. Pomegranate molasses can be found in most Middle Eastern groceries.

The cultivation of pomegranates predates written history. Although they probably originated in southwestern Asia, they are now grown in most of the world's warmer subtropical regions. (The most pomegranates I have ever seen at one time were in the marketplace in Tbilisi, Georgia, where all the pomegranate vendors seemed to have enormous black handlebar mustaches and deep black eyes and where all the sales pitches—at least to a non-Georgian speaker—seemed to be extraordinarily sensual and intimate. I wanted to buy every pomegranate in the place.) Pomegranates need a very hot and dry climate to ripen fully. Production is concentrated in the Middle East, but they are also a popular fruit in India, China, and Saudi Arabia. In this country pomegranates grow in all of the southern states, but most domestic commercial production is concentrated in the Central Valley of California, where midsummer temperatures routinely reach 100°F., witheringly hot for coastal city slickers like us but perfect for maturing sweet, juicy fruit.

The word "pomegranate" means "apple with many seeds," and when you cut through the leathery skin of a pomegranate and pry it open, you find the numerous juicy seeds bunched in large, almost randomly arranged clusters separated by creamy white membranes. No other fruit has this kind of structure, and botanists have given pomegranates their own family in the plant kingdom, Punicaceae. This family has only two species, one being the cultivated *Punica granatum* and the other a wild relative found only on an island in the western Indian Ocean.

Most pomegranates are the size and shape of a lumpy softball. The ones most commonly found in the market have bronzy red or purple skins, but the skin color of other varieties can be greenish ivory, gold, shocking pink, or deep maroon. (Skin color is not in any case a useful indicator of ripeness.) Seeds also vary in color, ranging from white to dark red. The most commonly grown variety, Wonderful, has brilliant wine-red seeds.

Extracting pomegranate seeds can be messy, but the following technique works well for us: Cut the fruit in half or in quarters with a sharp knife and immerse the pieces in a bowl of water. One by one, break the pieces apart, bending the skin side of the pieces inside out, opening up the membranes, and expelling the seeds into the bowl of water. Scoop off the membrane and skin that float to the top, collect the seeds in a strainer, and pick out any remaining bits of membrane. Use the seeds as the recipe directs. Seeds can be kept overnight in a covered container in the refrigerator.

There are several ways to juice pomegranates, but keep in mind that the white membrane is very tannic and bitter and you want to minimize its contribution to the final product. The best way to get tannin-free juice is to seed the fruit as described above, process the seeds in a blender or food processor, and strain the juice through a fine strainer. If you don't mind a little bitterness, an easier method is to roll the fruit on a hard surface, pressing down firmly with the palm of your hand, until the fruit feels slightly spongy. Hold the fruit over a bowl, and carefully poke a small hole in the side with a small knife. Be careful—juice may squirt out. Squeeze the juice into the bowl. Some recipes suggest cutting the fruit in half and using a citrus juicer, but this can be very messy, and some of that bitter membrane always gets ground into the juice.

You will find pomegranates at the market from September through December, but the main crop comes in October when the Wonderful harvest peaks. Pomegranates don't ripen after they're picked, and they give no external clues to their ripeness, so you have to trust the grower's judgment. Chose organically grown fruit that is heavy for its size; it will have more seeds and less membrane. The skin should look fresh, not dried out. Don't buy those with cuts or holes in the skin, but fruit that has started to split open is fine if you plan to use it right away; otherwise, pomegranates will keep for a week at room temperature or for several weeks in the refrigerator.

Pomegranates grow on large bushes or small trees and can be useful as ornamental plants in California and other southern climates, either pruned as a tree or shrub or trained as an espalier. They have brilliant orange-red flowers in spring, followed by the attractive fruit, and will give a garden a softly Mediterranean character.

Rocket Salad with Pomegranates and Toasted Hazelnuts

⅓ cup hazelnuts
1 pomegranate
  (about ½ cup seeds)
6 generous handfuls of rocket
  (arugula), washed and dried
½ tablespoon red wine vinegar
1½ tablespoons aged
  balsamic vinegar
6 tablespoons extra-virgin
  olive oil
Salt and pepper

Preheat the oven to 400°F.

Spread the hazelnuts out on a baking sheet and toast until golden, 12 to 15 minutes. Take them out when they are just golden brown in the middle; check by cutting a nut in half. They will continue to cook after they come out of the oven. Allow them to cool off a little, rub them between your hands to remove most of their skins, and chop them coarsely.

To get the seeds out of the pomegranate, cut it in half horizontally and smash the fruit onto a plate, cut side down. Most of the seeds will come out. Remove the remaining ones with a spoon.

Put the rocket in a large salad bowl and add the vinegars, olive oil, and salt and pepper to taste. Toss, making sure that all the leaves are evenly coated. Taste and adjust the seasoning as necessary. Add the hazelnuts and pomegranate seeds, toss again, and serve.

Serves 6.

Grilled Quail with Pomegranates and Curly Endive

Pomegranate molasses is pomegranate juice that has been cooked down to a thick syrup. It has a sweet-and-sour flavor that perfectly complements smokily grilled meats. Look for it in Middle Eastern markets.

12 quail
Salt and pepper
2 tablespoons pomegranate
    molasses
Splash of white wine or water
2 shallots, finely chopped
1½ tablespoons red wine
    vinegar

6 tablespoons extra-virgin
    olive oil
3 heads very young curly endive
    (frisée) no more than
    8 inches in diameter, with
    tender white centers
1 pomegranate
    (about ½ cup seeds)

Split the quail down the back along the backbone. Turn them over and press them flat with the heel of your hand. Season generously with salt and pepper. In a large bowl, combine 1 tablespoon pomegranate molasses with a splash of white wine or water. Add the quail and toss gently to evenly coat the quail with the marinade. Cover and marinate for a few hours in the refrigerator.

In a large heatproof bowl, mix the shallots with the vinegar and the remaining tablespoon of molasses and season with salt and a few grinds of black pepper. Allow the shallots to macerate for ½ hour, then whisk in the olive oil. Taste for salt and acidity and adjust as needed.

Remove the tough outer green leaves from the curly endive. Cut out the tough core, separate the leaves, and wash and dry them thoroughly. Roll the pomegranate firmly on the countertop to loosen its seeds. Cut it in half crosswise and, one at a time, invert the halves, cut side down, onto the palm of your hand. Hold over a bowl and pound on the back with a large spoon to dislodge the seeds, which will fall through your fingers. Pick out and discard any white pith that may have fallen out with the seeds. Reserve the seeds until you are ready to assemble the dish.

An hour before cooking, take the quail out of the refrigerator and build a wood or charcoal fire. Grill the quail over medium-hot coals (not too hot; the molasses in the marinade burns easily). Grill the quail, breast side down, for about 8 minutes, then turn and grill the other side for 2 to 3 minutes. The quail are done when the breast is springy to the touch and the juices run clear when a thigh is pierced with a sharp knife. Take the quail off the grill and let them rest for about 6 minutes in a warm place. Meanwhile, put the bowl containing the dressing on the grill to warm up. Add the curly endive and half the pomegranate seeds to the bowl and toss together to warm through. Arrange the salad on a platter with the quail on top and garnish with the rest of the pomegranate seeds.

Serves 6.

POMEGRANATE GRANITA

This luscious, brilliant red ice brightens many a winter dessert. Our favorite way to serve it is to scatter it over tangerine sherbet. It is also refreshing served by itself as a palate cleanser after a rich meal.

½ cup water
¼ cup sugar
1 cup fresh pomegranate juice

*Optional: A squeeze of
    lime juice*

Combine the water and sugar in a small saucepan. Simmer gently until the sugar is dissolved. Pour this sugar syrup into the pomegranate juice. Taste and adjust the acidity with a squeeze of lime, if needed. Pour the mixture into a bowl and freeze. After about 1 hour, stir the mixture so that it doesn't separate into juice and syrup. Once the mixture is frozen, chop it up with a knife or ice pick, transfer the ice to a smaller container, and store tightly covered in the freezer until time to serve.

Makes 1 pint.

POMEGRANATE SPRITZER

For a punchier grown-up spritzer, substitute vodka for one-half cup of the sparkling water.

⅔ cup sugar
⅔ cup water
2 cups fresh pomegranate juice

2½ cups sparkling water
1 lime

Dissolve the sugar in the water over low heat. Let the syrup cool. In a large pitcher, combine the syrup, juice, and sparkling water. Serve in large glasses over ice, with a last-minute squeeze of lime.

Makes 5 cups.

QUINCES &

Season: Fall

In *The Flavors of Sicily*, Anna Tasca Lanza writes vividly about making *cotognata*, quince paste, from the wild quinces that grow near her home amidst the Regaleali vineyards. In Sicily cotognata-making is a bit of an obsession. Everyone in the household may be called on to help prepare the fruit and stir the paste as it cooks and thickens over the fire; there are special molds to put it in; and then come four or five days of setting it out in the sun during the day and bringing it in at night to achieve just the right texture. The result is a beautiful dark red, jewel-like jelly that tastes like the most complex, aromatic, concentrated apple or pear you've ever had.

The French say *cotignac*; Spanish speakers call it *membrillo*. Quince paste is made from the Middle East to the Mediterranean to Latin America, but few people know it here. At Chez Panisse we have no special molds and we dry the paste in a low oven, but we make it in the traditional way, stirring the puréed fruit over heat until it is thick and concentrated. We cut sheets of the translucent paste into cubes or triangles and toss them in sugar for a special after-dessert treat, a revelation to those who have never had it before. We also serve quince paste with cheese, as they do in Italy and Spain; we particularly like to pair it with cow's- or sheep's-milk ricotta. And we mingle slices of poached quinces with apples or pears in galettes or add them to a compote of poached fall fruits. We also like to spread a little quince purée or jam on puff pastry to be topped with thin-sliced apples for a tart.

The quince has an intriguing fragrance, similar to that of ripe apples or pears but more complex, with hints of tropical fruits like pineapple and guava. A couple of quinces in a bowl will perfume an entire room. At one time quinces were common in American gardens, especially in

New England, and used for making jams and jellies and adding to apple butter. (Quinces make excellent preserves in part because of their high pectin content.) Now it is difficult to find a quince in the market, and many trees in backyards and country orchards alike are neglected and ignored. The decline of the quince may be explained by the fact that it is not a convenience food. The yellowish-white flesh of raw quince is inedibly hard, dry, and astringent and must be cooked before it becomes soft and flavorful and turns a lovely pink color. The few steps in preparation are quick and easy, but the cooking takes a long time.

Even small quantities of quince add flavor to other foods, and they work in long-cooked dishes because they hold their texture well. They are often cooked with meat in the Middle East and in North Africa; Persian cooks stuff them with a cinnamon-flavored beef mixture, and in Morocco they are stewed with lamb and chicken.

Anna Tasca Lanza's wild quinces are almost certainly domesticated varieties that have become naturalized to the countryside; the quince, *Cydonia oblonga*, has been grown in Sicily and all around the Mediterranean for thousands of years. The tree comes originally from western Asia, where it has an even longer history of cultivation. The quince is closely related to apples and pears; the small trees thrive in both subtropical and temperate climates. The fruit is roughly round or pear-shaped, often asymmetrical and scalloped, and has fuzzy skin that turns from green to golden when ripe.

A quarter of the world's quince crop is grown in Turkey; large quantities are also grown in China, Iran, Argentina, and Morocco. Quinces grow throughout Europe and in all the lower forty-eight states; market quinces come from several hundred acres of orchards in California and New York.

Quinces ripen in September and October, but fruit from storage can usually be found through December. You probably won't have a choice of varieties when you shop for quinces, but be alert for differences in appearance, texture, and flavor. Two fine-flavored quinces we often see in California are Smyrna and Pineapple. Another good variety available across the country goes by either of two names, Orange or Apple. Portugal and Champion are also good.

At the market, choose fragrant, organically grown quinces that have bright yellow or golden skin with few traces of green. They should be firm and have no soft spots or discoloration. The degree of fuzziness is a varietal characteristic, but riper fruit tends to be less fuzzy. Quinces will keep for a week or two at cool room temperature if they have good air circulation and much longer if refrigerated.

To prepare quinces for cooking, rinse them under cold water, rubbing off as much of the fuzz as you can. Cut away any brown areas. Don't bother to peel or core when making paste, jam, or jelly; the flavor is better, and the debris will get strained out anyway. Quarter, peel, and core fruit that will be poached or cooked with other ingredients.

Quince flesh oxidizes very quickly, but since it turns color when cooked, a little browning won't be noticeable. The final color of cooked quinces depends on the variety and degree of ripeness; most will turn pink or red, but a few stay resolutely beige. Cooking times vary widely too. Check carefully and often while cooking; quince flesh is cooked sufficiently when a knife slides in easily, but don't let the fruit get mushy.

Lamb Tagine with Quinces

3 pounds boned lamb shoulder, cut into 2-inch cubes
Salt and pepper
Olive oil
2 onions, peeled and grated
3 tablespoons unsalted butter
1 cinnamon stick
1 heaping teaspoon grated fresh ginger, or ½ teaspoon ground ginger
½ teaspoon saffron, crushed
2 pounds quinces
2 tablespoons honey
Juice of ½ lemon

Trim off and discard excess surface fat from the lamb. Season the meat with salt and pepper. Cover the bottom of a heavy stew pot with oil, heat, add the meat, and brown lightly on all sides over medium-high heat. Do this in batches, if necessary, to avoid crowding. When the meat is browned, reduce the heat and pour off the oil. Add the onions, butter, cinnamon stick, ginger, saffron, and 1 teaspoon salt and cook for about 5 minutes, stirring and scraping up any brown bits from the bottom of the pan. Pour in enough water to just cover the meat and cook, covered, at a gentle simmer until the meat is tender, about 1½ hours.

While the lamb is cooking, wash the quinces, rub off any clinging fuzz, cut each quince into 8 wedges, and core them. Do not peel: the peel contributes texture and flavor to the stew. Place the wedges in lightly acidulated water to prevent them from browning. When the lamb is tender, taste the stew for saltiness and adjust as needed. Add the quinces, honey, and lemon juice and simmer for another 15 to 30 minutes, until the quince wedges are tender but not falling apart.

Serves 4.

Quince and Apple Fritters

These fritters are best served quickly. They make a wonderful late break-fast or a satisfying dessert after a simple, informal supper or whenever else you can serve them as fast as you fry them. You can safely leave out the quince if you have to; use two apples and serve them drizzled with maple syrup rather than reduced quince poaching liquid.

½ cup poached quince
  wedges (page 266)
¾ cup quince poaching liquid
1 firm-fleshed apple
  (Golden Delicious or
  Sierra Beauty, for example)
2 tablespoons Calvados or
  Armagnac
Granulated sugar

⅔ cup water
1 pinch salt
2 tablespoons unsalted butter,
  cut into small pieces
⅔ cup unbleached
  all-purpose flour
3 eggs
Oil for frying (see Note)
Powdered sugar for dusting

Cut the poached quince into ¼-inch dice. Bring the poaching liquid to a boil in a small saucepan and reduce by half. Set aside until serving.

Quarter, peel, and core the apple. Cut into ¼-inch dice. Toss the apple with the Calvados and a tablespoon or so of sugar. (Add more if the apple is a tart variety.) Toss once or twice while making the batter.

Bring the water, ½ teaspoon sugar, salt, and butter to a boil in a small saucepan over medium heat. When the butter is melted, remove from the heat and add the flour all at once, stirring vigorously with a wooden spoon as the mixture pulls itself together. Return to the heat and keep stirring roughly until the batter is clinging together completely and its surface is shiny, about 3 or 4 minutes. Remove from the heat and allow the mixture to cool for 2 or 3 minutes. Then beat in the eggs one at a time, beating each egg until it is completely incorporated before adding the next one. Alternatively, instead of waiting for the mixture to cool and beating in the eggs by hand, transfer the mixture to the bowl of a standing electric mixer and use the mixer to incorporate the eggs one at a time. When all the eggs are beaten in, add the diced apple and its juices and the diced quince; beat well.

Heat the frying oil to 360°F. Scoop up tablespoon-size pieces of the batter with a fork and drop them carefully into the oil. Fry, turning several times, until they are a medium golden brown. Drain them on paper towels and keep them warm while frying the remaining fritters.

Serve immediately with a dusting of powdered sugar and a drizzle of the reduced quince poaching liquid.

Serves 6.

Note: You can fry fritters in any big, wide, heavy-bottomed pot or pan that will hold at least 1 quart of oil when half full (1 quart oil in a 10-inch skillet, for example, or 2 quarts in a 5-quart pot). Use good peanut oil.

QUINCE AND APPLE TART

1 pound tart apples (3 medium)	*10½ ounces puff pastry*
3 cups poached quince wedges	*(page 294)*
(page 266)	*1 tablespoon melted butter*
¾ cup apple cider	*2 tablespoons sugar*
	½ cup quince poaching liquid

Quarter, core, peel, and thinly slice the apples. Put a third of the sliced apples into a sauté pan. Add 1 cup of the quince wedges and ½ cup of the cider, bring to a boil, and simmer over low heat, stirring and mashing occasionally with a spoon, until the liquid has boiled off and the texture resembles applesauce, about ½ hour.

Preheat the oven to 400°F. Line a baking sheet with parchment paper.

Roll the puff pastry into an 8-by-16-inch rectangle, about ⅛ inch thick. Transfer the pastry to the baking sheet. With a sharp paring knife, trim off and save ½-inch strips from all 4 sides. With a pastry brush dipped in water, paint a ½-inch border around the outside edge of the pastry. Place the ½-inch strips of dough on the painted border to form a rim. Brush the rim with melted butter and refrigerate for 10 minutes.

Remove the shell from the refrigerator and spread the apple and quince sauce evenly on the bottom of the shell. Arrange the remaining poached quince slices and raw apple slices in alternating lines on top of the sauce. Sprinkle the fruit and the rim of the tart evenly with sugar.

Bake for 40 minutes, until the pastry edges are dark golden brown. When the tart is done, immediately slide it off the baking sheet and onto a cooling rack. Cook down the quince poaching liquid and the remaining cider until it is a thick syrup. Use the syrup as a glaze and sauce for the tart. Serve warm, with lightly sweetened whipped cream.

Serves 8.

POACHED QUINCES

As the quince wedges cook, they take on a lovely pink color. We serve these pretty wedges on tarts, in winter fruit compotes, and with fresh ginger cake.

2 cups sugar
6 cups water
2 pounds quinces (about 4 medium)
½ vanilla bean
½ lemon, sliced

Combine the sugar and water in a 4-quart pot, bring to a boil, and simmer slowly until the sugar is dissolved. Quarter, peel, and core the quinces and slice the quarters into ¼-inch-thick wedges. Split the vanilla bean and scrape the seeds into the sugar syrup. Add the bean pod, the lemon slices, and the quince wedges to the syrup. To keep the fruit submerged in the syrup while it cooks, cover the surface of the poaching fruit with a round of parchment paper and weigh it down with a plate. Simmer slowly until the quinces are tender, about 45 minutes.

Meanwhile, prepare five 8-ounce canning jars and self-sealing lids in boiling water, following the manufacturer's instructions.

When the quince wedges are tender, ladle the fruit and syrup into the prepared jars, allowing at least ¼ inch of headroom, and seal with the lids, following the manufacturer's instructions. (Or simply ladle fruit and syrup into clean jars, cool, and keep refrigerated, tightly covered, for up to 2 weeks.)

Makes 5 cups.

QUINCE PASTE

3 pounds quinces (about 6 medium)
3 cups water
2 cups sugar plus more for coating the pieces
Juice of 1 lemon

Wash the quinces and wipe off any clinging fuzz. Cut them in quarters, remove the woody core, and cut the quarters into roughly 1-inch pieces. Put the quinces in a 4-quart pot, add the water, bring to a boil, cover, and steam over medium heat, stirring occasionally, until the fruit is soft, about 20 minutes. When the fruit is completely tender and has started to break down, pass the mixture through a food mill or sieve.

Return the purée to the pot, add the sugar, and cook over low heat, stirring constantly, for about 45 minutes. The mixture will cook into a paste, bubbling thickly; when it's done, it should be thick enough to mound up, but still pourable. If the mixture starts to burn in the pan before it has completely thickened, turn off the heat and let it rest for a few minutes; the part sticking to the bottom will release when you start stirring again. When the mixture reaches the right consistency, stir in the lemon juice and remove from the heat.

Line a shallow pan measuring at least 8 by 10 inches with parchment paper. Lightly oil the paper with light vegetable or almond oil. Pour the paste onto the paper-lined pan, spreading it into an 8-by-10-inch rectangle, about ¼ inch thick. When it has cooled completely, invert the sheet of paste onto another piece of parchment paper. Carefully peel off the upper, oiled parchment paper. Let the paste dry uncovered overnight. (If it is not firm enough to cut at this point, try drying it out for an hour in the oven at 150°F. or the lowest setting.) Once the paste is cool and firm, cut it into 1-inch squares and toss them in sugar. Store uncovered in a dry place. When the paste is dry to the touch, it can be stored in an airtight container for as long as a year.

Makes eighty 1-inch-square pieces.

RASPBERRIES 🍂

Season: Late spring through early fall

The season's first raspberries, fresh from the garden, in a basket on the kitchen counter—aglow with color, flesh like soft velvet, giving off an intoxicating aroma… Can anyone doubt that summer has arrived? For these berries, the best treatment is the simplest: put them in a big bowl, sprinkle them with a little sugar, and drizzle good, thick cream over them. What more gratifying fulfillment of summer's promises?

Later in the season, combine raspberries with softer, sweeter fruits: raspberries and white nectarines, arranged in a bowl; or raspberries and peaches, baked in a crisp or cobbler. Or try making peach Melba the way we like to at the restaurant, with sliced fresh peaches (instead of a poached canned peach half), vanilla ice cream, whole raspberries, and a little fresh raspberry sauce. (Fresh raspberry sauce is delicious and easy to make: just purée raspberries with a little sugar to taste and strain through a fine sieve.) Or replicate Elizabeth David's incomparable summer pudding with raspberries and red currants.

Wild raspberries grow all across North America—from Newfoundland to Alaska and as far south as Mexico—and across much of temperate Europe and Asia as well. Cultivated raspberry varieties abound, and you should be able to grow your own almost anywhere—or at least succeed in finding fresh local berries at a roadside stand or farmers' market.

All cultivated raspberries belong to the genus *Rubus*, and many are descended from a wild European raspberry, R. *idaeus*. Most varieties of black raspberries, or blackcaps, are hybrids of one or both of two native North American species: *R. occidentalis* from the East and *R. leucodermis* from the West. In addition to red and black raspberries, there are cultivated varieties with yellow, golden, apricot, and purple-colored fruit. An inventory of mail-order sources of raspberry plants conducted in 1992 by the Seed Savers Exchange counted ninety-six varieties available for planting.

One of our earliest and most faithful raspberry growers was Mr. Hadsell, who lived on the other side of the coastal hills just east of Berkeley. Every spring Mr. Hadsell would arrive at the back door of the restaurant with a few baskets of the year's first raspberries. He returned week after week with more as the season progressed. The berries he brought—in all shades of red, black, and gold—were always perfect; we never refrigerated them, and we always used them that same day. Some became part of the night's dessert, some would always go out on plates to the diners completely unadorned, and many would be snatched and eaten by the waiters as they walked by the pastry kitchen table; they were that compulsively irresistible.

Organic growers in every part of the country have favorite varietals, with names that hint strongly of their geographical heritage. Favorites in the Northwest are the Willamette and Chilliwack; in the Midwest, Black Hawk and Redwing and Indian Summer; in the Northeast, Brandywine, Newburgh, and Fall Gold; and Cumberland in the South.

Because more and more raspberries are being imported from the Southern Hemisphere, you can find raspberries marketed at any time of year. But raspberries are one of the most fragile and perishable fruits, and they do not travel well, especially when picked fully ripe. Much of the fruit sent from Chile and New Zealand is harvested before it is mature and sweet. Do not disappoint yourself with out-of-season berries. Buy raspberries in the summer, when you can enjoy the rich flavor of fully ripe, sweet berries and feel the urgency of getting them to the table before they turn into so much beautiful red purée.

Raspberries are harvested during all the warmer months of the year and are especially plentiful early in their season, which begins in May in the South and West and as late as July in the cooler states. A second crop comes into production around mid-August and continues until the vines are killed by frost. We can sometimes pick raspberries for Christmas if the winter weather stays mild in our part of California.

Most raspberries are sold in shallow cardboard baskets. Do not buy those that are stained with the juice of crushed berries. Choose berries that look velvety and plump. Check carefully for mold, which often begins growing in the stem cavity and may be hard to detect until you taste. One moldy berry can ruin the flavor of a bowlful.

Because they are so fragile, raspberries cannot be stored for very long at home. And because they are usually too delicate to be washed, buy only those that have not been sprayed. At home, carefully empty out the baskets onto a shallow paper-lined tray. Look over the berries and discard any that show signs of mold. Pick off any clinging stems or leaves. Eat the raspberries immediately.

If you are lucky enough to be deluged with berries from your garden or the market, you can freeze them for future use in sauces or sherbet. Just lay the raspberries out on trays and freeze, then transfer them to plastic bags and return them to the freezer. Raspberries do have a small amount of natural pectin, and those not used right away can be crushed with sugar and boiled down to make jam.

RASPBERRY COULIS

2 cups (2 half-pint baskets) raspberries
¼ cup sugar
Optional: ¼ teaspoon framboise or kirsch
Optional: Lemon juice

Purée the raspberries, sugar, and framboise or kirsch, if you wish. Push the purée through a fine-mesh nonreactive strainer with a rubber spatula. Taste and adjust the sauce by adding more sugar or a few drops of lemon, if needed. Cover and refrigerate. Use within 3 days.

Makes 1½ cups.

Note: Other berry coulis are worth trying—blackberry, boysenberry, and olallieberry are all interesting.

Vanilla Custard with Raspberry Coulis

We bake these custards in individual gratin dishes that are 5 inches wide and about ¾ inch deep. The thin translucent layer of coulis poured over the custards makes them glow. The wide shallow dishes permit us to achieve the perfect balance of fruit to custard.

> 1½ cups heavy cream, chilled
> 1½ cups half-and-half
> ½ cup sugar
> One 1-inch piece vanilla bean
>
> 6 egg yolks
> ½ cup raspberry coulis
> (page 271)

Measure the heavy cream into a large mixing bowl. Measure the half-and-half and sugar into a medium-size saucepan. Split the piece of vanilla bean lengthwise and scrape out the seeds, stirring them into the half-and-half mixture. Add the scraped bean pods and heat the mixture to just under a boil. Briefly whisk the egg yolks in a bowl to break them up. Slowly pour in the hot half-and-half mixture, whisking constantly until thoroughly incorporated. Strain through a fine-mesh sieve directly into the cold heavy cream. Stir well. The custard mixture can be refrigerated for up to a day at this point.

When you are ready to bake the custard, preheat the oven to 350°F.

Place 8 individual small gratin dishes or eight 4- or 5-ounce ramekins in a deep baking pan. Fill the gratin dishes about three-quarters full with the custard. Carefully pour hot water into the pan until it reaches about halfway up the sides of the custard dishes. Cover the top of the pan tightly with foil and carefully place it in the oven. Bake for 30 to 40 minutes, until the custards are just beginning to set. To check for doneness, jiggle one of the gratin dishes a bit. The custard should be set except for a dime-size circle in center. Carefully remove the baking pan from the oven and remove the custards from the water bath. Let them cool completely in the refrigerator. The custards can remain there overnight or they can be served as soon as they are cool.

When you are ready to serve, ladle about 2 tablespoons of raspberry coulis on top of each custard. Tilt them back and forth to make the coulis cover the entire surface of each custard. Serve with crispy cookies for dipping.

Serves 8.

BRANDIED RASPBERRIES

These are like treasures to us in wintertime. The berries are folded into chocolate soufflé, spooned over bitter-almond ice cream, and scattered alongside cornmeal cake. The brandy we cook down and use for sauce.

Fill a 1-quart jar with raspberries. Pour in 1 cup sugar and cover with brandy or Cognac. Close the jar and let sit 4 days, shaking the jar occasionally to make sure that the sugar dissolves. Keeps 1 year.

RASPBERRY ICE CREAM

After straining the raspberries, you may want to add about a quarter of the strained seeds to the ice cream to give it a slightly different texture.

6 egg yolks
1½ cups whole milk
One 1-inch piece vanilla bean
½ cup sugar
½ teaspoon salt

2½ cups heavy cream, chilled
3 cups (about 3 half-pint baskets) raspberries
Kirsch or framboise eau-de-vie
Vanilla extract

Whisk the yolks briefly in a mixing bowl. Gently heat the milk, vanilla bean, sugar, and salt in a medium-size heavy-bottomed saucepan. When the milk mixture begins to steam, drizzle the warm milk into the yolks, whisking constantly as you pour. Pour the mixture back into the saucepan. Measure the heavy cream into the mixing bowl. Cook the mixture over low heat, stirring constantly with a wooden spoon or heat-resistant rubber spatula. When the mixture thickens enough to coat the spoon, immediately strain it through a fine-mesh strainer directly into the cream. Whisk together to cool the mixture, cover, and chill thoroughly.

Purée the raspberries in a food processor and press the purée through a nonreactive fine-mesh sieve. Add the strained purée to the chilled ice cream base and mix well. Add kirsch or framboise, 1 teaspoon at a time, until the raspberry flavor brightens, about 1 tablespoon in all. Stir in a few drops of vanilla extract. Freeze following the instructions for your ice cream maker. Serve the ice cream plain, with a sprinkling of toasted almonds, or with warm oven-roasted figs in their juices.

Makes about 1 quart.

Raspberry Soufflés

1 tablespoon unsalted butter,
    melted and cooled slightly
⅓ cup plus 2 tablespoons
    granulated sugar plus more
    for coating the ramekins and
    sprinkling on top
1½ cups raspberries
1 teaspoon lemon juice
½ teaspoon framboise or kirsch

3 egg yolks
⅛ teaspoon almond extract
6 egg whites
1½ teaspoons cornstarch
1 pinch salt
¼ teaspoon cream of tartar
Powdered sugar for dusting
1 cup raspberry coulis
    (page 271)

Preheat the oven to 450°F.

Brush the insides of six 5-ounce ramekins with the butter, leaving a generous lip of butter around the inner rim. Pour in some granulated sugar, coating the insides, and tap out any excess. Touch up any uncovered spots with more melted butter and sugar. Set the ramekins aside on a baking sheet.

Purée the raspberries with 2 tablespoons granulated sugar. Strain the sweetened purée through a fine sieve; you should have about ½ cup. In a large mixing bowl, whisk together the raspberry purée, lemon juice, framboise, egg yolks, and almond extract.

In another clean, dry mixing bowl, whisk the egg whites until they get frothy. Add the cornstarch, salt, and cream of tartar and beat until the whites are fluffy and hold soft peaks. Add ⅓ cup granulated sugar and keep whisking until the peaks are firm and glossy but not dry. Gently fold the whites into the raspberry mixture, deflating the whites as little as possible.

Spoon the soufflé mixture into the prepared ramekins, filling them just to the lip of butter. Sprinkle the tops with a thin layer of sugar. Drag your finger around the top and outer edge of the rim of each ramekin to clean up any splattered excess soufflé mixture; this ensures that the soufflé will rise straight up ½ inch or more without sticking to the sides.

Bake for 8 to 9 minutes, until the soufflés are tall, golden on top, and still slightly soft to the touch in the center. Remove the baking sheet from the oven and dust the tops of the soufflés with powdered sugar. Serve immediately on individual plates lined with napkins or doilies (to keep the ramekins from sliding around). At the table, pass a pitcher of raspberry coulis for the guests to pour into the center of their soufflés.

Serves 8.

RASPBERRY SYRUP

Raspberry syrup is a splendid concoction to make when berries are plentiful in the summer months. It is also a great way to use berries that are slightly soft and not perfect enough to eat fresh. The same recipe can be used with other bush berries, including blackberries, black raspberries, boysenberries, tayberries, huckleberries, and ollallieberries.

Take 1 half-pint basket of raspberries and pick over, removing stalks, leaves, and any moldy berries. (Washing berries is generally not recommended because they absorb too much water and begin to break down.) Put the raspberries in a saucepan and crush them thoroughly with a potato masher (or a whisk or a spoon).

Add 2 cups cold water to the berries and bring the mixture to a boil. Skim off and discard any scum that rises to the surface. Simmer the mixture for 15 minutes and remove from heat. Pour it through a fine nonreactive strainer, pressing on the fruit to drain out all the juices. Measure the hot liquid, pour it back into the saucepan, and add two-thirds as much sugar as there is liquid (e.g., to 1½ cups of liquid, add 1 cup sugar). Return the pan to the heat and stir until the sugar dissolves. Bring the mixture to a boil, remove from the heat, and pour the syrup carefully into a glass jar for storage.

An alternative method for making berry syrup is to save the seeds and fruit pulp left over after straining a berry purée for sherbet, mousse, curd, and other recipes that require no seeds. After puréeing the fruit through a sieve or in a food mill, use the seeds and fruit left behind and proceed as you would with crushed berries. To make the same quantity of syrup, you will need the seeds and pulp of about 2 pints of berries. This is a very efficient way to extract all the flavor from the berries.

The syrup can be kept in the refrigerator for a few weeks and will add color and fruitiness to many dishes. It can be mixed with sparkling water to make a refreshing fruit soda (add a sprig of mint and a twist of lemon to dress it up) or with white wine or Champagne to make an apéritif, or it can be mixed with spirits for fruity mixed drinks. Add it to lemonade (to make pink raspberry lemonade) or to tea (for raspberry iced tea). It is delicious spooned into plain yogurt for sweetness, swirled on top of ice cream for a quick ice cream sundae, or drizzled over pancakes and waffles.

Raspberry Jam

We use this to fill cakes (especially almond torte), tarts, and cookies. We also warm and strain it to use as a glaze for fresh fruit tarts, especially in the winter.

4 cups raspberries (about 3 baskets)
2 cups sugar
1 teaspoon lemon juice

Stir together the berries and sugar in a medium-size heavy-bottomed saucepan. Let sit for 15 minutes so that the berries start rendering their juice. Put a small plate in the freezer to use later to test the consistency of the jam.

Prepare two 1-pint canning jars and self-sealing lids in boiling water, following the manufacturer's instructions.

Bring the saucepan of berries to a boil over high heat, stirring occasionally to make sure there is no sticking (reduce the heat if there is). The mixture will bubble up dramatically, rising high up the sides of the pot. Skim off any light-colored foam as it collects on the edges. Soon the jam will boil down again, forming smaller, thicker bubbles. At this point, start testing the consistency by putting small spoonfuls of the jam on the cold plate. This will cool off the jam sample quickly so you can tell what the finished texture will be like. When the jam has cooked to the thickness you want, stir in the lemon juice. Turn off the heat and carefully ladle the jam into the prepared canning jars, allowing at least ¼ inch of headroom. Clean the lip of the jars with a clean, damp towel, and seal with the lids, following the manufacturer's instructions. The jam will keep for about 1 year.

Makes 2¼ cups.

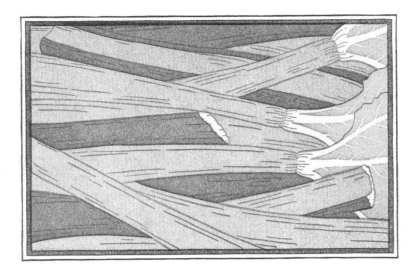

RHUBARB ❧

Season: Mid-spring through summer

Of course, rhubarb is technically a vegetable, but it appears here because we cook its leaf petioles as we do acidic fruits, for desserts and savory dishes. When field-grown rhubarb comes to market in the early spring, we say good-bye to the last of the apples and pears that wintered over with us. By mid-April, rhubarb is spotlighted in the crisps and open-faced galettes we serve in the Café, upstaged only by the cherries and apricots of late May. Rhubarb is the vegetable bridge between the tree fruits of winter and summer.

We use rhubarb in tarts, crisps, dessert soups, sherbet, ice cream, and fools. It makes delicious preserves and jam, especially combined with citrus. Its flavor complements rich meats such as pork or foie gras, and its tart acidity (it is related to sorrel) goes nicely with fish. According to Paula Wolfert, it is even eaten raw in a Middle Eastern salad.

The type of rhubarb cultivated as a fruit, *Rheum rhaponticum*, derives from several northern Asian species. For centuries rhubarb was cultivated chiefly for its root, an important medicine in China and elsewhere since at least 2700 B.C. The use of rhubarb as a food is much more recent. Seventeenth- and eighteenth-century experiments in the consumption of its leaves, which contain toxic amounts of oxalic acid, caused its reputation to suffer in Europe.

Only in the early nineteenth century, after the development of varieties with tender, juicy stalks, was rhubarb embraced as a food, particularly in England and America. American rhubarb cultivation began in Maine and Massachusetts in the 1820s. Rhubarb became known as pie plant, hardy and dependable despite the cold of North American winters. As settlers moved west, its cultivation spread as far as the Pacific.

Because it needs cold winters and cool weather during the growing season, only the northern United States and southern Canada are ideal for rhubarb; it does not thrive in the South. The northeastern states from Maine to Illinois, the Pacific Northwest, and northern California are the favored areas for field-grown rhubarb.

Growers in Washington and Michigan produce a small quantity of hothouse rhubarb in late winter and early spring. Plants that have experienced sufficient winter cold are planted in greenhouses, where they produce tender, pink shoots. The season for field-grown rhubarb starts in April and lasts until September. Field-grown stalks are firmer and more highly colored than the hothouse kinds. The harvest in the Northwest goes from late April through May, with a second harvest from late June into July. The best rhubarb from southern Canada, Michigan, and the East comes to market from late May into June, with the secondary harvest in August and early September.

Organic farmers who have deep, rich soil are very successful with rhubarb because it has few insect and disease problems. For the last several years our rhubarb has come from the Nisqually Produce Farm, a sixty-acre organic farm near Olympia, Washington, that harvests field-grown Ruby Red, a lower-acid variety with large, juicy, tender stalks.

At the market you will find more red or pink rhubarb than green, even though skin color is incidental to quality. Inside, the stalks may be pale green, pink, or, as in the case of several strains of Canada Red, red clear through. Be sure to choose stalks that are firm and turgid, with bright, glossy skin. Pass over those that are very thin or very thick; they may be tough and stringy. Avoid limp and flabby stalks. Late in the season be particularly mindful of pithy, tough, and fibrous stalks.

Rhubarb is ready to use as soon as it is harvested. To prepare for cooking, trim and discard all traces of leaves from the top of each stalk. Rinse the stalks quickly under cold water and wipe them clean with a damp towel. Trim away brown or discolored parts from the butt ends.

Cut into pieces as the recipe directs. Rhubarb should always be cooked in a nonreactive pot.

Rhubarb is often combined with strawberries and raspberries. Be careful that neither the flavors of the other ingredients nor the quantity of sugar overpowers rhubarb's subtle character, which reminds us of the smell of the earth in the spring.

BAKED RHUBARB COMPOTE

I have delightful childhood memories of rhubarb cooking on the stove, but I know that some people have unpleasant rhubarb flashbacks of fruit stewed to a purée. Baked rhubarb, however, stays in recognizable pieces and is juicy without being slimy. Valencia oranges are in season at the same time, and their juice and zest sweeten and temper the flavor of rhubarb. Try this with a little sweetened cream for dessert or as a side dish with pork.

1 pound rhubarb
1 Valencia or other juice orange
½ cup sugar

Preheat the oven to 350°F.

Rinse the rhubarb quickly under cold water and wipe dry with a clean towel. Trim and discard every bit of leaf and the tough inch or so at the bottom end of each stalk. Cut lengthwise into ⅓-inch-thick strips and then crosswise into 2-inch pieces. You should have about 6 cups.

Grate the zest of the orange into a 9- or 10-inch nonreactive baking dish and squeeze in about 3 tablespoons of its juice. Add the rhubarb and sugar and toss everything together until the rhubarb is coated with sugar and juice.

Cover and bake for 25 minutes. Remove the cover and continue baking for another 5 to 10 minutes, or until a knife slides easily into the rhubarb. Serve warm or at room temperature.

Serves 4.

Rhubarb Galette

When assembling this galette, give your imagination free rein and arrange the rhubarb in a lovely mosaic design. Serve it with orange ice cream (page 195), vanilla ice cream (page 301), or strawberry ice cream.

10 ounces galette dough (page 290), rolled into a 14-inch circle
1½ pounds rhubarb
1¾ cups plus 2 tablespoons sugar

2 tablespoons flour
¼ cup almond-amaretti powder (page 298)
3 tablespoons unsalted butter, melted

Preheat the oven to 400°F. Butter a baking sheet or line it with parchment paper.

Remove the galette dough from the freezer or refrigerator and place on the prepared baking sheet.

Rinse the rhubarb quickly under cold water and wipe dry with a clean towel. Trim and discard every bit of leaf and trim off and reserve the tough inch or so at the bottom end of each stalk. Cut lengthwise into ¼-inch-thick strips and crosswise into 3-inch pieces. Toss the rhubarb pieces with ¾ cup sugar and the flour in a nonreactive mixing bowl.

Sprinkle the almond-amaretti powder evenly over the pastry, leaving a 1½-inch border unsprinkled. Put the rhubarb pieces on top; the mound of fruit will be several inches high. Arrange the top layer of rhubarb in a whimsical pattern.

While rotating the tart, fold the border of exposed dough up and over itself at regular intervals, crimping and pushing it up against the outer circle of fruit, creating a containing rim that resembles a length of rope. Pinch off any excess dough. This rim must act as a dam, preventing juices from escaping while cooking, so make sure there are no folds or wrinkles that would permit such a breach. Brush the border gently with the melted butter and sprinkle it with 2 tablespoons sugar.

Bake in the center of the oven for about 45 minutes. Rotate the galette after about 15 minutes and push down the rhubarb with a spatula to flatten it. Rotate again after 15 more minutes to ensure even baking. When the galette is done, remove it from the oven and slide it off the parchment directly onto a rack to cool for at least 15 minutes before serving.

While the galette is baking, make a glaze by boiling the reserved butt ends of the rhubarb with 1 cup sugar and a splash of water until they are soft. Strain, then brush lightly over the baked galette.

Makes one 12-inch tart; serves 8 to 10.

RHUBARB GRAPEFRUIT PRESERVES

2 pounds rhubarb
2 grapefruit
4 cups sugar

Wash and dry the rhubarb and cut it into ½-inch dice. Peel the zest off the grapefruit and chop it very fine. Put the rhubarb, chopped zest, and sugar in a large heavy-bottomed stainless-steel pot. Juice the grapefruits into the pot. Let the mixture stand for 30 minutes (or overnight) to allow the sugar to dissolve and the rhubarb to release its juice.

Prepare five 8-ounce canning jars and self-sealing lids in boiling water, following the manufacturer's instructions. Put a small plate in the freezer to be used later to test the consistency of the jam.

Bring the pot of fruit to a boil over high heat, stirring occasionally to make sure it is not sticking to the bottom. The mixture will bubble high up the sides of the pot. Skim off any light-colored foam collecting on the edges. Soon the jam will subside, still bubbling thickly. Stir frequently and start testing for consistency by putting small spoonfuls of jam on the cold plate. This cools the samples quickly so you can tell what the finished texture will be. When the jam has cooked to the thickness you want, turn off the heat and carefully ladle the jam into the prepared canning jars, allowing at least ¼ inch of headroom. Seal with the lids according to the manufacturer's instructions. The preserves will keep for 1 year.

Makes 5 cups.

STRAWBERRIES 🍓

Season: Spring through summer

Almost all modern strawberry varieties are hybrids of two American species: *Fragaria virginiana*, the meadow strawberry, native to eastern North America from the Gulf of Mexico north to the Dakotas and Hudson Bay, and on the other side of the continent, *F. chiloensis*, the pine or beach strawberry, which is found along the Pacific coast from Alaska south all the way to Chile. But the twain never met until both species were brought to France.

French aristocrats and their gardeners have been passionate collectors, cultivators, and consumers of strawberries for centuries. Wild European strawberries were part of royal plant collections in Paris as long ago as the fourteenth century; it is said that Charles V had 5,000 strawberry plants in his gardens at the Louvre. The wild Virginia strawberry was introduced around 1600, and the wild Chilean species about a hundred years later. Not long after that, cross-pollination of the two wild parent species produced a plant bearing large, very flavorful berries, so superior in some ways to selections from the wild of either species that berry breeders have focused on cross-breeding these two ever since.

Cultivated strawberry varieties are classified according to their pattern of seasonal fruit production. June-bearing varieties produce one abundant crop in late spring or early summer; ever-bearing types set smaller crops throughout the summer and into the fall. Although strawberries can be grown anywhere in the United States, California produces the most: 80 percent of commercial strawberries come from here. Florida is the second-largest producer, and Oregon is a distant third. Berries from one or another of these commercial growing areas are usually available year-round; even in wintertime strawberries are shipped across the country from fields in California and Florida. But the sad truth is these berries are never as luscious and sweet as the ones local organic growers bring to market during the peak of the harvest from April through June. Furthermore, berries that are not grown organically are sprayed repeatedly with extremely noxious agricultural chemicals. Because of this and because of the backbreaking labor required to harvest them, strawberries are widely known to agricultural workers in California as *la fruta del diablo*—"the fruit of the devil." (Fortunately, many of the strawberries we serve not only are certified as organically grown but are also harvested by unionized, well-paid farmworkers.)

In the early twentieth century, as long-distance transport became more common, commercial varieties were bred for good shipping qualities and high yields, and considerations of flavor were slighted. Happily, many growers are now replacing the older, blander commercial standbys with tastier varieties, and backyard growers and small farmers continue to grow scores of other varieties, old and new, that are too fragile to be mass-marketed but have better flavor than the common commercial hybrids.

All strawberries are fragile and highly perishable, especially when perfectly ripe. Most commercial strawberries are therefore picked before they reach full maturity, and even the choicest varieties may disappoint when eaten underripe. Look for ripe, sweet berries from farms near you. Strawberries are grown in all fifty states. Check with your local produce store and farmers' market to find out which local varieties are best. If you buy California strawberries in the supermarket, look for the ones that are organically grown; Chandler, Seascape, and Quinault are all good varieties. Florida berry varieties with good flavor include Oso Grande and Selva.

In a very few farmers' markets you may encounter the fruit the French call *fraises des bois*, "strawberries of the woods." It is *F. vesca*, the European wild or Alpine strawberry. The berries are tiny, but their aroma is much more intensely pungent than that of conventional cultivated strawberries. Ripe wild strawberries must be used very fresh because their aroma fades fast after they are picked. You can look for them, but it may be more realistic to try growing them at home. Home gardeners should also try the rare but worthwhile musk strawberry, *F. moschata*, with its hauntingly complex flavor; the variety called Profumata di Tortona is available from several mail-order nurseries.

The Chino family ranch recently began sending us a new French hybrid strawberry, the exceptionally delicious and fragrant Mara des Bois, which produces large berries with a distinctly wild strawberry character. As of this writing, plants of this variety receive some commercial distribution, so check your local garden store or nursery for availability; it's worth looking for.

A freshly picked ripe strawberry is brilliantly shiny and plump; its calyx is a bright vibrant green and not wilted at all. Berry color alone is not always an indicator of good flavor, as color varies between varieties, but the darkest berries of any one variety will be the ripest. Baby the berries on the trip home and carefully lay them out on a paper-lined baking sheet as soon as you can. Berries that are very firm will improve and soften a bit if held overnight at room temperature. Only those very ripe berries that will not be used within a few hours need ever be refrigerated, and they should be eaten within a day or two; berries get moldy very quickly. Strawberries often don't need washing, but if there is sand or soil clinging to them, rinse them quickly in cold water just before stemming and using.

The texture of cooked strawberries is generally soft and uninteresting, although a few strawberries included in rhubarb pies or cobblers are good for flavor and sweetness, and preserves well made from perfectly ripe berries are irresistible. But perfectly ripe strawberries are best eaten raw: plain, sliced up into a glass of red wine, served alongside bowls of crème fraîche and sugar for voluntary dipping, or in a classic presentation such as strawberry shortcake. And in early summer, when the strawberry season is at its zenith, put up some jam to brighten the gray months when the berry bushes are bare and fruitless.

Many strawberries are low in acid; their flavor will be enhanced by slightly acid foods such as oranges, red wine, or balsamic vinegar. One of our most popular sherbets at the Café combines strawberries and the juice of Valencia oranges or tangerines. The sweet perfume of strawberries is also complemented by other aromatic ingredients, such as rose petals, lemon verbena leaves, and Muscat wine.

FANNY'S STRAWBERRY-ORANGE COMPOTE

This is an extremely simple and quick dessert, but you must use truly flavorful oranges and strawberries. If fraises des bois are available, add a few for their flowery perfume. The orange peel can be candied well ahead of time, and the rest takes only a few minutes.

2 small navel oranges
(about 10 ounces)
½ cup plus 2 tablespoons sugar

1 cup water
One 1-pint basket strawberries
(about 2 cups)

Remove about three-quarters of the zest from one of the oranges with a zester (the kind with tiny holes) or peel off strips of zest with a vegetable peeler and cut into a fine julienne. Measure ½ cup sugar and the water into a saucepan and bring to a boil to dissolve the sugar. Add the tiny strips of zest, reduce the heat, and simmer for about 30 minutes, until the peel is tender and the syrup has reduced and thickened slightly. Let cool.

Rinse the strawberries and dry them gently. Hull and slice them about ¼ inch thick into a bowl. Cut away all the peel from the oranges: slice off the tops and bottoms and cut away all the rind. Remove skinless sections of the oranges by sliding a sharp paring knife alongside the membranes and prying out the segments into the bowl with the strawberries. Squeeze the juice from the orange "carcasses," sprinkle with 2 tablespoons sugar, and mix gently.

To serve, spoon the compote into serving glasses or dishes, sprinkle some curls of the candied peel on top, and drizzle a teaspoon of the syrup from the peel over the compote.

Serves 4.

STRAWBERRY SHERBET

Two 1-pint baskets strawberries (about 4 cups)
¾ cup water
¾ cup sugar
Optional: A few drops of lemon juice or kirsch

Rinse, dry, and hull the strawberries. Purée them with the water and sugar. Taste and adjust the flavor with a few drops of lemon or kirsch if needed. Freeze according to the instructions for your ice cream maker.
  Makes about 1 quart.

STRAWBERRY SHORTCAKE WITH LEMON VERBENA CREAM

It takes a day for the cream to become infused with the complex perfume of lemon verbena, but it's worth the wait, because it adds a fragrant depth to the dish.

1 cup heavy cream
⅓ cup fresh lemon verbena leaves
Two 1-pint baskets strawberries (about 4 cups)
¼ cup plus 1½ tablespoons granulated sugar
6 baked 2-inch biscuits (page 291)
Powdered sugar for dusting

Pour the cream into a bowl. Tear the fresh lemon verbena leaves into the cream. Cover and refrigerate overnight.
  Slice the strawberries and toss with ¼ cup granulated sugar. Purée about ½ cup of the strawberries and stir into the bowl of sliced berries. Strain the cream through a sieve to remove the leaves. Whip the cream with 1½ tablespoons sugar until it forms soft peaks.
  To assemble the shortcakes, first slice the biscuits in half. Place a bottom biscuit on a plate, cover with a scoop of strawberries and a dollop of cream, top with the other half of the biscuit, and dust with powdered sugar. Serve immediately.
  Serves 6.

STRAWBERRIES WITH RED WINE

In the springtime wine-makers all over France enjoy the first strawberries of the season this way: sliced up and added to the red wine left in one's glass at the end of a meal. Wines that are a little lacking in fruitiness—either because they are well past their prime or from a not-so-good year—gain the most. And while you wouldn't want to do this to your thirty-year-old great Bordeaux, ordinary wines are inevitably enhanced. And so are the strawberries.

SUN-DRIED STRAWBERRY JAM

This method of jam-making requires a little patience, but it is among the best ways to preserve fresh strawberry flavor. We make it sometimes to capture the floral quality of wild strawberries.

5 cups strawberries
2 cups sugar
Optional: A few drops lemon juice

Rinse, dry, and hull the strawberries. Slice them in half and then into thin slices. Toss the slices with the sugar in a medium-size nonreactive pot and let them sit for 15 minutes while their juices are released and the sugar dissolves. Cook the berries over high heat for 10 minutes, skimming off any white foam as it rises. Immediately pour the hot jam into a flat-bottomed glass dish (or dishes) with a surface area large enough that the jam will spread to a thickness of no more than ½ inch in any one spot. Let the jam steam and cool uncovered. If the jam is thinner than you like at this point, let it sit out in a sunny spot to thicken. This can take a few days. Make sure the spot you choose is inaccessible to ants. If you want to put the jam outside, cover it with plastic wrap with a few holes punched in it to allow continued evaporation. When the jam has reached the desired texture, taste it and adjust the sweetness with lemon juice, if necessary. Transfer to clean glass jars, seal tightly, and keep refrigerated for up to a month.

Makes about 4 cups.

A BASIC DESSERT REPERTORY ❧

CRISP TOPPING

Ordinarily we disapprove of freezer storage and cooking in large quantities, but it is a great thing to have a container of crisp topping handy when summer fruits pour into the market. Quadruple this topping recipe and keep it in your freezer.

1¼ cups unbleached all-purpose flour	¼ teaspoon salt
6 tablespoons brown sugar, firmly packed	¼ teaspoon ground cinnamon
	⅔ cup ground pecans
2 tablespoons granulated sugar	12 tablespoons (1½ sticks) unsalted butter, chilled

Stir together the flour, brown sugar, granulated sugar, salt, cinnamon, and pecans in a mixing bowl. Cut the butter into small pieces and work it into the flour mixture with your fingers or an electric mixer, mixing until the topping starts to come together and has a crumbly but not sandy texture. The topping can be made ahead and refrigerated for a week or so or frozen for several weeks.

Makes about 3 cups; enough for 1 crisp.

GALETTE DOUGH

We make this dough every day at the restaurant, and we've included the recipe in our last three cookbooks. We use it for tarts both savory and sweet, of every shape and size. Jacques Pépin taught us how to make it— he calls it his "crunch tart" dough. The technique used to cut the butter into the flour is the key to good results with this recipe. We've altered our instructions a little to make this easier: in our last version, we recommended using your fingers, but this time we suggest using a pastry blender; instead of adding half the butter first, we now think you should start with just a third; and we are a little more precise about how much water to use and how to add it.

2 cups unbleached
  all-purpose flour
1 teaspoon sugar
¼ teaspoon salt

12 tablespoons (1½ sticks)
  unsalted butter, chilled, cut
  into ½-inch pieces
7 tablespoons ice water

Combine the flour, sugar, and salt in a large mixing bowl. Cut 4 tablespoons of the butter into the flour mixture with a pastry blender, mixing until the dough resembles coarse cornmeal. (Butter dispersed throughout the flour in tiny pieces makes the dough tender.) Cut in the remaining 8 tablespoons (1 stick) of butter with the pastry blender, just until the biggest pieces of butter are the size of large peas—or a little larger. (These bigger pieces of butter in the dough make it flaky.)

Dribble 7 tablespoons of ice water (that's ½ cup less 1 tablespoon) into the flour mixture in several stages, tossing and mixing between additions, until the dough just holds together. Toss the mixture with your hands, letting it fall through your fingers. Do not pinch or squeeze the dough together or you will overwork it, making it tough. Keep tossing the mixture until it starts to pull together; it will look rather ropy, with some dry patches. If it looks like there are more dry patches than ropy parts, add another tablespoon of water and toss the mixture until it comes together. Divide the dough in half, firmly press each half into a ball, and wrap tightly in plastic wrap, pressing down to flatten each ball into a 4-inch disk. Refrigerate for at least 30 minutes before rolling out. (The dough will keep in the freezer for a few weeks.)

When you are ready to roll out the dough, take one disk from the refrigerator at a time. Let it soften slightly so that it is malleable but still cold. Unwrap the dough and press the edges of the disk so that there are no cracks. On a lightly floured surface, roll out the disk into a 14-inch circle about ⅛ inch thick. Brush off excess flour from both sides with a dry pastry brush. Transfer the dough to a parchment-lined baking sheet and refrigerate at least ½ hour before using. (The rolled-out circles can be frozen and used the next day.)

Makes about 20 ounces dough, enough for 2 open galettes or tarts or 1 covered tart.

BISCUITS

This is the cream biscuit recipe we use for cobblers and shortcakes. (For examples, see the shortcake recipes on pages 214 and 287 and the cobbler recipe on page 50.)

1½ cups unbleached
* all-purpose flour*
1 big pinch salt
4 teaspoons sugar

2 teaspoons baking powder
6 tablespoons (¾ stick) unsalted
* butter, chilled*
11 tablespoons cream

Preheat the oven to 400°F.

In a medium-size mixing bowl, combine the flour, salt, sugar, and baking powder. Cut the cold butter into the flour mixture with a pastry blender until most of the pieces of butter are pea size or smaller. Stir in 10 tablespoons cream until the mixture just comes together. Turn the dough out onto a lightly floured surface and roll ½ inch thick. Cut into six 2-inch round or square biscuits, rerolling the dough scraps, if necessary.

To bake, place the biscuits on a baking sheet and brush the tops with the remaining 1 tablespoon cream. Bake for 17 minutes, until golden.

Serves 6.

Samantha's Pie Dough

A pastry blender (the little hand tool consisting of 5 or 6 bowed wire blades attached to a wooden handle) is the safest device for making small amounts of pie dough. It gives you control when you're incorporating the fat, and the dough won't heat up from overhandling (which can make it tough).

When you bake fruit pies, always use glass or ceramic pie plates; metal pans may react with fruit. Bake pies in the lower third of your oven, on top of a pizza stone if you have one; if you optimize the bottom heat of your oven, the crust will bake quickly and the pie won't develop a soggy bottom. Remember to line the oven rack or pizza stone with foil to contain any juices that may boil over. Bake pies thoroughly, until the crust is brown and any sugar on top is just beginning to caramelize.

2 cups unbleached
  all-purpose flour
½ teaspoon salt
½ cup (3 ounces) organic
  vegetable shortening

¼ pound (1 stick) unsalted
  butter, frozen and cut into
  ½-inch cubes
7 tablespoons ice water

Combine the flour and salt in a large mixing bowl. Drop the shortening into the flour mixture and work it in, using a pastry blender, until it has been cut into ⅓-inch pieces. Add the cubed butter and work it into the dough with the pastry blender until it is in pea-size pieces. Sprinkle the water over the mixture and toss with your hands, not squeezing at all, but letting the pieces fall through your fingers until it is evenly mixed. The mixture will be crumbly and seem dry.

Divide the dough in half and wrap tightly in plastic wrap, pressing the dough into disks. Let the dough rest in the refrigerator for at least 30 minutes before rolling out. You can leave it for up to 2 days in the fridge or a week in the freezer.

When you're ready to roll out the dough, unwrap it one piece at a time. If it still seems crumbly, first knead it slightly until it comes together. Press it into a 4-inch disk, smoothing out any cracks at the edges. Using as little flour as possible, roll out each disk into a circle about 13 inches in diameter and about ⅛ inch thick. Brush all excess flour off the dough with a dry pastry brush. Transfer the sheets of dough to a baking sheet, cover with plastic, and refrigerate until you are ready to use them.

Makes two 9-ounce pieces, enough for 2 shells or 1 double-crusted pie.

Cornmeal Dough

We have been using this recipe for a crisp dough for fruit tarts since it was published fifteen years ago by our friend Carol Field in her bible of Mediterranean pastry-making, *The Italian Baker*. It adds a pleasant crunch to peach and blackberry crostata (page 37), and we also like using it for double-crusted tarts filled with pears poached in white wine.

10 tablespoons (1 stick plus	*1½ cups unbleached*
2 tablespoons) unsalted	*all-purpose flour*
butter, room temperature	*½ cup yellow cornmeal*
¾ cup sugar	*¾ teaspoon salt*
3 egg yolks	*½ teaspoon vanilla extract*

Cream the butter and sugar together in a large mixing bowl. Add the egg yolks one at a time, mixing thoroughly after each addition. Sift the flour, cornmeal, and salt directly into the mixture. Add the vanilla and stir until the dough is thoroughly mixed. Divide the dough in half and gather it into 2 balls. Wrap the balls in plastic, press them into disks, and refrigerate for at least 30 minutes.

To roll out the dough, first cut four 14-inch-square pieces of parchment paper. Dust a piece of the parchment paper with flour. Take a disk of dough out of the refrigerator, unwrap it, and place on the floured paper. Dust the top of the dough with flour and cover with another piece of parchment. Roll out the disk into a 13-inch circle, about ⅛ inch thick. If the dough starts to stick to the paper while you are rolling, peel back the paper, dust again with flour, and replace the paper. Then flip the whole package over and repeat on the other side. If there is excess flour on the dough when you are done rolling, peel back the paper and brush it off. Chill the sheet of dough for at least a few minutes. Roll out the other disk the same way.

To make an 11-inch tart, generously brush the bottom and sides of an 11-inch tart pan with melted butter (so your tart won't stick to the pan). Remove 1 sheet of dough from the refrigerator and take off the top sheet of paper. Invert the dough into the tart pan and peel off the other piece of paper. Press the dough into the corners of the pan, pinching off any dough overhang. Use the dough scraps to patch any cracks. Let the tart shell rest in the freezer for 10 minutes before baking.

To prebake the shell, preheat the oven to 350°F. and transfer the tart shell directly from the freezer to the oven. Bake for about 15 minutes, until it is slightly golden. Halfway through baking, check the shell and pat down any bubbles that may have appeared. Let cool before filling.

Makes 20 ounces of dough, enough for two 11-inch open-face tarts or one 11-inch double-crusted crostata.

PUFF PASTRY

Puff pastry is such a wonderfully useful dough that you should learn to make it, even though it always takes time and, at least at first, a certain amount of concentration. But the rewards are great: Puff pastry makes a sublime base for any kind of fruit tart or tartlet; it makes a delicious vessel for all sorts of savory mixtures when shaped into vol-au-vents; and it makes a quick and delicious hors d'oeuvre when cut into strips, sprinkled with grated cheese, twisted, and baked.

This somewhat simplified version is sometimes called express puff pastry (or rough puff pastry) because it can be made faster than the traditional recipe and is easier to work. The result is virtually indistinguishable from puff pastry made the old-fashioned way, which starts with one large piece of butter wrapped in a piece of dough.

This recipe is easiest to make in a heavy-duty home mixer. Allow 4 to 6 hours from start to finish, including resting time, or make the dough over several days. The dough may be wrapped tightly in plastic and frozen for a month or so.

14 ounces (3½ sticks)
    unsalted butter
	1⅔ cups unbleached
	    all-purpose flour

1 teaspoon lemon juice	*½ cup unbleached bread flour*
⅔ cup ice water	*¾ teaspoon salt*

Cut the butter into ½-inch cubes and freeze for 30 minutes. Combine the lemon juice and water in a measuring cup. Measure the flours and salt into the bowl of a heavy-duty mixer fitted with the paddle attachment and begin mixing on slow speed. Add the chunks of cold butter a handful at a time, taking about 30 seconds to add it all. Mix for 30 seconds more, or until the edges of the cubes of butter have been rounded off. Slowly add the water and lemon juice, pouring along the inside edge of the bowl, and mix until the dough comes together roughly. The butter should still be in recognizable pieces and most of the flour should be moistened, but not wet. You may not need to add all the liquid.

Turn the dough out onto a lightly floured surface. With the heels of your hands, a pastry scraper, and a rolling pin, quickly shape it into an 8-by-14-inch rectangle, with an 8-inch side facing you and the long sides perpendicular to the near edge of your rolling surface. The dough may not knit together at this stage, but don't worry, it will eventually. With the help of a broad, rimless baking sheet or the false bottom of a large tart pan, fold the bottom one-third of the dough over the middle third. Brush off any flour, and then fold the top third over the middle. Lift the dough as you reflour the surface and turn the dough 90 degrees, so that the top flap is on your right, like the cover of a book.

Lightly flour the top of the dough and roll it again into an 8-by-14-inch rectangle. Fold in thirds as before. You have completed 2 "turns." Wrap the dough tightly in plastic wrap and refrigerate. Remove the dough from the refrigerator after 30 minutes, unwrap it, and give it 2 more turns. Rewrap the dough and refrigerate for 40 minutes. (You can also refrigerate the dough overnight at this point.)

Give the dough 2 more turns (6 turns in all) and refrigerate for at least 30 minutes before rolling out. The puff pastry can be frozen at this point or refrigerated overnight. (Frozen dough should be defrosted overnight in the refrigerator.)

Makes about 2 pounds.

Pâte Sucrée

This is the recipe we use for all the tarts and tartlets that we bake in fluted tin tart pans with removable bottoms. This dough is easy to make, it never gets tough from rolling, and it doesn't shrink when baked. We use the scraps to make jam-filled cookies for dessert plates in the restaurant.

¼ pound (1 stick) unsalted
   butter, room temperature
⅓ cup sugar
¼ teaspoon salt

¼ teaspoon vanilla extract
1 egg yolk
1¼ cups unbleached
   all-purpose flour

Beat together the butter and sugar in a medium-size bowl until creamy. Add the salt, vanilla, and egg yolk and mix until completely combined. Add the flour and mix until there are no dry patches. Wrap the ball of dough in plastic wrap and press into a 4-inch disk. Chill several hours or overnight, until firm.

To roll out the dough, first cut two 14-inch-square pieces of parchment paper. Remove the disk of dough from the refrigerator and unwrap it. Dust one of the pieces of parchment paper with flour, center the disk on it, and dust the top of the dough with flour. Cover with the other piece of parchment and roll out the disk into a 13-inch circle about ⅛ inch thick. If the dough starts to stick to the paper while you are rolling, peel back the paper and dust again with flour, and replace the paper. Then flip the whole package over and repeat on the other side. If there is excess flour on the dough when you are done rolling, peel back the paper and brush it off. Chill the sheet of dough for a few minutes.

To make an 11-inch tart, remove the top sheet of paper and invert the dough into the tart pan. Peel off the remaining piece of paper, press the dough into the corners of the pan, and pinch off any dough overhang. Use the dough scraps to patch any cracks. Let the tart shell rest in the freezer for 10 minutes before baking.

To make 4-inch tartlets, remove the top sheet of paper from the dough and cut out six 5-inch rounds. Transfer the rounds to 4-inch tartlet pans with a metal spatula. Press the dough into the corners and pinch off any extra dough from the edges. Let the tartlets rest in the freezer for 10 minutes before baking.

To prebake tart or tartlet shells, preheat the oven to 350°F. Transfer the shells directly from the freezer to the oven. Bake until slightly golden, about 15 minutes. Check the pastry halfway through baking and pat down any bubbles that may have formed. Let cool before filling.

To make cookies filled with jam or lemon curd, preheat the oven to 350°F. Roll the dough or dough scraps into 1-inch balls. Roll the balls in sugar and place them on a baking sheet, 1 inch apart. Press a dent into the top of each cookie with your thumb or forefinger. Bake for 12 minutes and remove from the oven. Fill each dent with a bit of jam or curd and return the cookies to the oven for about 5 more minutes, until they have turned a light golden color. Let cool completely before serving.

Makes 11 ounces of dough, enough for one 11-inch tart, or six 4-inch tartlets, or 30 cookies.

AMARETTI

Sometimes we use these cookies to garnish ice creams and custards, but more often we grind them up into the almond-amaretti powder we use in fruit tarts and fruit stuffings and layer into semifreddi and ice cream bombes.

1 cup almonds
¼ cup apricot kernels
  (noyaux, see page 19)
½ cup powdered sugar
1 teaspoon unbleached
  all-purpose flour

2 egg whites, room temperature
⅓ cup granulated sugar
½ teaspoon vanilla extract
⅛ teaspoon salt

Preheat the oven to 300°F. Line a baking sheet with parchment paper.

In a food processor, pulse together the almonds, noyaux, powdered sugar, and flour until the nuts are finely ground and the mixture has the granularity of fine-grained sea salt. Whisk the egg whites (either by hand or with an electric mixer) in a dry, preferably copper bowl until they are foamy. Add the granulated sugar and whisk until they hold soft peaks. Fold in the vanilla, salt, and the nut mixture.

Use a teaspoon to drop the batter onto the baking sheet in 1-inch mounds about 1 inch apart. Bake for 30 minutes, until the amaretti are just beginning to brown, then turn off the oven, leaving the cookies to dry and crisp for another 20 minutes. Remove from the oven and let cool. Store the cookies in an airtight container for up to 1 month.

Makes 30 cookies.

ALMOND-AMARETTI POWDER

One of our pastry cooks coined the name "moondust" for the mixture of ground almonds and crushed amaretto cookies that we sprinkle around so liberally in desserts, and started so labeling its containers. Unfortunately, the coinage caught on, despite the efforts of another pastry cook who countercoined, labeling the containers "lunar lint." Now "moondust" is common dessert kitchen usage, although some of us still cringe when we hear the name.

We always keep the stuff on hand in summertime, when we make so many tarts with apricots, nectarines, peaches, and plums. We use it under the fruit when assembling galettes because it absorbs some of the excess juice that stone fruits release when they're baked while imparting its own subtle almond flavor. We use about ¼ cup per galette.

¼ cup ground almonds
¼ cup unbleached all-purpose flour
¼ cup sugar
¼ cup amaretti (see page 297), pulverized

Toss all the ingredients together. Stored in an airtight container in the refrigerator, this keeps for a few months.

Makes 1 cup.

SABAYON

Sabayon is the French word for zabaglione. It names the same dessert: sweetened egg yolks flavored with rum or eau-de-vie or Madeira or any good sweet wine and whisked vigorously over low heat until they turn into a thickening pale yellow cumulus cloud.

⅓ cup dark rum (or Cognac or eau-de-vie) or Muscat de Beaumes-de-Venise (or other sweet or fortified wine)

3 tablespoons sugar
4 egg yolks
¾ cup heavy cream

Gently heat together the spirits or wine and 1 tablespoon of the sugar in a saucepan. Have ready a stainless-steel mixing bowl in an ice bath and another saucepan of simmering water on the stove. Whisk the egg yolks in another stainless-steel bowl with the remaining 2 tablespoons sugar until they are pale yellow and form a ribbon when you lift the whisk. Whisk in the warm rum and set the bowl over the pan of barely simmering water. (Don't let the water touch the bottom of the bowl.) Whisk constantly over low heat until the mixture begins to thicken and mound up slightly. Immediately pour into the bowl in the ice bath, but do not scrape out any cooked egg that may have congealed on the bottom of the hot bowl. Whisk over ice until cool. In another mixing bowl, whip the cream until it forms soft peaks and fold into the egg mixture.

Makes 2 cups.

FRANGIPANE

Frangipane is a culinary term of complicated history and imprecise meaning ("almond-flavored mixture" comes close). This frangipane recipe is for a fluffy almond butter that the Chez Panisse dessert kitchen finds indispensable, using it as a base for plum, fig, orange, apple, and pineapple tarts. Our founding dessert chef, Lindsey Shere, in her essential *Chez Panisse Desserts*, gives a recipe for frangipane cream—a delicious almond macaroon–flavored pastry cream that also makes a fine tart base.

3 ounces (⅓ cup) almond paste	*1 tablespoon flour*
2 teaspoons sugar	*1 egg*
2 tablespoons unsalted butter,	*½ teaspoon kirsch*
room temperature	*1 pinch salt*

Blend together the almond paste and sugar with an electric mixer or beat together by hand. Beat in the butter. Mix in the flour, egg, kirsch, and salt and beat until fluffy. Keeps for 1 week, refrigerated.

Makes ½ cup.

SPONGE CAKE

We owe this recipe to our friend the food writer Shirley Sarvis. It makes an unusually moist and light sponge cake that we use for all sorts of things: gâteaux glacées (layers of fruit sherbet, ice cream, and sponge cake), semifreddi and similar Italian desserts (fruit, custards, whipped cream, liquor-soaked sponge cake, etc.), and variations on baked Alaska (layers of sponge cake and ice cream or sherbet encased in meringue and baked), as well as the blood orange tart on page 193 and the domed berry cake on page 49.

Sponge cake crumbs are useful for lightening nut stuffings, such as the pistachio stuffing for nectarines on page 181. To make them, take leftover sponge cake that's at least a day old, cut it into 1-inch cubes, and process into coarse crumbs by hand or by pulsing briefly in a food processor.

5 eggs, separated, room temperature	*1½ cups sugar*
½ cup cold water	*1½ cups cake flour*
½ teaspoon vanilla extract	*½ teaspoon baking powder*
¼ teaspoon almond extract	*¼ teaspoon salt*
	¾ teaspoon cream of tartar

Butter and flour a 9-inch round pan, 3 inches deep (such as a spring-form pan), or a 12-by-18-inch sheet pan; line the bottom with parchment paper. Preheat the oven to 350°F.

Whisk the egg yolks for about 5 minutes. Beat in the water and vanilla and almond extracts. Add the sugar and beat about 5 minutes more. The mixture will form a faint ribbon when the whisk is lifted.

Sift together the flour, baking powder, and salt. In another bowl, beat the egg whites with the cream of tartar until they form soft peaks.

Gradually and gently fold the sifted dry ingredients into the egg yolk mixture. When the flour is incorporated, fold in the beaten egg whites with a rubber spatula.

Pour the batter into the prepared pan and spread evenly. Bake for 30 to 40 minutes in a round cake pan or 15 to 20 minutes in a rectangular sheet pan, until the cake is lightly browned and springy to the touch. Let cool on a rack. The cake can be made in advance and kept at room temperature or wrapped well and frozen.

Makes one 9-inch round or one 12-by-18-inch rectangular cake.

Vanilla Bean Ice Cream

The texture of this ice cream is wonderful when it is served just after it has been frozen. It is our lighter version of vanilla ice cream, the one we prefer for fruit desserts. Once it is frozen, you can stir in a swirl of candied, brandied, or fresh fruit—orange peel, chopped dates, cherries, peaches, nectarines—or leave it plain and serve it alongside a fruit pie or crisp or cobbler.

6 egg yolks	*1 pinch salt*
1 cup whole milk	*1 vanilla bean*
⅔ cup sugar	*2 cups heavy cream, chilled*

In a mixing bowl, whisk the egg yolks just enough to break them up. Gently heat the milk, sugar, and salt in a medium-size saucepan. Split the vanilla bean lengthwise, scrape out the seeds with a paring knife, and put them into the milk mixture along with the bean pod. Stir slowly over low heat until the milk is steaming and the sugar is dissolved. Drizzle the warm mixture into the egg yolks, whisking constantly as you pour. (This is called tempering the egg yolks.)

Return the milk and egg yolk mixture to the saucepan. Measure the heavy cream into the mixing bowl. Cook the mixture over low heat, stirring slowly and scraping the bottom of the pan with a wooden spoon or heat-resistant rubber spatula, until the mixture thickens enough to coat the spoon. (This happens at a temperature of about 170°F.) Immediately remove from the heat and strain through a fine-mesh sieve into the bowl with the heavy cream. Whisk together to cool the mixture, cover, and chill thoroughly.

Freeze the mixture following the instructions for your ice cream machine. Transfer the frozen ice cream to a clean dry container, cover, and store in the freezer for several hours before serving to firm up.

Makes 1 quart.

Variation: To make coffee ice cream, use half-and-half instead of milk and steep ¾ cup coffee beans in it; add the coffee beans with the sugar and steep for an extra 15 minutes.

Pastry Cream

Old-fashioned pastry cream is still one of the most important components of our pastry kitchen; we use it as a base for fresh fruit tarts and soufflés and to fill cream puffs.

3 tablespoons unbleached all-purpose flour	One 1-inch piece vanilla bean
3 tablespoons sugar	3 egg yolks
1¼ cups whole milk	1 tablespoon unsalted butter, chilled
1 pinch salt	

Mix the flour and sugar together. Put the milk and salt in a small saucepan and warm gently over low heat. Split the vanilla bean and scrape out the seeds with a small knife. Add the seeds and the pod to the milk, and when the milk starts to steam slightly, whisk in the flour and sugar mixture. Over medium heat, whisking slowly and continually to make sure nothing sticks to the bottom of the pan, cook the mixture until it is thick and glossy. It is done when the raw flour taste is gone, about 10 minutes.

Whisk the egg yolks enough to break them up, then whisk them into the milk mixture. Cook for another minute. Remove the pastry cream from the heat and whisk in the cold butter. Strain through a fine sieve into a bowl. Cover immediately with a piece of plastic wrap pressed onto the surface of the pastry cream so that is does not develop a skin as it cools. Refrigerate immediately. Keeps for 1 week. To use pastry cream for filling tarts or cream puffs, lighten it by folding in a little whipped cream.

Makes 1½ cups.

Variations: For tangerine-, lemon-, or orange-flavored pastry cream, grate the zest from two or three citrus fruits into the milk before cooking. For bitter almond–flavored pastry cream, add 3 tablespoons of pulverized noyaux (page 19) to the milk before cooking.

CANDIED GINGER

This recipe is for good-quality fresh young ginger, which is often available. Choose bulbous, firm, heavy roots with bright, clear, unwrinkled skin. More rarely, usually in the early summer, you can buy "baby ginger" from Hawaii—thin-skinned, cream-colored, immature, almost translucent rhizomes with bright rosy shoots. Baby ginger can be candied too, with excellent results. However, being younger, more tender, and less spicy, it needs fewer blanchings.

2 pieces fresh young ginger, about 6 inches long
3 cups water
1½ cups sugar, plus ½ cup for tossing

Scrape the skin off the ginger with a sharp-edged spoon or small knife. Cut the root into ⅛-inch-thick slices against the grain. Put the slices in a medium-size nonreactive saucepan and cover with cold water. Bring to a boil and cook for 15 minutes. Drain, cover with fresh cold water, boil, and again cook 15 minutes. Repeat this blanching process 2 more times, for a total of 4 blanchings in all.

After the last blanching, drain and return the ginger to the pan with 3 cups water and 1½ cups sugar. Slowly bring the syrup to a boil, stirring occasionally, and simmer about 20 minutes, until the ginger is translucent and the syrup is boiling in a rapid upsurge of small bubbles. Its temperature should reach 230°F. on a candy thermometer. Turn off the heat and let stand for 30 minutes, for the ginger to absorb more syrup. Drain. Save the syrup, if you wish; it has a strong ginger flavor and can be used to sweeten drinks, for example.

Spread the ginger slices out on a nonreactive surface (a baking sheet lined with parchment paper, for example) or on a rack; the slices should not touch one another. Let them dry overnight, uncovered, at room temperature. The next day put the ginger slices in a bowl or on a baking sheet with ½ cup sugar and toss with your fingers to separate them, coating all their sides with sugar. Store in an airtight container, refrigerated, for up to 6 months.

Makes 2 cups.

BIBLIOGRAPHY ❧

Bertolli, Paul, with Alice Waters. *Chez Panisse Cooking*. New York: Random House, 1988.

Bocuse, Paul. *Paul Bocuse's French Cooking*. New York: Pantheon Books, 1977.

Brennan, Georgeanne. *The Glass Pantry: The Pleasures of Simple Preserves*. San Francisco: Chronicle Books, 1994.

Buying Guide for Fresh Fruits, Vegetables, Herbs, and Nuts, The. Montebello, Calif.: Blue Goose, 1976.

Casas, Penelope. *The Foods and Wines of Spain*. New York: Alfred A Knopf, 1991.

Chez Maxim's: Secrets and Recipes from the World's Most Famous Restaurant. New York: McGraw-Hill, 1962.

Child, Julia. *The Way to Cook*. New York: Alfred A. Knopf, 1989.

Citrus Industry, The. Vol. 1. Berkeley: University of California, 1967.

Coombes, Allen J. *Dictionary of Plant Names*. Portland, Ore.: Timber Press, 1994.

Darrow, George M. *The Strawberry: History, Breeding, and Physiology*. New York: Holt, Rinehart and Winston, 1966.

David, Elizabeth. *Elizabeth David Classics*. New York: Alfred A. Knopf, 1980.

Davidson, Alan. *Fruit: A Connoisseur's Guide and Cookbook*. New York: Simon & Schuster, 1991.

———. *The Oxford Companion to Food*. New York: Oxford University Press, 1999.

Escoffier, A. *The Escoffier Cook Book*. New York: Crown Publishers, 1969.

Facciola, Stephen. *Cornucopia II: A Source Book of Edible Plants*. Vista, California: Kampong Publications, 1998.

Field, Carol. *The Italian Baker*. New York: Harper & Row, 1985.

Fruit, Berry and Nut Inventory. Decorah, Iowa: Seed Saver Publications, 1993.

Girardet, Fredy. *The Cuisine of Fredy Girardet*. New York: William Morrow, 1982.

Greene, Janet, and Ruth Hertzberg and Beatrice Vaughan. *Putting Food By*. New York: Plume Books, 1991.

Grigson, Jane. *Jane Grigson's Fruit Book*. New York: Atheneum, 1982.

Guérard, Michel. *Michel Guérard's Cuisine Gourmande*. New York: William Morrow, 1979.

Herbst, Sharon Tyler. *The New Food Lover's Companion*. Hauppauge, New York: Barron's, 1995.

Lanza, Anna Tasca. *The Flavors of Sicily*. New York: Clarkson N. Potter, 1996.

———. *The Heart of Sicily*. New York: Clarkson N. Potter, 1993.

McGee, Harold. *On Food and Cooking*. New York: Charles Scribner's Sons, 1984.

Montagné, Prosper. *Larousse Gastronomique: The New American Edition of the World's Greatest Culinary Encyclopedia*. New York: Crown Publishers, 1988.

Morton, Julia F. *Fruits of Warm Climates*. Miami: Julia F. Morton, 1987.

Olney, Richard. *Lulu's Provençal Table*. New York: HarperCollins, 1994.

———, and the editors of Time-Life Books. *Preserving*. Alexandria, Virginia: Time-Life Books, 1981.

———. *Simple French Food*. New York: Atheneum, 1974.

Plagemann, Catherine. *Fine Preserving: M. F. K. Fisher's Annotated Edition of Catherine Plagemann's Cookbook*. Berkeley, Calif.: Aris Books, 1986.

Reich, Lee. *Uncommon Fruits Worthy of Attention: A Gardener's Guide*. New York: Addison-Wesley, 1991.

Root, Waverly. *Food: An Authoritative and Visual History and Dictionary of the Foods of the World.* New York: Simon & Schuster, 1980.

Saunt, James. *Citrus Varieties of the World.* Norwich, England: Sinclair International, 2000.

Schneider, Elizabeth. *Uncommon Fruits & Vegetables: A Commonsense Guide.* New York: Harper & Row, 1986.

Shere, Lindsey Remolif. *Chez Panisse Desserts.* New York: Random House, 1985.

Specialty and Minor Crops Handbook. Oakland: University of California, Division of Agriculture and Natural Resources, 1998.

Stobart, Tom. *The Cook's Encyclopedia.* New York: Harper & Row, 1981.

Sunset Western Garden Book. Menlo Park, Calif.: Sunset Publishing Corporation, 1995.

Townsend, Doris McFerran. *The Cook's Companion.* New York: Crown Publishers, 1978.

Walheim, Lance. *Citrus.* Tucson, Arizona: Ironwood Press, 1996.

Wolfert, Paula. *Couscous and Other Good Food from Morocco.* New York: Harper & Row, 1973.

———. *Mediterranean Cooking.* New York: Times Books, 1977.

INDEX 🐝